ISREAL HOROVIT
field, Massachusett
FIELD PLAYS. He completed a nover
his first play, THE COMEBACK, at age 17, and
has been writing plays continuously since then.
Among his more than thirty produced plays to
date are THE INDIAN WANTS THE BRONX,
LINE, IT'S CALLED THE SUGAR PLUM,
MORNING, DR. HERO, THE PRIMARY EN-
GLISH CLASS, SHOOTING GALLERY RATS,
THE REASON WE EAT, MACKERAL, THE
WIDOW'S BLIND DATE, SUNDAY RUNNERS
IN THE RAIN and an adaptation to Dickens'
A CHRISTMAS CAROL: SCROOGE and MAR-
LEY. For film, he wrote THE STRAWBERRY
STATEMENT; for television, PLAY FOR
GERMS [for VD BLUES], BARTLEBY, THE
SCRIVENER [from the Melville novel], and a
cycle of plays for Canadian television called
GROWING UP JEWISH IN SAULT STE.
MARIE. Prose fiction includes a novel,
CAPPELLA, and a novella, NOBODY LOVES
ME. He has won numerous awards, including
two OBIEs, for best plays off-Broadway, the
EMMY for television plays, the French Critics
Prize, the Prix du Jury of the Cannes Film Festi-
val, an Award in Literature of The Academy of
Arts and Letters, plus Guggenheim, Fulbright
and National Endowment Fellowships. He was
one of the founding playwrights of the Eugene
O'Neill Memorial Theatre Foundation and is
Artistic Director of The New York Playwrights'
Lab at the Actors Studio. Horovitz plays have
been translated into and performed in more than
twenty languages, worldwide. He divides his
time between homes in New York's Greenwich
Village and the seaport city of Gloucester,
Massachusetts.

THE WAKEFIELD PLAYS

ISRAEL HOROVITZ

 A BARD BOOK/PUBLISHED BY AVON BOOKS

AVON BOOKS
A division of
The Hearst Corporation
959 Eighth Avenue
New York, New York 10019

BAF 8 -2 -80

CONTENTS

THE WAKEFIELD
PLAYS

The Wakefield Plays, Part I

HOPSCOTCH
A Play in One Act

For Paul Simon.

The People of the Play

ELSA: Calls herself Lorali, thirtyish, youthful body, blond hair, fair.
WILL: Calls himself Earl, thirtyish, tall, dark-haired, dark-complexioned, thin.

The Place of the Play

Park playground, overlooking Lake Quannapowitt, Wakefield, Massachusetts.

The Time of the Play

September, sunny afternoon.

A Note on the Music

Paul Simon's song "Was a Sunny Day" should be used to begin and to conclude play.

Lights out in auditorium.

Music fades in.

Lights fade up.

Asphalt patch, small park playground.

Small traditional green park bench, baby carriage set at bench's outermost corner, facing upstage.

ELSA *is discovered, drawing hopscotch grid on asphalt with yellow chalk. She throws a pebble into the first square and hops to it, picks it up, continues hopping to end of grid, turns, returns to starting position: her game has begun.*

Music plays to completion.

As ELSA *plays, we sense she is bothered by something or someone offstage, beyond auditorium.*

As music fades out, ELSA *calls out into and above auditorium.*

ELSA: You like what you're seein'?
  [*No response. She returns to her game. When she reaches the end of the grid, she turns, stops, calls out again.*]
ELSA: Hey, c'mon now, will ya! If you're gonna gawk, gawk from where I can gawk back! Fair's fair!
  [*No response. She throws pebble; plays.*]
ELSA: I'll turn my back, I won't watch. You can either come out and show yourself . . . or go away. . . . [*Pause; calls louder.*] Either way's okay with me! You gotta do one or the other, *okay?* [*She turns her back to auditorium.*]
  [*A moment of silence passes.*
  A young man, WILL, *appears in auditorium. He will stop a moment and then walk swiftly and directly onto stage, directly to* ELSA. *He will never alter his course, once he begins to move to her.*
  She turns; sees him. She is obviously frightened.]
ELSA: I'm not frightened, you know. . . .
  [WILL *continues his move to her.*]
ELSA: This place is crawling with people, you know that?
  [ELSA *is frozen in fear.* WILL *continues to move to her.*]
ELSA: You better just back down, huh? This place is crawling with people. . . . I mean, there's no danger here, right? . . .
  [WILL *reaches* ELSA. *He takes her in his arms and kisses her on the lips. She is overwhelmed by his size and acquiesces, at first, to his embrace and kiss. She then responds with noticeable strength and emotion.*
  They hold their kiss awhile.
  They break apart, holding a fixed stare between them.]
ELSA: That was a good one. . . . [*She smiles. She throws pebble.*] Strong silent type, huh? [*Hops.*]
WILL: [*Looking in baby carriage*] Where's the baby?
ELSA: Playing. Why?
WILL: Yours?

ELSA: Sure. [*She throws the pebble and begins her hopscotch game again.*]

WILL: Where's your husband? Working?

ELSA: It's daytime, isn't it? [*Points to sky.*] That big round bright thing up there's the sun. When you can see it, you can pretty much figure it's daytime. And when it's daytime, people are working. . . . [*Smiles.*] *Most* people.

WILL: This what you do for a living?

ELSA: [*Smiles.*] Naw. Not yet. I'm not turning pro till after the next Olympics. . . .
[*She throws pebble again and plays.* WILL *sits and watches a moment.*]

ELSA: You married?

WILL: Me? Naw.

ELSA: Ever close?

WILL: To being married? [*Pauses.*] Naw. Not even close.

ELSA: How come?

WILL: I looked around me. All my married friends were spending their weekends playin' softball. Their wives were home spending their weekends complaining about bein' left alone . . . while their husbands were playin' softball.

ELSA: That's why?

WILL: Sure. I hate softball. All's I needed was to get married and haveta start bullshit like *that!* You know what I mean? [*He smiles.*]

ELSA: You've got a lota charm and a wonderful sense of humor.

WILL: You noticed?

ELSA: MMMmmm. I never miss a trick. [*She begins to play again.*]

WILL: I see you waited. . . .

ELSA: For what?

WILL: Babies.
[*She stops. She looks at him, suddenly. He nods to carriage.*]

WILL: I could tell from the age. Still in a carriage and all.

ELSA: [*She plays.*] Oh, yuh. I waited. [*She smiles.*]

WILL: Boy or girl?

ELSA: Well, now. It's gotta be one or the other, right?

WILL: Nine chances outa ten, yuh.

ELSA: Girl.

WILL: Name?

ELSA: Lorali.

WILL: How's that again?
  [*She throws.*]

ELSA: Lorali. [*She plays.*]

WILL: That's pretty. Yours?

ELSA: [*Stops; looks at him.*] My name?
  [*He smiles.*]

ELSA: The same: Lorali. [*She resumes play.*] I'm Lorali the
  Second, she's Lorali the Third. My grandmother was
  Lorali and my mother was Lorali, Junior. . . . [*Smiles.*]
  Very common name around these parts. [*She throws.*]

WILL: No kidding. I never heard it in my life before, now
  I hear of four of them. . . . And in a jerk town like
  Wakefield, too. . . .

ELSA: Very well known and very well respected name, too.
  . . . [*She plays.*]

WILL: Around these parts, huh? [*Stands.*] Wakefield, Mas-
  sachusetts, United States of America, North America,
  Western Hemisphere, Earth, Universe, Infinity . . . New
  England. [*Smiles.*] I'm very deep.

ELSA: Oh, yuh. So's the lake.

WILL: What d'ya call it?

ELSA: The lake?

WILL: Yuh. The lake.

ELSA: Janet. I call it Janet. [*She turns to him.*] See these
  shoes? [*Points to her shoes.*] These are the twins. [*Nods
  to bench.*] The bench is Nanny Mary Poppins and you
  are what we see of Silver as he rides off into the sunset:
  a horse's ass! [*Stops; controls her anger by turning away
  from him.*] Unbelievable! [*Faces him again.*] Lake Quannapowitt. Named for the local Indians . . . a tribe that
  vanished.

WILL: Oh, right . . . I forgot.
  [*Silence. Ten count.*]

ELSA: [*She plays.*] You wanna know about my husband?
  [*Stops at 10.*]

WILL: Sure. What does he do for a living? Break backs?

ELSA: Naw. Not for a living; he just breaks backs as a
  weekend hobby kind of thing. . . .

WILL: He sounds nice. . . .

ELSA: He's a minister.

WILL: No kidding?

ELSA: No kidding.

WILL: What kind of minister?

ELSA: Protestant.

WILL: A Protestant minister. You don't say? What denomination?

ELSA: [*She will hop backward one square as she speaks each word or phrase.*] Baptist. [*Pauses.*] Blond. [*Pauses.*] Blue eyes. Both of them. . . . [*Pauses.*] Six-five-and-a-half . . . [*Pauses.*] Square jaw, thick neck . . . [*Pauses.*] He's a hunk. [*She crosses to* WILL.]

WILL: He is?

ELSA: Mmmm . . .

WILL: A hunk?

ELSA: Mmmmm . . .

WILL: Of what?

ELSA: Huh?

WILL: A hunk of what?

[ELSA *returns to grid; resumes game.*]

ELSA: You just passing through . . . or are you planning to start a business here? Hey! Maybe pizza. [*Smiles.*] Santoro hit it big with subs—maybe you could be pizza. Wakefieldians eat a hell of a lot of pizza. A pizza palace with a real gimmick could be a real hot-shit success!

WILL: Anybody ever tell you you've got a mouth like a toilet?

ELSA: [*Stops.*] Oh, yuh. Coupla guys. They didn't get too far with me, though . . . not with an obvious line like that. [*Smiles.*] You know . . . maybe a quick feel, but nowhere solid. [*Pauses.*] I've never been a sucker for an obvious come-on line. I like something more subtle. . . .

WILL: [*Stands.*] A gun, a knife? That sort of thing?

ELSA: No. Uh uh. [*Smiles.*] Money's more what I had in mind.

WILL: [*After pretending to fish in his pockets*] Jeez . . . what a shame! [*He crosses to the grid; smiles.*] I used all my spare change on the train from North Station. . . .

ELSA: [*She plays to 10 and back, stops.*] Hey, well, listen! You can't win 'em all! I had a guy here just the other aftanoon . . . a real blowah . . . real bullshit ahtist type, ya know. . . . He tried to pay me with magic beans. . . .

WILL: No kidding?

ELSA: No kidding.

WILL: Was he youngish?

ELSA: Yuh, youngish. . . .

WILL: Sho't?

ELSA: Yuh. Wicked sho't. Nearly teensy. . . .

WILL: Was he leading a cow on a rope?

ELSA: That's him!

WILL: [*Sits on bench.*] Never heard of 'im! [*Pauses; changes attitude suddenly.*]

ELSA: [*Plays again.*] You do night work, huh?

WILL: Huh?

ELSA: You work anywhere?

WILL: Yuh. I work.

ELSA: What kind?

WILL: I work for a big company. . . . Construction.

ELSA: Oh, really? You construct things?

WILL: Me, personally? Nope. Opposite. I tear things down. I'm in the destruction end. . . . Wrecking.

ELSA: [*She moves to* WILL *at bench.*] Gee, it, well, sounds like you've done really well with yourself . . . very successful. [*Pauses.*] Wrecking, huh? [*Pause.*] They pay you a lot of money to do that? [*She sits beside* WILL *on bench.*]

WILL: Money? Sure, well . . .

ELSA: Sounds like it took a lot of schooling. . . .

WILL: Schooling? Well, I . . .

ELSA: You have a big desk? . . .

WILL: C'mon . . .

ELSA: . . . a big *position!*

WILL: You s'posed ta be *cute* now or somethin'?

ELSA: Me? Cute? Uh-uh.

WILL: [*Forces a calm pitch to his voice.*] I have a middle-sized position. . . . Middle management, they call us. [*Smiles.*] It's a middle-sized position.

ELSA: Do you like it?

WILL: [*Yells.*] My position? Do I like my middle-sized position???

[*There is an embarrassed pause.*]

WILL: I'm still awful tired from traveling. My nerves are all edgy. . . .

ELSA: Don't sweat it. [*Hops.*] I can understand that. . . . [*Pauses.*] I meant "the town." [*Stops.*]

WILL: Huh?

ELSA: When I asked "Do you like it?" I meant "Do you like the town?" [*Smiles.*] Being here.

WILL: Oh, I getcha. You wanted to know if I liked being here. [*Smiles.*] I love it.

ELSA: I figured you did. [*Hops.*] Most everybody here was born here. . . .

WILL: Really? . . .

ELSA: [*Stops.*] . . . And stayed! [*Pauses.*] You know what I mean?

WILL: Your parents? Are they still . . . ?

ELSA: My parents, are they still? Sure. Still as they come. [*Smiles.*] Two days apart. [*Pauses.*] Happens.

WILL: I was gonna ask about their house and all. . . . I never even guessed . . .

ELSA: *That* happens, too. . . .

WILL: How long ago?

ELSA: How long ago what?

WILL: How long ago did you lose them?

ELSA: [*Hops.*] Lose them? You mean, like in Filene's Basement. . . . [*Pauses.*] You make it sound as though I were careless! [*Pauses. Pretends to be talking to third person.*] Excuse me, but I seem to have lost my parents. . . . [*To* WILL *again; timbre of voice suddenly changed*] Last month. Four weeks ago. You just missed the excitement . . . the hustle and the bustle. . . .

WILL: I'm sorry. . . .

ELSA: Don't be.

WILL: I am . . . I really am.

ELSA: Long time comin'. Just as well. . . .

WILL: I'm really very sorry to find out. . . .

ELSA: Yuh, I was, too. . . . [*Looks directly at* WILL.] I'm not scared of you at all anymore, not at all. So, just don't get that into your head, okay? [*Hops.*] I used to hate boys. . . . [*Stops.*] I grew up. . . . [*Throws pebble.*] Things changed. [*Hops.*] Now I hate men. [*Stops.*]

WILL: His heart?

ELSA: Huh?

WILL: Your father. Was it his heart?

ELSA: What do *you* think?

WILL: And your mother? She was sick long, too?

ELSA: Take a wild guess. . . .

WILL: [*Angrily*] *Aren't you getting tired of this???*

ELSA: *Where . . . have . . . you . . . been???*

WILL: I . . . dunno. . . .

ELSA: That outa state? [*Pauses.*] I don't hear an answer!

WILL: Newport News.

ELSA: Where's that?

WILL: Virginia.

ELSA: What'd ya wreck there? Men? Women? Buncha kids?

WILL: Navy yard. Tore it down.

ELSA: [*After a pause; she stops the game.*] He had his heart attack, finally. Waited long enough, worryin' . . . [*Pauses.*] Shot outa his chair like he'd been kicked by a mule. . . . Watching Miss America.

WILL: Were you there?

ELSA: Sure.

WILL: That musta frightened you.

ELSA: I don't know. I s'pose . . .

WILL: Your husband?

ELSA: What about him?

WILL: Was he . . . with you . . . Then?

ELSA: Then? No. Just me.

WILL: And your mother?

ELSA: On display. Being waked. In the living room.

WILL: Oh . . . I see. [*Walks to her.*] And you were . . . alone, huh?

ELSA: That's what I said, right? You've got yourself a sho't-memory problem, don'tcha? [*Hops. Throws the pebble; hops to it.*] You know who won? You maybe know her. [*Pauses; no reply.*] Miss Virginia. A brunette with mushy big brown eyes, a wicked dumb drawl, mouth always open real slutty-like, and a pair of tits shot, no doubt about it, full of sand. . . .

WILL: C'mon . . .

ELSA: Your type . . .

WILL: Don't be vulgar!

ELSA: [*Hops throughout speech.*] But I am! Born vulgar, grow up vulgar, die vulgar; it's kinda a tradition around here . . . among those who stay and miss out on the sophistication of world travel. . . . [*Pauses; then quietly*] Must be nice. [*No reply.*] Your life.

WILL: [*Smiles.*] It's the greatest.

ELSA: You speak any languages?

WILL: Jeez, I thought I'd been doin' it since I got here . . . fact is, I thought we'd both been!

ELSA: [*Flat, childish reading.*] Ho. Ho ho. Ho ho ho. Some rapid-fire slashing wit ya got there! [*Pauses; throws pebble.*] Foreign tongues is what I meant.

WILL: Nope. You?

ELSA: What da *you* care?

WILL: I don't. I really don't.

ELSA: I know. I really know.

WILL: You ever been outa here? Outa Wakefield?

ELSA: [*Throws pebble; hops.*] Too happy ta wanna leave! Everything I'll ever want is right here . . . right in Wakefield . . . squashed in between Reading, Stoneham, Greenwood, and Lynnfield. . . . [*Smiles.*] Everything I'll ever need is right here. Always be'n, too. . . . [*Pauses.*] Everythin' else is bullshit. That's the way I see it.

WILL: You finish college?

ELSA: [*After a long pause; quietly*] Noop. . . .

WILL: How come?

ELSA: I was busy!

WILL: Oh, yeah? Doin' what?

ELSA: You own anything?

WILL: You always answer questions with questions?

ELSA: I try to. Okay with you?

WILL: Fine with me. Sure.

ELSA: You own anything special?

WILL: What, exactly?

ELSA: How about weird belts? I always notice that men who travel around, like you do, get to wearin' a lot of weird belts. . . . You know. . . . Hand-carved stuff . . . sometimes with studs. . . . The kind quee-ahs sometimes wear. . . . [*She smiles.*] You know what I mean?
[*There is a long pause.*
WILL *slowly lifts his shirt and displays his waist to her. There is no belt around his waist.*]

ELSA: You've lost weight. You're skinny.

WILL: I'm not skinny. I'm thin. You get tired of airport food. You get thin.

ELSA: I use'ta be skinny, till high school. I got a big stomach in high school. [*Pauses.*] Gone now, but it used to worry me a lot. In high school. [*Pauses.*] Sometimes I used to wake up worrying, in the middle of the night. Sometimes

I used to wake up maybe two or even three times a night.
[*Pauses.*] I used to have to go into the bathroom. We
had a full length mirror on the door. I use'ta stand in
front of it and hoist up my nightgown, about to my chin,
and stare at my stomach. [*Pauses.*] It really worried me
a hell of a lot! It sorta . . . well . . . it sort of ruined me,
you might say. My twirling. [*Pauses.*] I used to twirl. I
was very good at it. Some people used to think I could
twirl wicked. . . . I still could . . . if I had to. [*Pauses.*]
You're pretty weird, you know that?

WILL: Do we *have* to???

ELSA: I'm gonna be thirty soon. You know that? Next
month . . .

WILL: You look younger. . . .

ELSA: Yuh, that's what they tell me. . . . [*Stops; looks at
him. She throws the pebble.*] You ever been anywhere
that you actually thought was . . . you know . . . exciting? Worth stayin' at, maybe?

WILL: I guess . . .

ELSA: Someplace where you might send somebody like me?

WILL: You might like cities. . . .

ELSA: I've seen cities!

WILL: I think I've seen 'em all; every city. [*Pauses.*] My
line of work. It's indigenous.

ELSA: What's that supposed to mean?

WILL: Indigenous? "Peculiar to."

ELSA: I'm not stupid!

WILL: I never said you were!

ELSA: You travel a lot, huh? [*She plays again.*]

WILL: Sure, wherever they have a big demolition job, I
have to go there first and estimate the costs. . . .

ELSA: Sounds really crappy.

WILL: It's pretty bad. [*Pauses.*] Do you think I'm dull?

ELSA: Yes. I really do.

WILL: I don't talk to people much.

ELSA: It does show a little, yuh. [*She throws pebble, plays
awhile; stops. She turns to him.*] Here's a fact about me
you probably missed: Did you know that I was very
nearly Miss America?

WILL: C'moff it, will ya?

ELSA: It's true! [*Pauses.*] I came really close. I did! [*Pauses.*]
I twirled for my specialty.

WILL: How close?

ELSA: Very. [*Pauses.*] Fourth. [*Pauses.*] State runoffs. . . .

WILL: You get any money?

[*No reply.*]

WILL: What did you get?

ELSA: [*Suddenly angry again*] You've got no right to just come around and stare at people and start up all sorts of bullshit, ya know!!! [*Pauses.*] What the hell do you think ya get for fourth in the goddam state runoffs!??? [*More softly now*] I got nothing.

WILL: I bet you were cute.

ELSA: [*Carefully*] The things . . . they . . . promise . . . you. [*Silence.*]

WILL: I've personally always found twirlers to be . . . you know . . . a little *stupid*, but . . . you know . . . stimulating.

[*She looks up. He smiles.*]

WILL: It's true! It always turned me on. Maybe it's the way you fingered the aluminum stick. . . .

ELSA: Thanks a lot.

WILL: But it's true! You are!

[*She looks at him, tight-lipped.*]

WILL: Cute. [*He smiles.*] You're more than that. You're really pretty . . . beautiful.

ELSA: [*Looks at him, directly.*] You got feelings like the side of a hill, you know that?

WILL: I keep hearin' that. Yuh.

ELSA: [*Smiles.*] Did it ever occur to you that I might be special?

WILL: Special? [*Smiles.*] No, never. [*Pauses.*] Not at all.

ELSA: [*She plays.*] I do a lot of special things. . . . I have special talents. . . .

WILL: [*He moves to her.*] Like what? Acrobatic dancing? Musical saw? Oh, *this*! You mean *this*? [*He looks at grid.*]

ELSA: I'm good at voices. Especially on the telephone. [*Smiles.*] You ever make any dirty phone calls?

WILL: [*He goes to bench; sits.*] A few. Maybe twenty, thirty. That's about it.

ELSA: I mean really *filthy* phone calls. The kind you don't even read about. . . . The kind you just sort of muse over. . . . Really *filthy* phone calls. . . .

WILL: Oh, I thought you just meant *dirty* phone calls.

Filthies? Oh, sure, I guess I've done several hundred
filthies . . . [*Pauses; adds quickly*] This month!

ELSA: I did thirty-one straight days in a row.

WILL: I think I read about it.

ELSA: I called the butcher.

WILL: What the hell are you talkin' about anyway?

ELSA: I called the butcher. [*Pauses.*] Every time I use'ta
walk by his butcher shop, he use'ta call out ta me . . .
usual things like "Hey, blondie, you want some of my
meat?" or "How about some nice loins, cutie?" That kind
of thing. [*Smiles.*] I called him every night from the first
of July right through till the thirty-first, inclusive. Gave
him something to think about! [*She crosses to bench and
sits beside* WILL: *quite close to him, in fact.*]

WILL: You like it?

ELSA: I loved it! [*Pauses; smiles. She touches his leg;
lightly.*] At first he was really made nervous, you know,
by my language and all. . . . But by the middle of the
month . . . even earlier . . . by the tenth, or so, he'd
calmed down really quite a lot. By the twentieth, he'd
worked it out to get his wife and family to stop picking
up the phone. He worked it out most of the time to get
them right outa the *room!* [*Pauses.*] He started whole
conversations! [*Pauses; excited.*] You know what he said
on July twenty-eighth?

WILL: If I knew, it's somehow slipped my mind!

ELSA: I love you.

WILL: What?

ELSA: [*She stands; moves upstage of* WILL *and bench.*] That's
what he said: "Miss, I want you to know that I really love
you." That's what he told me. I asked him if he wanted
to meet me, but all he wanted was my telephone number.
. . . [*She blows in* WILL's *ear, lightly; she giggles.*]

WILL: C'mon, will you. . . .

ELSA: It's true! He kept avoiding the question. He just kept
asking for my number. . . .

WILL: What time of day did you call him?

ELSA: What the hell kind of weird question is that?

WILL: I just wondered. . . .

ELSA: Time of *night.* Five minutes to eleven. . . . Just before the news.

WILL: Every night?

ELSA: Religiously.

WILL: How could he get his family out of the room, every night, five to eleven?

ELSA: He was dedicated.

WILL: *You're* the weird one here!

ELSA: [*She touches his hair; smiles.*] How come you're all jittery?

WILL: Me?

ELSA: [*She sits close to him again.*] On the thirty-first, I walked into his shop and asked him if he liked my halter top. . . . It was hot and I had a halter that was kinda loose-fitting, wicked thin . . . no bra or anything . . . and shorts that were kinda wrecked from bein' washed so much. . . . You know . . . holey. [*Smiles.*] Nothin' underneath them, either. . . . [*Pauses.*] He pretended he didn't know me. Even when I did the same sentences I did on the phone, over and over again to his face, he pretended he didn't know me. He said he'd have to call the cops if I didn't shut my dirty mouth. Can you imagine? We were all alone in the shop. . . . Me, just talkin' the sentences over and over to his face. Him, standing there with his bloody hands and apron. *A look of honest-to-God shock on his face!*

WILL: [*Suddenly*] This is an awful thing, but it's on my mind . . . I've forgotten your name!

ELSA: What?

WILL: I know it was pretty, but I can't remember it exactly. . . . [*Pauses.*] I'm sorry.

[*She stands; goes to grid.*]

ELSA: [*Furiously*] *What the hell do you want from me, anyway?* [*She plays.*]

WILL: I don't want anything from you. It was a sunny day, I was walking, I saw you, I thought it might be interesting. . . .

ELSA: Bullshit! You've been following me for a week now!

WILL: [*He goes to her.*] I saw you over here by yourself . . . hopping around like some kind of weird kind of retarded hooker, you know . . . and I estimated that it might be interesting—

ELSA: [*Interrupts.*] Drop dead!

WILL: [*Yells.*] *—to pick you up!*

ELSA: *Was it???*

WILL: *Was it what???*

ELSA: *WAS . . . IT . . . INTERESTING???*

WILL: [*After a long pause; softly*] No. Not very. [*Pauses.*] Not *bad.* [*Pauses.*] You're not stupid. Just not very . . . [*Smiles.*] . . . interesting.

[*She throws pebble and misses mark.*]

WILL: You missed. [*He picks up pebble: pretends to hand it to her; drops it at her feet.*] I wasn't concentrating.

[*She picks up pebble, throws it into square, hopping to it. Again and again, in succeeding squares.*

WILL *picks up her yellow chalk, writes "ELSA" quite visibly on top slat of bench. Adds a heart and arrow.*]

ELSA: It's Lorali. [*Spells the name aloud.*] L–O–R–A–L–I is the way we spell it.

WILL: I don't think that's correct. [*Smiles.*] Okay. I'm . . . Earl. Earl the Third. My grandfather and father were both Earls.

[WILL *suddenly writes "EARL" in large letters scrawled over her hopscotch grid. He suddenly grabs her and pulls her down onto the hopscotch field with him, pinning her arms behind her, holding her down to the ground with him.*

WILL: [*Yells angrily.*] I'm Earl the Third! [*Pauses.*] Maybe even Earl the Fourth! Who's keepin' score, huh? [*Screams.*] *How about Mister Earl???* [*He forces her to kiss him.*] Is that any better?

ELSA: Let me up!

WILL: When I want to!

ELSA: *You let me up!*

WILL: When I *decide* to!

ELSA: *YOU LET ME UP!!!*

[*He kisses her again, roughly, forcing her into a somewhat docile state.*

ELSA *is quite visibly shaken; frightened. Their difference in size is unquestionable.*

WILL *breaks the kiss.*]

WILL: Is that any better?

ELSA: Yuh. [*Quietly*] Just what I've be'n waiting for. It must take a lot of courage to throw around somebody who's half your size.

WILL: I'm ready to hear about this frocked and collared

husband of yours. . . . [*Pauses.*] Do you two enjoy each
other?

[*No reply.*]

WILL: I expect an answer here *please.* . . .

ELSA: Yes, we do.

WILL: How? I'd really like to know how. Speak to me. Tell
me . . . some of the good things you do together.

ELSA: You're hurting me!

WILL: Good. . . .

ELSA: Son of a bitch!

WILL: C'mon, Lor-ah-*liar*! Let's hear what you and the
Reverend do for your jollies! [*Leans even closer, bending
over her.*] I'm really curious. [*Lets loose of her arm now.*]
You're free. [*Sits back, watches, as she weeps.*] You gonna
tell us?

ELSA: [*Weeping*] You've got no right. . . . [*Pauses.*] Rides. . . .

WILL: You say "rides"?

ELSA: We . . . take rides . . . together. . . .

WILL: Horses?

ELSA: In our car. We take rides. That's what we do. . . .
[*Quietly; weeping*] That's what we do around here. We
ride up one-twenty-eight to the shopping centers . . . up
in Burlington . . . down in Peabody . . . usually after
they're closed. . . . We sit in our car and look at the out-
sides of the stores. . . . [*Pauses.*] Everybody does it. [*She
sobs a moment.*] We don't talk much. Hardly at all. If he
died during the rides, we'd crash. If I died, nothing much
would happen. . . . [*She regains her composure.*] You've
really got no right . . . no more . . . [*Pauses; then deep-
throated, carefully*] I . . . am . . . so . . . unhappy.

[*There is a long pause.*]

WILL: [*Smiles.*] Is he a good driver?

ELSA: Who?

WILL: Your husband. Does he like trying new roads?
Branching out . . . being . . . inquisitive?

ELSA: This isn't fair. . . .

WILL: What is it? I'd really like to give it a try. . . .

ELSA: What are you talking about?

WILL: Your number. What is it? I'll give you a ring, huh?
Here. Write it down. . . .

[*He throws a piece of chalk at her. She takes it and writes*

her number in huge letters on the asphalt.
She stands; her attitude changed, composed.]

ELSA: I should call a cop!

WILL: [*Pauses.*] You invited it. [*Pauses.*] You forget so
    soon? A week ago, Park Square, outside the Greyhound
    station. [*Smiles.*] I couldn't believe my goddam eyes!
    [*Pauses; attitude changed now.*] You forget? Ahhhh,
    that's too bad. [*Leans in; he is quite angry.*] I just got
    off the bus. Still carrying my suitcases. You were leaning
    against the building . . . with the others . . . a real pro,
    huh? Wicked awful tough.

ELSA: You're crazy!

WILL: Oh, yuh, really crazy. [*Pauses.*] You smiled, I smiled.

ELSA: I never saw you outside of any bus station! What the
    hell are you talking about?

WILL: Who was he?
    [*No reply.*]

WILL: *Who was he?*

ELSA: Who was who?

WILL: Answer me who were you waiting for?

ELSA: You're making this all up!

WILL: [*Yells.*] *Come off the shit!*

ELSA: Okay, fine. That's what you need. That's what you
    get! I don't know who he was! Just somebody passing
    through! Okay.

WILL: "Somebody passing through"? What the hell is *that*
    s'posed ta mean?

ELSA: It just means . . . somebody. [*Turns to him; sud-
    denly.*] *I have to have somebody!*

WILL: You could leave.

ELSA: I can't.

WILL: *I* did.

ELSA: But you're back! How come?

WILL: Just passing through, believe me. Nothing here that
    interests me enough to stay in this jerk town.

ELSA: I loathe you.

WILL: You're really a tramp, aren't you? I mean, when you
    get right down to the bottom of things, you just whore
    around, don't you? Isn't that right?
    [*No reply.*]

WILL: How many?

ELSA: [*Yells.*] How many what?

WILL: [*Same volume.*] How many men? How many men do you have to have?

ELSA: [*Spits her words.*] As many as I can get! [*She plays again.*] My husband . . . he went to Baptist Clergy Council meeting in Worcester, to give a speech on family planning. Family planning . . . that's his specialty. He likes to use Peter Pan buses instead of driving, gives him time to study his notes. He likes his speeches perfect. [*Silence.*]

WILL: Your mother . . . how'd she die?

ELSA: She just did.

WILL: That's no answer. . . .

ELSA: What's the goddam difference to you, huh?

WILL: I'd like to know. . . .

ELSA: She's *my* mother, not yours!

WILL: I'd like to know.

ELSA: You shoulda stuck around! You woulda known!

WILL: Elsa. . . .

ELSA: Fourteen years! Nothing! Not a word! You marry me on a Tuesday and by Friday you're gone! Not a call, not even a pigeon with a note, not even a bottle floating in the lake with a message. Fourteen years and not a word. [*Pauses.*] *Nothing! What do you want?*

WILL: Want?

ELSA: Here? Now? What do you want?

WILL: A look.

ELSA: A look? Okay, fine: look! [*She spins once around; faces him again.*] You had your look. Now leave!

WILL: I don't know anybody here anymore, just you. . . .

ELSA: [*Screams.*] *Join a club!*

WILL: Elsa, please. . . . [*He reaches for her. She pulls away, slapping his face, sharply.*]

ELSA: Don't you *for Jesus Christ's sake! ever* put your hands on me again!

WILL: I was seventeen!

ELSA: I was sixteen!

WILL: I'm sorry.

ELSA: You've got no *right* to be sorry. [*Faces him.*] Sixteen years old and pregnant and terrified and you just fucking leave me here to . . . to *what*? To die? To what? What did you figure I was gonna do? Run the bank? Drink the lake? I'm really curious, Wilbur. I really am!

WILL: I was seventeen. I was scared.

ELSA: How about when you were nineteen? How about when you were twenty-five? How about when you were twenty-seven? [*Pauses.*] I'll tell you what's really on my mind right now, Wilbur . . . what's really right on the tip of my tongue as I stand here lookin' at you face to face. . . . [*Clearly*] I wasted so much of my time worrying about you and you're nothing! I've had dozens more interesting boys than you right here in town. Practically *all* of them!

WILL: Shut it up, now, okay? [*He moves away.*]

ELSA: Can't take it, huh? [*She chases him.*]

WILL: I don't give a fat shit about you *or* your boys. . . .

ELSA: I gave yours away.

WILL: What's *that* tidbit s'pose'ta mean? [*He stands his ground.*]

ELSA: I was pregnant, remember? [*Pauses.*] Did you forget? I gave it away.

WILL: Boy or girl?

ELSA: Which d'ya want it ta be?

WILL: Don't be stupid!

ELSA: But I am!

WILL: Elsa!

ELSA: Boy?

WILL: Boy?

ELSA: Girl!

WILL: Which?

ELSA: Both. Twins. Triplets. A litter! I had a litter! You shoulda stuck around. It was quite a show. . . .

WILL: Listen to me—

ELSA: Nope. Sorry. . . .

WILL: Listen to me!

ELSA: Nope.

WILL: *Listen to me!* If you had a son . . .

ELSA: [*Quickly; correcting him.*] Daughter!

WILL: *Listen!* If you had a son . . . and he were seventeen . . . and he got a local girl knocked up . . . and he could either stay here and . . . be married to her . . . or he could get the hell outa Wakefield! . . . *which would you want him to do???*

ELSA: [*She lunges at him. He throws her down onto the hopscotch grid.*] You filthy rotten son of a bitch!

WILL: Elsa, listen!

ELSA: You filthy rotten bastard!

WILL: Elsa!

ELSA: There's no son! I killed it! I couldn't take his crying. I couldn't take his noise. [*Pauses.*] He had your face. That's what I *really* couldn't stand. . . . That's what I *really* couldn't take. He was you! [*Pauses.*] It's true. [*There is a long pause—as he stares at her.*]

WILL: I didn't make a mistake at all, did I? I did just the right thing, didn't I? [*Pauses; then suddenly*] I think you're a *monster!*

ELSA: Swell. Great. That's just great. Is that what you came back here for? To tell me that?

WILL: [*Touches baby carriage.*] Whose is this?

ELSA: It's not mine. You said that, not me. It probably belongs to somebody young. Town's full of young families. The town's crawling with young families.

WILL: I'm sorry about your mother and father. I really am. . . .

ELSA: Save it, okay?

WILL: I'd hoped to see them . . . to talk to them. . . .

ELSA: To what? To get them to forgive you? They didn't. They never would've, believe you me. [*Pauses.*] That's a fact.

WILL: I would've liked to have tried to explain. . . .

ELSA: Hey, listen, be my guest. Try. Explain. They're buried right over there in Lakeside. You know the spot, don't you? Right next to yours. . . .

WILL: I never guessed you'd still be so . . . involved.

ELSA: Now what's that s'pose'ta mean, hmmm?

WILL: You just seem so . . . involved . . . with me. Still so passionate. . . .

ELSA: You're really unbelievable, Will. You were an unbelievable kid and you ran away and saw the world and grew up and now you're back here and I can see you've become just an unbelievable middle-aged adult. It's all just unbelievable. [*Pauses.*] I'm really happy to see the way you've turned out . . . to see what a stupid little asshole you turned out to be. . . . [*She sits.*] I can see exactly what you are. I . . . am . . . so . . . lucky. [*Suddenly*] *I wish you were dead!*
[*There is a substantial silence.*

WILL *moves to her, faces her, but cannot touch her.*
She stands facing him.
He is suddenly eloquent; precise. He is somewhat aloof.]
WILL: I'm getting married. [*Pauses.*] I've met a girl. She's
very nice. I think you'll like her. [*Pauses.*] I've decided
to stop . . . you know . . . moving around. [*Pauses.*]
I'm coming back. [*Suddenly angry*] We're settling here.
. . . Home. [*Pauses. Yells.*] Aren't you going to say anything? [*Pauses. No reply.*] We'll talk. I'll call you. [*Moves
away from her, stops; turns and faces her from new dis-
tant position.*] I'm sorry it's so . . . awkward . . . so awkward between us . . . still. [*Pauses.*] I was sure you'd
. . . well . . . you'd understand. [*He moves away from
her, to edge of stage, at point from which he entered
play. He stops there a moment, silently. Then he speaks,
angrily.*] I never played hopscotch with you! I don't know
what the hell you think you're doing!
[*He exits the play.*
*The music fades in. (Note: Paul Simon song cued to lyric
"Her name was Lorali" through end of song.)*
ELSA *sits on bench, alone, in front of her name and the
heart and arrow. Graffiti written with her yellow chalk,
all around; her telephone number, his name. She looks
at the marks on her hopscotch grid; she is weeping.*
Music plays to completion. She bows her head.
Lights fade, with music.]

THE PLAY IS OVER.

Wakefield, New York City, Paris, Gloucester—
October 1973–August 1978

The Wakefield Plays, Part II

———— •·• ————

THE 75TH
A Play in One Act

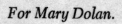

For Mary Dolan.

The People of the Play

AMY CHAMBERLAIN: Thin, well-groomed, attractive, ninety-three.

ARTHUR "COOKIE" SILVERSTEIN: Tall, thin, well-groomed, handsome, ninety-three.

The Place of the Play

Small private dining room in restaurant overlooking Lake Quannapowitt, Wakefield, Massachusetts.

The Time of the Play

September, evening.

A Note on the Music

John Hall's song "Still the One" should be used to start, interrupt, and conclude the play. The music source should be the onstage jukebox. Note: "Still the One" is recorded by Hall's group, Orleans.

Darkness in auditorium.

Up-tempo popular music is heard at substantial volume.

Garish lights of coin-operated jukebox switch on, revealing jukebox onstage.

A human figure, back to audience, leans over front of machine, thumping same with her hands.

It should appear that figure is beating time to rhythm of music.

Lights to soft glow, revealing section of small-town small restaurant. Figure is woman, AMY CHAMBERLAIN. *She is extremely old, thin. She wears a long overcoat. Her back is still to auditorium, but it has become evident that she is trying to stop jukebox from playing. She is now kicking the machine, as well as beating same with her hands.*

There are two round tables onstage: four small chairs surround each. Stage otherwise clear.

AMY: [*Yells.*] *How d'ya stop this goddam racket??* [*She kicks machine again; nothing happens.*]
   [AMY *moves to table, chooses chair, removes coat, folds same over back of chair; sits.*
   She looks about for a waiter. There is none.
   Another record begins to play on jukebox. This one is even louder and more raucous than the first.
   AMY *is amazed.*]
AMY: *Anybody here??? This music is a bit sonorous.*
   [*No response.*]
AMY: [*She stands and moves to jukebox, kicks and whacks same several times.*] *Hello!* [*She looks about for ladies' room; sees door. She exits, leaving her coat on chair.*]
   [*The stage is empty awhile, but for furniture, jukebox and coat.*
   The music continues.
   ARTHUR "COOKIE" SILVERSTEIN *enters. He is, like* AMY, *nearly ancient. He, too, wears a long overcoat. He carries brown bag.*
   He looks about the room and, seeing no one, moves to jukebox and tries to stop same from playing loud music. Unable to stop same, he kicks machine and soon begins to whack same with hands and brown bag.
   Music continues.
   SILVERSTEIN *goes to second table and removes coat, sets down brown paper bag, folds coat over back of chair, and sits in chair next to coat.*
   He searches through brown bag and removes rolled banner.
   He stands, goes to jukebox, carrying rolled banner. He kicks jukebox several times.
   He yells.]

COOKIE: *Anybody here???* [*No response; he continues to kick jukebox.*] *Anybody know how to shut this goddam thing off???* [*He screams now.*] THIS IS OFFEN-SIVE!!! . . .

[*Music ends abruptly, as song is completed.* COOKIE's *scream is now in the clear.*]

COOKIE: *I SAID THAT THIS IS OFFENSIVE!!!* . . . [*Realizes his screams have not been covered by music.*] . . . Thank you very much. Thank you.

[*Looks about room. Sees he is still alone.*

He fastens banner to wall, after unrolling same. Lettering on banner reads:

WELCOME 75TH

He stands back and looks at banner.

AMY's *coat catches his eye. He walks to same and touches it, then lifts it to look at it closely.*

AMY *pokes her head onto stage again. Watches a moment.*]

AMY: Alan Roberto?

COOKIE: [*Turns and faces her.*] Eleanor Fritz!

AMY: No.

COOKIE: Me, neither. . . .

AMY: Frank Lazzaro?

COOKIE: I'm not Italian. . . .

AMY: Oh, my God! Jimmy Kiley!

COOKIE: Nope! [*Pauses.*] Annie MacGlennon!

AMY: Not at all. . . . Edgar Lancing?

COOKIE: Nope.

AMY: Philly Drinkwater?

COOKIE: Nope.

AMY: Wilbur Lynch?

COOKIE: He's dead.

AMY: I thought not. [*Pauses.*] Are you Wakefield High?

COOKIE: Yup.

AMY: Don't tell me. Let me guess. [*Smiles.*] You wouldn't be Hannah's cousin Adrian?

COOKIE: Right. I wouldn't be.

AMY: Everybody else is . . . well . . . accounted for, in terms of men.

COOKIE: Silverstein.

AMY: A what?

COOKIE: Silverstein. Arthur Silverstein.

28 Israel Horovitz

AMY: I'm sorry . . .
COOKIE: *Cookie* Silverstein . . .
AMY: Oh, of course, *Cookie* Silverstein! That's you!
COOKIE: [*Smiling*] Yup.
AMY: Cookie!
COOKIE: And you're . . . ?
AMY: Amy.
COOKIE: Amy?
AMY: Chamberlain . . .
COOKIE: Amy *Chamb*erlain!
   [*There is a pause in which they both smile at each other.*]
AMY: I don't think I remember you at all.
COOKIE: Nor I you.
AMY: Where did you live?
COOKIE: In high school? Elm Street.
AMY: Elm Street? West Side?
COOKIE: Elm Street. Runs up from the tracks on North
   Avenue all the way to Reading. . . .
AMY: Well, I know that. It's just that . . . well . . . I know
   everybody on Elm Street and . . . Silverstein?
COOKIE: Cookie!
AMY: I beg your pardon?
COOKIE: Me. Cookie. That's my name.
AMY: Well, listen, at my age, why do I doubt *any*thing?
   [*Pauses.*] Silverstein, you say?
COOKIE: Silverstein. My father was Samuel Silverstein . . .
   the mover. . . . He had his shop in Medford and another
   one later in Stoneham. Silverstein the Mover. You re-
   member?
AMY: Well, listen. At my age. [*After a pause*] How have
   you been?
COOKIE: Oh, very well, very well.
AMY: Cookie?
COOKIE: Cookie.
AMY: What an odd name for a boy!
COOKIE: You were up Lynnfield way, right?
AMY: When?
COOKIE: High school.
AMY: No. We were up the park. West Side. Parker Road,
   in fact. . . .
COOKIE: Parker Road?
AMY: Number twenty-seven. . . .

COOKIE: White house with green trim.

AMY: Yellow. Bright yellow.

COOKIE: There's no yellow house I can remember on Parker. . . .

AMY: There was a Taffy.

COOKIE: A taffy *house?*

AMY: Taffy *Turner*. But never a Cookie. . . . [*Pause.*] Tuffy, I mean. Tuffy Puddle! You remember?

COOKIE: Do I remember Tuffy Puddle? Do I remember Tuffy Puddle? Didn't we play together every day on the West Ward hill?

AMY: You did?

COOKIE: Every day.

AMY: Tuffy.

COOKIE: Tuffy.

AMY: Wonderfully good-natured boy . . .

COOKIE: Salt of the earth . . .

AMY: Never wanted much . . .

COOKIE: Never got much . . .

AMY: What became of Tuffy?

COOKIE: Tuffy? [*Pauses.*] Dunno. . . . [*Pauses.*] Probably quite successful.

AMY: No doubt. [*She pauses; sits. Leans back.*] Just us?

COOKIE: I suspect so.

AMY: How many were we?

COOKIE: Then? [*Pauses.*] Eighty-one.

AMY: Eighty-one?

COOKIE: *If* we count the Reilly girl. . . .

AMY: Carol?

COOKIE: Her sister: Helen.

AMY: Why wouldn't we count Helen?

COOKIE: She never actually graduated with us—with our class. She had . . . trouble.

AMY: Ah, yes. [*Pauses.*] What sort of trouble?

COOKIE: Family.

AMY: With her family?

COOKIE: Excuse me?

AMY: She had trouble with her family?

COOKIE: Who?

AMY: Helen Reilly? Family trouble?

COOKIE: Family *way*: she was in it.

AMY: Ah, yes. Did we know the father?

COOKIE: There was none.

AMY: There *had* to be one. There always is. . . .

COOKIE: Not from us: from our graduating class. [*Pauses.*] She always turned her affection away from our year. Either above us or beneath us. [*Pauses.*] She was fond of my brother.

AMY: Was she?

COOKIE: Very fond. You might even say she was *keen* on him.

AMY: Was she?

COOKIE: *He* said so. . . . [*Pauses.*] I suppose she was. [*Pauses.*] He was a full head taller than me.

AMY: Was he?

COOKIE: I can vouch for that myself. A full head. Two years younger, too. One of those flukes of genetics. . . .

AMY: I'm sure.

COOKIE: My entire family was flukish, genetically speaking.

AMY: Were they?

COOKIE: Not my mother and father. They were normal. I mean, who *knows* if they were? It's just that the genetic fluke I'm speaking of was found out in their children: me and my brothers and sister.

AMY: Bald?

COOKIE: Short.

AMY: Really?

COOKIE: I was nearly a foot shorter than my younger brother. . . .

AMY: Helen Reilly's friend?

COOKIE: Right. Him. And he was nearly a head taller than me, but a foot shorter than my father. . . .

AMY: That would make you a head and a foot shorter than your father. . . .

COOKIE: At the minimum.

AMY: That *is* strange!

COOKIE: Oh, yes. A fluke. My sister, poor thing, she was incredibly short.

AMY: Was she?

COOKIE: Nearly a legal midget.

AMY: *Was* she?

COOKIE: Becky—poor Becky . . . incredibly short, really. . . .

AMY: Little Becky Roberto?

COOKIE: Excuse me?

AMY: Was that the way we knew your sister?

COOKIE: Little Becky Silverstein.

AMY: I don't think so.

COOKIE: I *know* so!

AMY: I don't think I remember her. . . .

COOKIE: Couldn'ta forgot her, once you saw her. Tiny little thing, but very well formed, for her size and all. Very attractive to the multitude of men here in town. . . .

AMY: Was she?

COOKIE: Oh, very much so. The Lazzaro boys couldn't keep their hands off her. . . . [*Pauses; embarrassed.*] . . . I hope you pardon my bein' so blunt.

AMY: Oh, well. Times have changed, haven't they?

COOKIE: And for the better, too, I'd have to say!

AMY: I knew the Lazzaro family quite well. Funny, you should mention them in relation to your poor stunted sister.

COOKIE: They lived close by. On Eustis Avenue. . . .

AMY: They did indeed. And I on Parker. Number twenty-seven. . . .

COOKIE: And we were thirty-three Elm. [*Smiles.*] You place us now, do you?

AMY: I suppose.

COOKIE: It was an enormous gray house with a Dutch-shaped roof. My uncle built it for my grandfather. . . . [*Smiles.*] Very wealthy.

AMY: Your grandfather?

COOKIE: My uncle.

AMY: Your *grandfather* lived in Wakefield?

COOKIE: Born here. Same house as me.

AMY: Native Wakefieldians?

COOKIE: We were very nearly Yankees . . . *Puritans*, almost.

AMY: Goldstein?

COOKIE: Silverstein.

AMY: And your sister married a Lazzaro?

COOKIE: Excuse me?

AMY: Your sister married a Lazzaro. You said that. Am I getting it bollixed up? I do that. . . .

COOKIE: Oh, not bollixed badly. You're very close to what

I said. [*Smiles.*] I said, my sister Becky was tremendously bothered by the Lazzaro brothers' sexual advances to her body. . . .

AMY: Was she?

COOKIE: Something terrible!

AMY: I am simply amazed! Simply amazed! *Sexual?*

COOKIE: With their hands.

AMY: I don't completely understand. . . .

COOKIE: [*He gestures with his hands.*] While walking . . . on the street . . . their hands!

AMY: In an acrobatic fashion, you mean?

COOKIE: No, you've made a major bollix of it now. Now you have. [*Pauses.*] My sister, the stunted one, was tremendously bothered by the Lazzaro boys fondling her breasts when she took walks. . . .

AMY: *Are you serious???*

COOKIE: Deadly so.

AMY: I am simply amazed!

COOKIE: Italians.

AMY: I am simply amazed.

COOKIE: So was she, the first dozen or so gropes. . . .

AMY: I can well imagine!

COOKIE: It made her a bit frightened to take walks. . . .

AMY: Which brother in particular?

COOKIE: All of them.

AMY: There were five or six. . . .

COOKIE: Six. And we suspected the father as well. . . .

AMY: You *can't* be serious???

COOKIE: Is the Pope Catholic?

AMY: He certainly is!

COOKIE: Then there you are.

AMY: I would have to say shocked and amazed. I am simply shocked and amazed. . . .

COOKIE: Sorry to have brought it up. . . .

AMY: Not at all. These things are good to know. . . . [*Pauses.*] Which brother, in particular? Did she say?

COOKIE: It was always difficult for her to be sure. . . . She bein' so short . . .

AMY: . . . and they bein' so tall!

COOKIE: Exactly.

AMY: Poor little thing.

COOKIE: It was horrible . . . for her . . . first dozen or so times . . . until she learned.

AMY: To stop them?

COOKIE: Opposite. To just let them do it. [*Pauses; tight-lipped.*] It was the only way. [*Pauses.*] Get it over with, quickly.

AMY: I am simply beside myself.

COOKIE: As were we all.

AMY: Why, do you suppose, am I hearing this for the first time?

COOKIE: Oh, well, you can understand *that*. . . .

AMY: I suppose I can. . . .

COOKIE: You knew the Lazzaro family well then, did you?

AMY: Well, my God! Not *that* well!

COOKIE: I wasn't insinuating.

AMY: Of course not. I'm just a bit shaken from the news.

COOKIE: Oh, Christ, it was more than sixty years ago. . . .

AMY: I suppose, but the sting's still there. . . . [*Pauses; smiles.*] I had quite a crush on a Lazzaro. You might even say I was . . . you know . . .

COOKIE: Keen?

AMY: Oh, that, too. . . .

COOKIE: Which one of them?

AMY: Alan.

COOKIE: Alan?

AMY: He pitched a no-hitter against Reading . . . and a one-hitter against Melrose.

COOKIE: Of course, Alan . . . the pitcher. [*Pauses.*] I remember him well . . . Lefty. Left-handed, right? [*Pauses.*] Oh, I don't think Alan hardly groped her at all. . . . Maybe once or twice, just to keep up the family image, but that's all.

AMY: I shouldn't think so. Alan wasn't very happy in that family.

COOKIE: You don't say?

AMY: Couldn't wait to leave town.

COOKIE: Did he?

AMY: For the war.

COOKIE: Of course.

AMY: Came back very well decorated, too.

COOKIE: I think I'd heard that. . . .

AMY: But never really happy again. . . .

COOKIE: Did you see him?

AMY: Excuse me?

COOKIE: *Date* him, I suppose you'd say?

AMY: Oh, no. [*Pauses.*] An occasional dance. A walk . . .
[*There is a pause.*] He was quite tall. A six-footer, I think.

COOKIE: Oh, I don't think so. Not Alan Lazzaro. Maybe
Angelo . . .

AMY: Really, Mr. Silverstein, I should know. . . .

COOKIE: Cookie.

AMY: Oh, no, thank you . . . stuffed.

COOKIE: My name. My name is Cookie.

AMY: Your given name?

COOKIE: Nick.

AMY: This is very confusing.

COOKIE: My given name is Arthur. My nickname is Cookie.
[*Smiles.*] I prefer Cookie. I don't know why. It suits
me. . . .

AMY: I wish I could say I remember you. I don't.

COOKIE: May I be truthful?

AMY: I wish you would.

COOKIE: I don't remember you, either.

AMY: But that's just ridiculous!

COOKIE: But it's the truth!

AMY: I was a cheerleader, for goodness' sake!

COOKIE: You were?

AMY: K.

COOKIE: You were K?

AMY: Senior year. I was L, junior year. . . .

COOKIE: [*Trying to remember*] L, junior year . . . K, senior
year . . . [*Squinting now*] K, K, K . . .

AMY: Martha Beebe was W. . . .

COOKIE: Carol what's'ername was A. . . .

AMY: And I was K!

COOKIE: I can do no more than draw a blank on K. . . .
[*Pauses.*] Christ! [*Squints. He visualizes and points to
each imagined cheerleader in line, on the air between
him and* AMY.] W . . . A . . . a blank . . . E . . . F . . .
I . . . E . . . L . . . [*Remembers*] Let's just wait a minute! L! Junior year! [*Sings, to melody of "My Old Ken-
tucky Home"*] "Oh, the moon shines bright . . ." [*Points
to* AMY, *who completes the song by singing the final line.*]

AMY: ". . . on my Quannapowitt home." [*She laughs.*] You remember!

COOKIE: [*Laughing as well*] Ah, yes. You were L . . .

AMY: Between E and D . . .
[*They both laugh.*]

COOKIE: Elaine Hawkins was E, and Maud what's'ername was D. . . .

AMY: [*Stops laughing.*] Not at all. . . .

COOKIE: Huh?

AMY: Not at all! It was Maud Anderson and she was a majorette, not a cheerleader. Elaine Hawkins was neither a cheerleader nor a majorette. She was quite hefty, if I recall correctly.

COOKIE: [*Stunned*] Christ! She was more than hefty! She was a battleship. . . .

AMY: Could you please not use that expletive?

COOKIE: What?

AMY: I've never taken to people just saying "Christ!" like Christ was just a word. I'm sorry.

COOKIE: Oh, God! I'm really sorry.

AMY: No, *I'm* sorry. I don't mean to embarrass you. . . .

COOKIE: I'm embarrassed. . . .

AMY: There, you see? [*Pauses.*] I'm sorry. I apologize. [*Looks about the room.*] Where are the others?

COOKIE: The others?

AMY: There are supposed to be twelve of us. Alice and Rosemary Simon . . .

COOKIE: Oh, no . . .

AMY: What?

COOKIE: There's just us, I think. . . .

AMY: No, there are twelve of us. [*Looks for her coat and pocketbook.*] There's a letter with the ticket. . . .

COOKIE: It's from me.

AMY: There's a list in with the ticket: those lost, those . . . well . . . gone . . . and those found. There are twelve of us.

COOKIE: I sent the letter.

AMY: Rosemary . . . [*Hears.*] You what? You sent the letter?

COOKIE: I did.

AMY: Oh. [*Pauses.*] Did you? [*Finds letter by now and looks at it.*] Arthur "Cookie" . . . [*Looks at* COOKIE.] You?

COOKIE: Me.

AMY: Then you should know. About the others. . . .

COOKIE: I do.

AMY: *All* of them?

COOKIE: Our class had a bad year. [*There is a silence.*] One of the worst.

AMY: Rosemary?

COOKIE: Car wreck. Horrible.

AMY: A car wreck? At her age?

COOKIE: Ironical.

AMY: I should say. Rosemary?

COOKIE: Route one-twenty-eight, down near the Manchester exit in North Beverly. [*Smiles.*] Read it in the *Globe*. A very nice-sized notice.

AMY: Large?

COOKIE: Oh, very large. Excellently thought out, too. At least *I* thought so.

AMY: Well, then. I can just stop waiting for the others, can't I?

COOKIE: I was quite relieved to find you here. I didn't get your form back.

AMY: I don't understand.

COOKIE: There was a personal history form. I didn't get yours back.

AMY: Were you a class officer?

COOKIE: Me? [*Laughs.*] No.

AMY: I should think not. [*Pauses.*] Oh. Not to cast any insinuendos, but I do remember our officers. . . .

COOKIE: John and Janette . . .

AMY: Lovely couple . . .

COOKIE: Did they date?

AMY: John and Janette? Oh, more than that. They married.

COOKIE: Did they?

AMY: They reunited at our own reunion. It was a beautiful thing to see.

COOKIE: I can imagine. . . .

AMY: Dancing, cheek to cheek and all. . . . It was our fortieth. . . .

COOKIE: I missed that one.

AMY: His first marriage, her fourth, I believe. . . .

COOKIE: They must have been fifty-five, maybe fifty-six.

AMY: Fifty-eight.

COOKIE: Must have been.

AMY: Precisely.

COOKIE: I was off fighting. . . .

AMY: For whom?

COOKIE: For us! For whom? Whom did you think? There was no time for me to be dancing cheek to cheek, I'll tell you that!

AMY: That old and fighting still?

COOKIE: I reenlisted after the Second War. . . .

AMY: Did you?

COOKIE: I was piss and vinegar. . . Ex*cuse* me!

AMY: Not at all. Don't you worry. . . .

COOKIE: I missed our fortieth. . . . Couldn't get the weekend. I remember it well. . . .

AMY: You would have won "Traveled Longest Distance." . . .

COOKIE: Oh, no. I was just up at Devens. . . .

AMY: England?

COOKIE: Fitchburg. Fort Devens. Out route two, west, past Concord, Acton, through Ayer, Shirley and into Leominster, where you pick up twelve–north, into. . . .

AMY: [*Interrupts him; completes his list.*] Fitchburg.

COOKIE: Not much of a town.

AMY: Never was.

COOKIE: I tried for the weekend, but I couldn't get it. Paid for my tickets, too. . . .

AMY: Tickets, were they? In the plural?

COOKIE: Married, no children. Married late for children. She was sixty. . . .

AMY: Local girl?

COOKIE: No. Gloucester. A spinster, but very nice. Taught English . . . at the O'Malley School, the junior high. . . . A Gloucester spinster.

AMY: *I* taught English. . . .

COOKIE: Oh, I didn't mean . . . [*Pauses; embarrassed.*] Nothing wrong with not marrying. I think not-marrying is a fine institution!

[*He laughs; pleased by his small joke. No response at all from* AMY.]

COOKIE: That was a play on words.

AMY: I married twice.

COOKIE: Did you?

AMY: Once to a Frenchman and once to a Californian.

COOKIE: You've seen the world, then, haven't you?

AMY: I have some memories.

COOKIE: Sounds like it. Sounds like it. [*Smiles.*] In France, then, with the Frenchman?

AMY: Providence.

COOKIE: Ah, yes. Rhode Island French. Quite a few of them in Providence, aren't there?

AMY: Oh, thousands. Even still. . . .

COOKIE: Children?

AMY: No.

COOKIE: Neither time?

AMY: No.

COOKIE: *There's* something in common, then . . . between us, I mean.

AMY: Yes.

[*There is a silence.*]

COOKIE: Do you remember Evelyn whosis?

AMY: Who could forget?

COOKIE: She won the award for "The Most Children" every reunion. Nobody could catch up.

AMY: Catholics.

COOKIE: Insanely so, I'd say. . . .

AMY: She stayed in town, didn't she?

COOKIE: Married a Lynch.

AMY: Never moved from town, did they? Even after that awful scandal. They never moved.

COOKIE: They couldn't, could they? Fourteen screaming children all around them all the time. . . .

AMY: Shocking way to waste your time!

COOKIE: I agree.

AMY: Cleaning noses . . .

COOKIE: Wiping up spilled milk . . .

AMY: Packing lunches . . .

COOKIE: Sunday meals . . .

AMY: Telephone calls from long distance . . .

COOKIE: Tragedy befalling . . .

AMY: [*After a pause*] Yes. That would've be'n the worst. [*There is a silence.*]

AMY: Who wins the award for "Distance Traveled," then? You or me?

COOKIE: I'm down from Burlington. . . .

AMY: Vermont?

COOKIE: No, Burlington . . .

AMY: Just up here? [*He nods.*] Burlington's only four miles from here.

COOKIE: As the crow . . . you know . . .

AMY: . . . flies?

COOKIE: Flies. [*Looks down; embarrassed.*] I did live once, for a month, in D.C. . . . [*Pauses.*] But that was a hotel. Hotels don't really count. [*Pauses.*] Very little traveling done. I guess I never wanted to, because, I . . . well . . . I didn't. [*Looks up.*] You?

AMY: What?

COOKIE: In from the Coast?

AMY: Oh, no. He passed on almost immediately after we married. [*Pauses.*] Very soon after. [*Pauses.*] Within the week, in fact.

COOKIE: Did he?

AMY: Very sudden.

COOKIE: Tragic business. Heart?

AMY: Lungs. They both collapsed. . . .

COOKIE: Simultaneously?

AMY: Spontaneously, as well.

COOKIE: Tragic business. No warning?

AMY: He coughed.

COOKIE: Not much warning in a cough. . . .

AMY: One never knows.

COOKIE: That's the truth.

AMY: I had a great deal of trouble locating his family. [*Pauses.*] I'd not yet actually met them. [*Pauses.*] Californians.

COOKIE: You mentioned that.

AMY: We were living up Stoneham way. . . .

COOKIE: Were you?

AMY: Do you know Gould Street?

COOKIE: Near the junk shop?

AMY: Scrap yard.

COOKIE: Oh, yes, I do. I'm very interested in that. . . .

AMY: In junk?

COOKIE: In the phenomenon. . . .

AMY: I don't completely understand. . . .

COOKIE: Those of us who move away . . . far away . . . from birthplaces . . . and those of us who . . . you know . . . don't.

AMY: Ah, yes, I see. [*Smiles.*] I've always quite liked it here. . . .

COOKIE: As do I.

AMY: Never saw the need to move about. . . .

COOKIE: Nor I. . . .

AMY: I've had my work. . . .

COOKIE: Teaching English?

AMY: Precisely.

COOKIE: In Stoneham?

AMY: Not for a while. Not since my retirement. Oh, I still live there. I just no longer teach.

COOKIE: [*Smiles.*] Well, it looks as though I win. I must say, this is a surprising victory. . . .

AMY: I would call it a tie myself. . . .

COOKIE: Nonsense. In order to reach Burlington, you have to pass through Stoneham *and* Woburn. . . . [*Smiles; shrugs.*] No question who wins "Longest Distance Traveled." . . .

AMY: *Longer* distance traveled.

COOKIE: I see. Yes.

AMY: If there were three of us, it could be longest. . . .

COOKIE: I remember that, now that you bring it up. [*Smiles.*] Do you remember Miss Caswell?

AMY: Remember her? She started me out!

COOKIE: All of us! Wonderful teacher, wonderful woman as well. . . .

AMY: On my career, I mean! I actually taught English!

COOKIE: Oh, yes. I see what you mean.

AMY: I remember the day she took me aside. [*Smiles. Imitates still older woman.*] "Amy Chamberlain, you have a talent." [*Pauses.*] "For what?" I asked. I was young. [*Pauses; smiles. Changes vocal pitch to older woman's timbre.*] "For teaching the language, its rules and uses." And she was right. . . .

COOKIE: Nearly always.

AMY: I do have a talent. . . .

COOKIE: A way with words. . . .

AMY: Do you think so?

COOKIE: Very certainly so.

AMY: Thank you . . . Cookie.

COOKIE: It's something I notice in an English-speaking person. . . .

AMY: You're very kind.

COOKIE: Would you have any interest in dancing?

AMY: The ballet?

COOKIE: With me.

AMY: Oh, I see. [*Smiles.*] It's been a while. [*Pauses.*] I would. Yes. I think we should. It's an occasion, after all. . . .

COOKIE: We're the seventy-fifth . . .

AMY: Together again . . .

COOKIE: We're the lucky ones . . .

AMY: I should say!

COOKIE: [*Fishing in his pockets*] Do you have a favorite? [*She stares at him blankly. He nods to jukebox.*]

COOKIE: Song?

AMY: I doubt if it's there.

COOKIE: You might be surprised.

AMY: "Don't Fence Me In."

COOKIE: Is it?

AMY: It is. Never known why. [*Sings.*]
"Give me land,
lots of land,
'Neath the starry skies above . . ."
[*Sings, with strong voice.*]
". . . Don't fence me innn . . ."

COOKIE: Let me have a look. . . .
[*He stands and moves to jukebox. She continues to sing song.*]

AMY:
"Let me wander over yonder,
Where the West commences . . .
I can't stand dah-dah and
I can't stand fences . . .
Till I da-dah da-dah . . ."

COOKIE: It's been years since I've played one of these things. . . . [*Jiggling coins; reading price*] My Christ! It's certainly risen from two-for-a-nickel, I'll tell you that!

AMY: [*Trying to remember*]
"I can't stand dah-dah . . .
and I can't stand fences . . ."
[*Pauses*] I've lost it! [*Sings again.*]
"Where the West commences . . .
I can't stand dah-dah and

I can't stand fences!"

[*To* COOKIE] Do you remember what comes in between
fences and *commences*?

COOKIE: [*Drops coin in slot and lights on machine flash
signal for him to choose a song.*] Let's just have a peek
here. . . . [*Puts on his eyeglasses.*] Right!

AMY: I've lost it completely.

[*Sings.*]

"Where the West commences . . ."

[*Speaks.*] Like a sieve . . . [*Sings.*]

"Where the West commences . . .

I can't stand dah-dah . . .

and I can't stand fences . . ."

[*Speaks.*] Well, that's gone now! All gone!

COOKIE: I don't see the song here. I'm afraid it's not on the
machine. . . .

AMY: It doesn't matter. . . .

COOKIE: It was so popular, too. . . .

AMY: Play anything you like. . . . Play one of *your* fa-
vorites. . . .

COOKIE: Mine? Oh, well, I never knew too much about
music. . . . [*Looks over selection list.*] I always admired
"Those Wedding Bells Are Breaking Up That Old Gang
of Mine."

AMY: Oh, good, then. Play that.

COOKIE: I don't see it.

AMY: [*Sings.*]

"Let me wander over yonder where the West commences
. . . I can't stand dah-dah / and I can't stand fences . . ."
[*Speaks.*] Gone!

COOKIE: I don't think it's here!

AMY: Surprise us, then!

COOKIE: You mean just pick any number that comes to
mind?

AMY: Certainly.

COOKIE: Oh, well, then . . . [*Smiles.*] Fifty cents.

AMY: For a song?

COOKIE: That's what it costs now.

AMY: It's all relative, isn't it?

COOKIE: Relative to what you've got, you mean. . . .

AMY: [*Smiles.*] That's very good, yes. [*Pauses.*] I've got my pension. I foxed them on that one, didn't I? Worked thirty years, pensioned for twenty-eight.

COOKIE: So far. . . .

AMY: Right! So far! They'll change the retirement dates one day when they smarten up, won't they?

COOKIE: I've been pensioned nearly forty-seven years now.

AMY: You're not serious?

COOKIE: Imagine if I'da quit at forty, like they wanted?

AMY: You went straight in after high school, did you?

COOKIE: Many of us did. Things were different then.

AMY: Never any thought of college?

COOKIE: College of Life and Hard Knocks. That's me. [*He smiles; she doesn't.*]

COOKIE: College of Life and Hard Knocks.

AMY: I suppose.

COOKIE: And you? Radcliffe, I suppose.

AMY: Smith.

COOKIE: [*Amazed*] Did you? I was making a joke there. I really thought you'd come back with "Salem Normal." I never dreamed you'd be comin' back with "Smith." [*Pauses.*] You've been beautifully educated, haven't you?

AMY: Miss Caswell's the wonder behind all that.

COOKIE: I'm sure she is. Wonderful woman. Wonderful teacher and a wonderful human being to boot. [*Pauses; suddenly upset.*] Oh, God!

AMY: What's the matter?

COOKIE: You remember old Mrs. Nicker . . . Warren School?

AMY: Fourth grade?

COOKIE: That's her.

AMY: Died when we were in fifth. . . .

COOKIE: *You* were Warren School, too?

AMY: Parker Road . . .

COOKIE: Do you remember old Nicker, then?

AMY: Certainly.

COOKIE: She had a problem with flatulency, so to speak. . . . [AMY *looks down.*]

COOKIE: Sorry. Anyway, you remember her?

AMY: Yes, of course. She died when I . . . we . . . were in the fifth. . . .

COOKIE: My fault.

AMY: What?

COOKIE: My fault. In fourth grade, I kicked her. Her leg never healed and she died from it. My fault. It was my fault.

AMY: You're not serious?

COOKIE: She took us out for recess. We were playing kick-ball, when the bell rang. I was up. I'd been waiting for my up about ten minutes, about half the recess. The pitcher pitched . . . I kicked . . . Miss Nicker stepped in to stop me from kicking and end the game. . . .

AMY: And you kicked her?

COOKIE: Kicked her? Damn near flew her into the trees!

AMY: You can't be serious?

COOKIE: Deadly so. She was in her grave within the year. Her leg never healed. I think they took it off before she finally went, nothing could've saved her. . . .

AMY: You've got it all wrong!

COOKIE: Would that I did!

AMY: But you do! She lived right next to us. . . .

COOKIE: Parker Road . . .

AMY: Right next to us. Twenty-nine!

COOKIE: That's a fact!

AMY: It was her stomach that killed her. Some sort of tumor. . . . They were Christian Scientists. I heard the screams for weeks. Terrible thing. I'll never forget.

COOKIE: Emily Nicker, fourth grade, H. M. Warren School?

AMY: Twenty-nine Parker Road. Flatulency problem . . . so to speak. . . .

COOKIE: My God!

AMY: I remember it like yesterday. . . .

COOKIE: All these years . . .

AMY: Poor old thing . . .

COOKIE: What a relief!

AMY: I can imagine! . . .

COOKIE: You can't. You really can't. . . . [Pauses.] I . . . am . . . so . . . relieved!

AMY: I'm very happy for you. . . .

COOKIE: I'd like very much to dance. Would you?

AMY: I wouldn't mind.

COOKIE: I say number six. How's that sound?

AMY: Fine.

COOKIE: [Inspecting machine] That doesn't seem to be the

way this works. Would you choose six-A, six-B, six-C, six-D, E, or F?

AMY: F.

COOKIE: Really? _

AMY: F.

COOKIE: [*Pushes buttons.*] Here goes.

[*Machine clicks into action.*

He goes to her.

She rises.

They assume ballroom dance position in each other's arms.

Up-tempo music crashes in, loudly.

They stare awhile at one another.

They attempt a few steps of a waltz. It is impossible.

AMY *sits.*

COOKIE *goes to machine and pushes all buttons, then kicks and whacks same.* AMY *stands, goes to machine, removes plug. Music and lights on machine fade out together.*]

COOKIE: I thought I would lose my senses! [*He is exhausted from whacking the machine. He leans against chair.*]

AMY: [*Suddenly screams.*] *That's it!*

COOKIE: [*Amazed; he sits at other table.*] What's it?

AMY: *Lose my senses!* [*Laughs.*] Isn't that ironical? Lose my senses?

COOKIE: I've missed the context, I think. . . .

AMY: It fits . . . between *commences* and *fences.* . . .

COOKIE: It does?

AMY: It rhymes. With *commences* and *fences. Commences, fences, lose my senses.*

COOKIE: There's rhyme there. That's true enough.

AMY: I . . . am . . . so . . . relieved.

COOKIE: Glad to have helped out. . . .

AMY: It's the biggest fear I have.

COOKIE: Fences?

AMY: [*Laughs; whoops.*] You are so *clever*, Cookie! You really are! [*Laughs.*] I haven't had a laugh like this in Christ knows how long! [*Laughs again; stops. Dries eyes.*] That was a good one.

COOKIE: [*Begins to laugh.*] I see. [*A deep laugh here.*] Whewwww!

AMY: [*She joins his laugh with her own.*] My sides!

COOKIE: Our sides!

[*They both whoop again with laughter, looking across the space from table to table at one another.*
The laughter ends.
They dry their eyes.
There is a silence. They are lost in a memory.]

AMY: [*Breaking the long, frozen silence*] How were your grades?

COOKIE: [*Quickly*] Not much.

AMY: Weren't they?

COOKIE: I didn't click into real concentration until . . . later on. . . . Later on in life.

AMY: Yes.

COOKIE: Your grades were excellent?

AMY: Quite good, yes.

COOKIE: B pluses and A minuses? That sort of thing?

AMY: Oh, yes. And then some.

COOKIE: Higher?

AMY: A bit.

COOKIE: A minuses and A's?

AMY: A's and A pluses, mostly.

COOKIE: Were you the . . . ?

AMY: No. . . .

COOKIE: I didn't think so. . . .

AMY: . . . Bruce B. Webber . . .

COOKIE: . . . I remember that. . . .

AMY: Every A I got, he got an A plus. Every A plus I got, he matched. . . .

COOKIE: Always higher . . .

AMY: On the average . . .

COOKIE: Must've bothered you. . . .

AMY: Not at all.

COOKIE: Must have.

AMY: Not any more. . . .

COOKIE: Course not. . . .

AMY: Sixty years now. . . .

COOKIE: Seventy-five!

AMY: Ah, yes. . . .

COOKIE: That's why we're here. . . .

AMY: Seventy-five . . . [*A pause.*] I remember being two.

COOKIE: Two years old?

AMY: I do. I have a memory. My mum . . . cuddling me.

COOKIE: Extraordinary mind you have.

AMY: Do you think so?

COOKIE: Oh, I do.

AMY: So much fed in.

COOKIE: Must be a burden. . . .

AMY: Old age is supposed to dull it all. . . .

COOKIE: Blend it together. . . .

AMY: Not I.

COOKIE: Me, neither. . . . [*Pauses.*] Hell of a burden. [*Smiles.*] Whatever became of him?

AMY: Bruce B. Webber?

COOKIE: I'd heard Tech. . . .

AMY: Tech?

COOKIE: MIT . . .

AMY: Oh, no! He quit there. . . .

COOKIE: Really?

AMY: Quit during his first year. They say he was failing . . .

COOKIE: His *health*?

AMY: His grades!

COOKIE: You're joking!

AMY: Small fish, big pond. . . . That sort of thing.

COOKIE: Bruce B. Webber? Failing? Doesn't seem possible, does it?

AMY: Smith girls often spent a weekend in Cambridge. Harvard or MIT. Clara Ellison, from Great Neck, Long Island, New York, dated Bruce B. Webber's brother Alfred, also a W.H.S. man. . . .

COOKIE: Poor Alfred.

AMY: Oh, yes. Poor Alfred, indeed. . . . You may remember . . .

COOKIE: Which of us could forget?

AMY: Clara brought the news of poor Alfred's brother, our own Bruce B. Webber. . . .

COOKIE: And he was in fact failing?

AMY: And despairing, too!

COOKIE: Not drinking as well?

AMY: I don't think so. . . . [*Pauses.*] Clara didn't mention any drinking. . . . [*Pauses.*] Perhaps . . .

COOKIE: Who would have guessed?

AMY: Small fish.

COOKIE: But you certainly did well at Smith. . . .

AMY: Quite well.

COOKIE: Same pond for both of you. . . .

AMY: That's true enough. [*Smiles.*] Lake Quannapowitt.

COOKIE: Terrible, the pollution formed in that lake in seventy-five years!

AMY: Do you take walks?

COOKIE: I do. I do.

AMY: I do, as well. . . .

COOKIE: Now, of course, with route one-twenty-eight cutting right into my property, it's . . . well . . . it's not as nice, not as relaxing.

AMY: Noise can bury you!

COOKIE: You needn't say *that* above a whisper, I can tell you that! [*Leans in.*] I've foxed them.

AMY: Mmm?

COOKIE: The route one-twenty-eight commission. I've foxed them. [*Looks around room before he speaks.*] I requested, procured, and installed an absolutely official, state-provided sign for the road at my property edge: "BLIND CHILD." [*Smiles.*] Isn't that wicked clever?

AMY: [*Smiles.*] Blind child?

COOKIE: [*Chortles awhile.*] Cut the noise to half. . . .

AMY: Really?

COOKIE: You can see the cars and trucks visibly lose speed the moment they see the sign. . . . Feet loosen right off their accelerators! [*He chortles again.*] I'm very proud of *that* idea!

AMY: Do you own a great deal of property?

COOKIE: A modest amount.

AMY: How lucky for you.

COOKIE: I planned.

AMY: Good for you!

COOKIE: I bought the original parcel back about forty years now. At the time I first bought, I insisted on taking options on five adjoining parcels. . . . [*Pauses.*] Or would I say "adjacent"?

AMY: You might. You might even say "contiguous." . . .

COOKIE: Ah, yes, contiguous parcels. That has a nice ring!

AMY: How clever of you! And you've managed to buy them all?

COOKIE: And then some.

AMY: Have you?

COOKIE: Twelve parcels in all.

AMY: My Lord!

COOKIE: It's an eyeful.

AMY: All near the highway, is it?

COOKIE: Oh, no. Just the tip of two. The bottom edges, you might say. . . .

AMY: I see.

COOKIE: I've got a pond. . . .

AMY: On your property?

COOKIE: It's very nice.

AMY: I love a small pond.

COOKIE: I wouldn't exactly call it a *small* pond. It's quite large. . . .

AMY: Really?

COOKIE: Half a mile across in width; three quarters of a mile in length. . . .

AMY: Sounds enormous!

COOKIE: Very pleasant, I should say.

AMY: I should think so!

COOKIE: Stocked with pickerel. . . .

AMY: Pickerel?

COOKIE: Pickerel are young pike. They like the deep, cool, fresh water. . . . [*Smiles.*] They're quite a large, long fish.

AMY: How marvelous for you!

COOKIE: [*He returns to her table; sits. He talks quickly, confidentially.*] A bit saved every year and, by the time you hit *my* age . . .

AMY: Not I.

COOKIE: I'm sorry. . . .

AMY: Never had a business head. . . .

COOKIE: But you've got your pension. . . .

AMY: Yes, that. But I never used it well. . . .

COOKIE: Do you own or rent?

AMY: Rent.

COOKIE: Oh, I see. [*Pauses.*] Renting can be nice.

AMY: Not the same as owning.

COOKIE: I know many a happy renter. . . .

AMY: I know a few. . . .

COOKIE: I know many an unhappy owner. . . .

AMY: Yes, I suppose. . . . [*Smiles.*] You have a very pleasant way.

COOKIE: Do you think so?

AMY: I do.

COOKIE: Well, aren't you nice to say it. . . .

[*There is a pause.*

COOKIE *reaches across the table and touches* AMY's *hand. She smiles.*

Tableau.

COOKIE *withdraws his hand.*

He smiles.]

COOKIE: Bruce B. Webber never impressed *me* much, I can tell you *that*!

AMY: Oh, I wouldn't sell him short. . . .

COOKIE: I don't. I don't. But he did have an arrogant streak!

AMY: You have to in this life. If you want to get ahead . . .

COOKIE: I don't agree!

AMY: I'm afraid it's true. . . .

COOKIE: And where did it get Mr. Bruce B. Webber? . . .

AMY: I suppose . . .

COOKIE: All that drinking and despairing! . . .

AMY: I suppose . . .

COOKIE: As if that family didn't have enough trouble and grief, with poor Alfred's untimely end. . . .

AMY: [*Shakes her head.*] There's no word invented for what that family did to Alfred L. Webber. . . . Not in Greek, not in Italian, probably not even in the Irish tongue. . . .

COOKIE: Were you friendly with Alfred?

AMY: . . . L. Webber? Yes, I suppose I should say yes. . . .

COOKIE: Were you close friends?

AMY: [*Pauses.*] Which of us was, really. He was so . . . well . . .

COOKIE: Odd?

AMY: Odd's too harsh. . . .

COOKIE: Despairing?

AMY: Yes, that too. And, of course, his problem . . .

COOKIE: The drinking . . .

AMY: Like a fish. . . .

COOKIE: Awful to see. . . .

AMY: Tried to stop him. . . .

COOKIE: I'm sure you did. . . .

AMY: Never could. . . .

COOKIE: [*After a pause*] You were *that* close, were you?

AMY: We took walks. In the afternoons. Not many, but they had quality. . . . [*Smiles.*] He knew the lake like a friend . . . the wildflowers . . . by name . . . butterflies . . . by name, as well . . . the trees . . . [*Pauses.*] He was the first to make me see the beauty of the old headstones. . . .

COOKIE: [*Amazed*] In the cemetery?

AMY: Can you imagine? I was squeamish at first. . . .

COOKIE: [*Increasingly amazed*] The headstones in the cemetery?

AMY: We made rubbings.

COOKIE: [*Shocked*] Of the headstones in the cemetery?

AMY: Some of them were quite beautiful. . . . Seventeenth-century. . . . Very early Wakefield families. . . .

COOKIE: This is a little difficult for me to follow. . . . [*He is clearly amazed.*] You and Alfred . . . together . . . took walks in the cemetery? . . . And made rubbings of tombstones?

AMY: Yes, we did.

COOKIE: Christ!

AMY: I know it sounds a bit odd. . . .

COOKIE: Odd? Weird, you mean.

AMY: Well, I . . .

COOKIE: [*Interrupting her*] My entire family's buried there. . . .

AMY: Not *that* cemetery.

COOKIE: Huh?

AMY: We did our rubbings in the other cemetery.

COOKIE: Oh, yes.

AMY: Near the Congo church. . . .

COOKIE: Back of the Hartshorne House. . . .

AMY: Precisely.

COOKIE: Alfred's as weird as they come.

AMY: [*Sudden anger, after a pause.*] I think we've carried this subject to a conclusion, Mr. Silverman. [*Pauses.*] I think this conversation of ours is . . . exhausted.

COOKIE: I didn't realize . . .

AMY: That we were close? [*Smiles.*] Yes, we were.

COOKIE: I'm really sorry.

AMY: I'm sure you are. [*Smiles.*] Alfred L. Webber was the gentlest man I have known in my entire ninety-three

years of knowing men . . . and I have known many, sir,
many. [*Pauses.*] I think we have touched, as they say, a
ticklish spot.

COOKIE: I'm really sorry, Miss Chamberlain. I hope you can
forgive me. . . .

AMY: I do. I do. . . . [*Pauses.*] I'm a bit overprotective with
my memories. . . .

COOKIE: I understand. . . .

AMY: So much of it has been so difficult. . . .

COOKIE: Tragedy befalling you, over and over again. . . .

AMY: [*Looks about room.*] Well . . . [*Smiles.*] I'm feeling a
bit tired. . . . [*Pauses.*] No one else expected. Just us,
I suppose. . . . [*Smiles.*] We didn't get an awful lot for
our money, did we?

COOKIE: Oh! I have your money! [*Reaches in his pocket;
finds check.*] Here!

AMY: Oh, not at all!

COOKIE: No, it's your check. I never cashed it. [*Pauses.*]
Please.

[*She takes check.*]

COOKIE: When you failed to return the form, I assumed
. . . [*Pauses.*] I only came myself on an outside chance
that someone . . . [*Smiles.*] I'm very pleased I did. . . .

AMY: [*Pocketing check*] Yes. As am I.

COOKIE: I didn't order a meal, because . . .

AMY: I understand. . . .

COOKIE: I canceled the caterer. . . .

AMY: There was a caterer?

COOKIE: Oh, yes. I thought there might be as many as ten
of us. . . .

AMY: Really?

COOKIE: Tragic year for our class. . . .

AMY: Perhaps next time . . .

COOKIE: What's that?

AMY: We'll keep the caterer.

COOKIE: And a proper dancing band!

AMY: A dancing band?

COOKIE: Easily arranged!

AMY: Dance band. I'm sure that's what you mean: dance
band.

COOKIE: Precisely!

AMY: Perhaps next time.

COOKIE: Should we wait the five years?

AMY: It's the tradition.

COOKIE: We might bend the tradition a bit. . . .

AMY: In which way?

COOKIE: Why not wait just *one* year?

AMY: And have a seventy-sixth? I suppose. We could call it "The Spirit of Seventy-six."

COOKIE: It certainly has a ring. . . .

AMY: I wouldn't mind at all, really. Not at all. . . . [*She stands.*] You have my address, don't you?

COOKIE: Twenty-seven Parker Road . . .

AMY: No, Thirty Gould . . .

COOKIE: Oh, yes!

AMY: Will you remember?

COOKIE: Etched on my brain already!

AMY: [*He helps her into her coat.*] Next year, then? [*She smiles; extends her arm for a handshake.*]

COOKIE: [*Takes her hand; holds it awhile.*] Could we do it next week?

AMY: Next week?

COOKIE: Next week. I would like that very much, Miss Chamberlain.

AMY: I suppose so. What would we call it?

COOKIE: Seventy-Five-*A*.

AMY: Yes. Do you have a telephone?

COOKIE: I do. I do. I'll write out my address and number for you. [*He fishes for and finds a wallet with pad and gold pen, in his jacket's inside pocket.*] Here. I'll write it down.

AMY: [*She is looking through her pocketbook.*] I'm afraid I haven't a pencil. . . . [*Sees his.*] Isn't that elegant?

COOKIE: [*Hands paper to her.*] That's my address and telephone there. . . . May I ask yours?

AMY: I'll write it for you. . . . [*She takes pen and paper and writes her address and telephone number upon paper.*] Wonderful pen. . . .

COOKIE: Thank you. . . .

[*She hands pen and paper to him.*]

COOKIE: Ah, yes. Gould Street, Stoneham. I know it. . . .

AMY: Just past where the scrap yard used to be. . . .

COOKIE: You have lovely handwriting. . . .

AMY: Do you think so?

COOKIE: Perfect Palmer Perfect. . . . Wonderful to see.

AMY: Not quite so perfect as it was. . . .

COOKIE: Lovely . . . [*Pockets her address, his wallet, etc.*]
I'll call you . . . when? . . . day after tomorrow? What's
a good time of day for you?

AMY: Late afternoon. I've always enjoyed a telephone call
in the late afternoon.

COOKIE: Four-thirty, day after tomorrow. You'll hear my
ring.

AMY: I look forward to it.

COOKIE: Do you have a ride now? . . . I could have my
driver take you . . .

AMY: You have a driver, do you?

COOKIE: Been with me for years now. Excellent driver.
Highly skilled.

AMY: Do you have a limousine?

COOKIE: I do.

AMY: My goodness! [*She giggles.*] What a small world. . . .

COOKIE: Could I arrange, then, for you to be driven . . .
[*Smiles.*] I could ride along, if you'd like.

AMY: Thank you, but my ride is arranged. [*Looks at her
watch.*] Well done by now, I should think. I'm nearly
twenty minutes late. [*Smiles.*] Good company.

COOKIE: You're very kind to say that. . . .

AMY: I can't promise you we'll meet next week, but we
can discuss it . . . the possibility of our meeting . . .
when you call.

COOKIE: I understand. Four-thirty, day after tomorrow.

AMY: [*Extends hand again.*] Well, then . . .

COOKIE: I'll walk you to your car. . . .

AMY: Please, don't! [*Smiles.*] I'm perfectly capable . . .

COOKIE: I know that. I just thought it would be nice. . . .

AMY: I'd rather you didn't!

COOKIE: Fine. We'll say good night here, then. . . .
[*They shake hands.*]

COOKIE: I'm very pleased to have met you . . . to have seen
you again, I mean.

AMY: As am I. . . . Pleased to have met you again . . . Mr.
Silverstein.

COOKIE: . . . Cookie.

AMY: Yes. [*She smiles.*] Cookie. [*She exits the play.*]
[*There is a silence.*

COOKIE *walks to the jukebox and replugs electrical join to the wall outlet.*
The jukebox lights relight.
The music fades in again, winding up to full sound and speed, at the precise spot on the recording at which the plug was pulled earlier in the play.
COOKIE *crosses to the chair, collects his coat, puts it on, stops a moment.*
He begins to exit, thinks better of it, returns to chair, sits.
The music continues.
COOKIE *sits at table, staring straight out, listening to music, lost in a fantasy.*
He taps his fingers on the tabletop, to the rhythm of the music.
The lights fade out.]

THE PLAY IS OVER.

Gloucester, New Haven, Milwaukee, New York City—July 1976–May 1978

The Wakefield Plays, Part III

ALFRED THE GREAT
A Play in Three Acts

For Samuel Beckett.

The People of the Play

MARGARET: Forty, small, pretty, Irish.
ALFRED: Forty, handsome, tends to the elegant.
WILL: Forty, wholesome good looks, tough, not muscular.
EMILY: Forty, handsome, tends to the elegant.

The Place of the Play

Living room of early-nineteenth-century New England home; owned by Will and Margaret, Wakefield, Massachusetts.

The Time of the Play

Start of fall.

. . . but when I think of all the books that I have read and of the wise words I have heard spoken, and of the anxiety I have given to parents and grandparents, and of the hopes that I have had, all life weighed in the scales of my own life seems to me a preparation for something that never happens.

—William Butler Yeats, *The Autobiography of William Butler Yeats*, "Reveries over Childhood and Youth" (1914)

ACT I
Scene 1

Living room. Saturday, midafternoon. Stage in darkness.

Three sharp knocks are heard. Same sound will precede each scene of play.

*First words of play—*ALFRED'S—*are heard.*

ALFRED: So. We begin?
   [*Lights to full, suddenly.*
   MARGARET *stands in living room, facing* ALFRED, *who has just arrived in room.*
   Room is of classically New England architectural lines and furnishing, except surprisingly sparse, nearly without furniture or decoration.
   An essential stuffed sofa set center stage; heavily stuffed armchair set downstage right, thronelike.
   Coffee table is used in front of sofa; cigarettes, ashtray, and cigarette box, on top.
   Pedestal ashtray is set stage right of chair.
   A hooked rug may be used, but no other stage dressing wanted.
   No windows but for stained-glass panes in staircase wall and smoked-glass panel in front door, perhaps surrounded by small stained-glass panes.
   Kitchen door on swing hinge, stage-left wall; front door set opposite, stage-right wall.
   Cellar door nonfunctional, but visible, under staircase balcony.

*Upstage wall oversized, passes offstage, either side, into
infinity. Infinite height as well.*

ALFRED *faces downstage, head bowed; he is nervous. He
wears suede shirt jacket, buff-colored trousers, loafers,
deep-colored shirt, open at neck.*

MARGARET, *equally nervous, fidgets, faces him. She wears
pastel peignoir, puff slippers, a smile.*]

ALFRED: Shall we, Margaret? Shall we begin?

MARGARET: Yes, I suppose. [*Pauses.*] It's not that I'm not
delighted to see you. It's just that I'm really . . . well . . .
surprised. There are knocks . . . I go to the door . . . and
it's you: Alfred! What are you doing here?

ALFRED: [*Angrily at first*] I don't know. [*Pauses; quietly*]
I don't know. I wanted to see you . . . to see my old
house . . . see the town . . . see Wakefield . . . I wanted
to see you.

MARGARET: [*Embarrassed*] I'm happy to see you, too. It's
been ten years. . . .

ALFRED: [*Correcting her*] Fifteen.

MARGARET: Really?

ALFRED: [*Smugly*] Fifteen.

MARGARET: It's been fifteen years. That's a long time. I'm
happy to see you again. You're cute, Alfred . . . cute.
You never were. If you were, I didn't notice. But you
certainly are now. Cute.

ALFRED: [*He turns away from her.*] Don't play with me,
Margaret. Really. I know what I look like. Okay.

MARGARET: Alfred . . .

ALFRED: Please.

MARGARET: [*Suddenly. Her scream will not be acknowledged by* ALFRED.] Will you, for Jesus Christ's sake, sit
down? [*Silence.*] Fifteen years? Really?

ALFRED: [*Smiling*] You were twenty-five. Just. Me too. You
were heavier. Not heavy. Heavier.

MARGARET: [*As an apology*] That's a long time.
[*He looks at her. They smile. They kiss.*]

MARGARET: [*Making conversation*] How's Emily?

ALFRED: Oh, fine. Same as ever. Will? How's Will?

MARGARET: Will's become a model father. I know it's hard
to believe, but it's true. Will's become a model father.

ALFRED: [*Surprised*] You've had children?

MARGARET: Well, no. There was Will, Jr. . . . and the little girl. . . .

ALFRED: Oh, yes, the little girl. Forgive me. I'm sorry. For a moment, I forgot. . . . Will, *Jr.*?

MARGARET: Yes. Remember Will and Ruby had . . . well, Alfred . . . trouble?

ALFRED: Trouble?

MARGARET: Trouble. Senior year.

ALFRED: I'm afraid I don't follow. . . .

MARGARET: Do you remember Ruby? She was F, junior year. . . .

ALFRED: "F" in what sense, Margaret?

MARGARET: Cheerleader lineup.

ALFRED: Oh. "F"! I see. . . . [*Thinks.*] W . . . A . . . K . . . E . . . Ah, yes, Ruby. Skinny, wrenlike, sad-eyed . . . ?

MARGARET: Will got her in trouble.

ALFRED: You don't say? Trouble? Family-way sort of thing?

MARGARET: Will, Jr.

ALFRED: Of course. I must have known that and forgotten. . . . [*He walks from* MARGARET; *changes the subject.*] Nice room. Good-size room. Nice dimensions, nice proportions. Just right. Nice. Nice. Nice room. I always liked this room. . . .

MARGARET: [*Quickly*] Damn it, Alfred, I know you're rich. I've read the papers.

ALFRED: It's . . . uh . . . nothing.

MARGARET: Will works a twelve-hour day. Eight to eight. Hasn't had a raise in seven years now.

ALFRED: It's nothing. I was lucky.

MARGARET: Will and I are very happy, Alfred. I warn you. We are very happy. Happier than I ever thought I could ever be.

ALFRED: I'm happy to hear that.

MARGARET: Will's become quite a gentleman. Quite a gentleman. No more of the rough stuff you remember.

ALFRED: I don't remember any rough stuff.

MARGARET: The school psychiatrist said he was angry because he was a foundling. Those foundling days were the seeds of the rough stuff. All passed now. Night school. Eight-to-eight and then night school. Quite a gentleman, Will is. Very hardworking and *very* well liked around these parts now, I can tell you *that*.

ALFRED: Margaret, this may shock and amaze you, but . . .
I don't really remember Will well. . . .

MARGARET: Stoneham High . . . played left end . . . also
ran the hundred . . . 10-2½ . . . fast, wiry, quite
cute . . . ?

ALFRED: Oh . . . *Stoneham* High. . . . Perhaps I didn't
really know Will at all. It's hard for me to separate what
I've forgotten from what I never knew: very little difference as the years fly by. He's how old now: Will?

MARGARET: Forty.

ALFRED: He's forty and he still goes to school?

MARGARET: After work, in the evenings. Self-help is Will's
middle name.

ALFRED: You must be proud. . . .

MARGARET: I certainly am. . . .

ALFRED: I can understand. . . .

MARGARET: Will and I have a great deal in common. . . .

ALFRED: Really?

MARGARET: My not knowing exactly who my father was
and Will's being a foundling. . . .

ALFRED: Oh, in *that* sense. . . .

MARGARET: Those are the ties that truly bind.

ALFRED: What are?

MARGARET: I beg your pardon?

ALFRED: The ties?

MARGARET: That bind? Family. Origins. . . .

ALFRED: Oh. Right.

MARGARET: Let's take you, for example. After all these
years and all that success, look at you.

ALFRED: How so?

MARGARET: Right back here: in your old town, in your old
house.

ALFRED: Everybody I've got's buried here . . . in this town.
By the lake. Quannapowitt. Ever see the cement bench?

MARGARET: The what?

ALFRED: The cement bench on my family plot. It's got my
name stamped right on the back of it. Ever see it?

MARGARET: We're in the other cemetery.

ALFRED: I know that! Christ, I know that! I just thought
you might have taken a walk through and seen the bench.

MARGARET: No, I haven't. Not yet, anyway. I might,
though: someday. . . . Cement?

ALFRED: It's a white cement bench. It's got my name—our family name—etched right into the back of it. [*Pauses.*] Who sits on it?

MARGARET: That's true enough.

ALFRED: [*Quickly, clearly*] Everybody I ever had is lying right there: foot of the bench. Right in the dirt. Excuse me. The soil. I should have said "the soil." Fresh soil. And fresh roses. On the soil, not in it. Somebody has been putting cut roses on my brother's grave. I wish I hadn't stopped smoking. I haven't thought about a cigarette for two years.

MARGARET: You want a cigarette?

ALFRED: Nope. Quit.

MARGARET: Mind if I smoke?

ALFRED: Nope. Smoke.

MARGARET: I won't. If you don't want me to, I won't.

ALFRED: Smoke.

MARGARET: You're right. It'll kill me.

ALFRED: Smoke. Don't worry about me. Really. I'm okay.

MARGARET: I really shouldn't . . . [*Lights a cigarette.*] That's better.

ALFRED: [*Clipped; a command*] Put it out.

MARGARET: What?

ALFRED: Put it out. If Will wants you to die, that's his business. I don't want you to die. Put it out.

MARGARET: Will wants me to stop smoking.

ALFRED: I don't care. Put it out.
[*She does.*]

ALFRED: Good. Did that hurt? I mean, did that kill you not to have the cigarette??? It's a piggy habit. Really piggy.

MARGARET: Did Emily quit?

ALFRED: In what sense, Margaret?

MARGARET: [*Smiling*] Your own wife? You couldn't stop her?

ALFRED: Stop her?

MARGARET: From smoking.

ALFRED: Emily's a big girl. If she wants to kill herself, that's her concern, not mine.

MARGARET: Piggy.

ALFRED: Hmmm?

MARGARET: Piggy. You said, "It's a *piggy* habit."

ALFRED: I did?

MARGARET: Always. Always did. That's one of your very favorite words.

ALFRED: Piggy? I suppose.

MARGARET: God.

ALFRED: [*Overlapping*] Piggy?

MARGARET: God.

ALFRED: [*Overlapping*] You shouldn't smoke.

MARGARET: God.

ALFRED: [*Overlapping*] It's really dumb.

MARGARET: God.

ALFRED: [*Overlapping*] *I* think it's dumb.

MARGARET: No wonder Emily hates you.

ALFRED: Emily doesn't hate me.

MARGARET: Of course she does.

ALFRED: She *does*?

MARGARET: She always *did*. I know. I've read the papers. I think Emily's very sophisticated.

ALFRED: When did you meet Emily?

MARGARET: Meet who?

ALFRED: Emily.

MARGARET: Well, never.

[*Silence.*]

ALFRED: Why did you say, "she did"?

MARGARET: Did what?

ALFRED: Hate me.

MARGARET: She did. She went three years without talking to me.

ALFRED: Three years?

MARGARET: Three years and three months. She talked to everyone else, of course, but to me she said nothing. I know. I saw it in the papers.

ALFRED: Then it *must* be true!

MARGARET: That's very difficult.

ALFRED: What's very difficult?

MARGARET: [*With deliberation*] To say nothing: it's very difficult to say nothing. At least, I *think* it would be difficult to say nothing. I've never said nothing. [*Smiles timidly.*] I've never said nothing.

[ALFRED *walks to* MARGARET, *stares straight at her face, then drops his eyes down the front of her body. When*

his eyes return to her eyes, MARGARET *pulls away, back
from him, smiling bravely.*]

MARGARET: I often wonder, don't you?

ALFRED: Course I do. [*Pauses; smiles.*] I'm surprised that
you and Will never had any children together. Didn't
Will want any?

MARGARET: It's not Will. It's me. I can't . . . have any.

ALFRED: Well, that doesn't sound right. Have you seen a
good doctor?

MARGARET: Just the locals . . . you know . . . Flynn and his
son. . . .

ALFRED: There. You see. Inconclusive. You need to see
Mass. General men. Top specialists. You should assume
nothing. For all you know, Will might have had it once
and lost it.

MARGARET: Lost it?

ALFRED: It happens. [*Pauses; embarrassed.*] Happened to
me. I went impotent once. Twice, really.

MARGARET: Impotent is different.

ALFRED: I know, but it frightened me all the same.

MARGARET: Don't most men go . . . impotent?

ALFRED: How do you mean?

MARGARET: Well, impotent.

ALFRED: But how, exactly?

MARGARET: [*Nervously*] Impotent. Impotent. Can't get it
up.

ALFRED: I don't know.

MARGARET: I'm sure they do. Are you worried?

ALFRED: I'm terrified.

MARGARET: Are you still?

ALFRED: Terrified?

MARGARET: Impotent.

ALFRED: I don't know.

MARGARET: When was the last time you . . . tried?

ALFRED: Last night.

MARGARET: And you couldn't?

ALFRED: I could. I did.

MARGARET: Oh. And before that?

ALFRED: Before *what?*

MARGARET: God, Alfred. When did you try before that?

ALFRED: Before last night? [*Pauses.*] Yesterday morning.

[*Pauses.*] And I succeeded. [*Pauses.*] But you never know
when it's going to hit again. [*There is a long pause.*] How
do you know expressions like "get it up"?

MARGARET: I don't know. I heard it.

ALFRED: [*Controlled anger*] Does Will say things like "get
it up"?

MARGARET: [*She probably giggles.*] I don't know. He might
have. I've heard it in jokes. Old men can't "get it up."

ALFRED: I was thirty-two when it happened.

MARGARET: That was eight years ago.

ALFRED: That's not old, thirty-two. [*Pauses.*] How would
I know about "most men"? I don't sleep with men.

MARGARET: God.

ALFRED: I would be frightened with you in bed right now.
Frightened it would hit.

MARGARET: No wonder Emily hates you.

ALFRED: She'll never let me forget it.

MARGARET: You couldn't get it up for Emily? [*She enjoys
her question.*]

ALFRED: Twice. She only knew about the first time.

MARGARET: That doesn't make sense.

ALFRED: She was asleep the second time. I waited until she
was asleep. I figured that if it hit, she wouldn't know.
[*Pauses.*] It hit. [*Pauses.*] She didn't know. I don't sleep
well, Margaret. It's difficult.

MARGARET: For you.

ALFRED: To sleep.

MARGARET: I'm sure.

ALFRED: I can't close my eyes.

MARGARET: I'm sure. [*Pauses.*] You can't what?

ALFRED: Close my eyes. I never blink. Didn't you notice?
I can force a blink. Watch. [*He blinks.*] I just did. [*He
blinks again.*] See? It's really no problem, if I *force* them
down. But the natural normal state of my eyes is . . .

MARGARET: Wide open . . .

ALFRED: . . . wide open.

MARGARET: It must be difficult.

ALFRED: It was hell for the first nine or ten years.

MARGARET: Now?

ALFRED: Now? Oh it's much better. I have to force things
a bit, but it's much better. You have to work at getting
what you really want. I've actually been quite successful.

MARGARET: I know. I've read the papers.

ALFRED: I've had my picture in the papers.

MARGARET: I've seen them.

ALFRED: I was in bed with Emily.

MARGARET: In the paper?

ALFRED: When it hit. [*Too quickly at first*] I kept thinking that the door was going to open. I couldn't put it out of my mind. I kept thinking that the door was going to open and everybody I knew was going to burst into the room. They were at the door. I couldn't stop thinking that.

MARGARET: Was I there?

ALFRED: Were you *where*?

MARGARET: At the door?

ALFRED: Oh. Yuh. I suppose.

MARGARET: I wasn't, was I? I wasn't there.

ALFRED: My God! That's a very complicated idea.

MARGARET: Who was at the door?

ALFRED: [*Angrily*] Just people from the city. Nobody from here. . . .

MARGARET: [*Correcting him*] From *home*.

ALFRED: From home. Nobody from home. Just city people.

MARGARET: Sophisticated.

ALFRED: Huh?

MARGARET: The group. Probably a very sophisticated group.

ALFRED: It was just a daydream.

MARGARET: A daydream?

ALFRED: It wasn't real.

MARGARET: It happened in the daytime?

ALFRED: In the morning.

MARGARET: You and Emily?

ALFRED: When we woke up . . . I *think* it was morning!!! . . . It doesn't matter. [*Pause.*] I can't remember.

MARGARET: Did it begin then?

ALFRED: The terror?

MARGARET: The three years of no-talking?

ALFRED: [*Softly*] No.

[*Silence.*]

MARGARET: "Never let it get into your mind."

ALFRED: I beg your pardon?

MARGARET: That's what Will says: "Never let it get into your mind."

ALFRED: Has Will ever gone . . . you know . . .

MARGARET: Well . . . Alfred! That's really *personal!*

ALFRED: I'm really terrified. I mean, it would help to know.
Has he???

MARGARET: No. No, he hasn't.

ALFRED: God damn! . . .

MARGARET: Will is an unusual man.

ALFRED: God damn! . . .

MARGARET: Stop it. Don't be ridiculous. We don't do it
every five minutes.

ALFRED: God damn! . . .

MARGARET: Sometimes we don't do it for weeks. Once we
went four months without doing it. One whole summer.

ALFRED: No wonder your marriage is shaky.

MARGARET: My marriage isn't shaky.

ALFRED: It isn't perfect.

MARGARET: It's close.

ALFRED: It's shaky.

MARGARET: You can't come back here after all these years
and . . . and pass judgments like that. Everybody isn't
rich, you know. There are certain privileges you have
that everybody doesn't have. God knows how you got
them. I mean, it certainly is ironic that out of all the kids
in our class, you, Alfred L. Webber, the very *least* likely
to succeed, succeeded. [*Pause.*] I happen to be very
happy.

[*Silence.*

ALFRED *walks to her. They kiss. They break apart from
each other. Each looks down, avoiding eye contact.*]

MARGARET: Why did you think otherwise?

ALFRED: My mother and my father were born in this town.
Their mothers and fathers, too. Imagine that.

MARGARET: The same for all of us . . . mostly.

ALFRED: They're buried side by side, every one of them,
down at Lakeside. My father hated the lake. He never
let me swim in it. Said it was full of dangerous weeds.
Pull you down and hold you under. Every summer, we
packed up the whole house—everything we owned, on
the back of his truck—and went twenty miles down the
road, to Hamilton, our summer house. A place for the
winter, a place for the summer. A place to be poor, a
place to be poorer. [*Pauses.*] Oh, Margaret . . . seeing

you now. Standing here in the house in which I grew
up . . . seeing you now . . . still so pretty . . . so pretty . . .
[*They smile at each other. They do not touch, do not kiss,
but stand frozen instead, each watching the other's eyes.*
WILL *enters. He is ill-clad in sport jacket or gabardine
suit.*

He carries two bags of groceries.

MARGARET *and* ALFRED *pull away from each other, violently.*]

WILL: [*Very, very hostile*] Company?

MARGARET: This is Alfred.

WILL: [*Still hostile*] Honest to God???

ALFRED: Honest to God.

MARGARET: I've told Will a lot about you, Alfred. [*Pauses.*]
This is Will.

[*The men shake hands.*]

WILL: [*Dryly*] Pleasure.

ALFRED: Pleasure.

WILL: Mag's told me all about you.

ALFRED: Don't believe it.

WILL: [*Suppressing anger*] Seen all your clippings. Mag's
got a scrapbook full of your clippings. You get a lot of
media. She's filled up a good couple of scrapbooks over
the years. Used to get me jealous. Not so much as the
letters: they used to drive me *crazy*, first nine or ten
years, watching Mag sit down to write you a letter every
night. She hardly ever mentioned my name in them. Like
I didn't exist.

MARGARET: He used to read them.

WILL: Hell of a thing, at the end of a day, when you need
company most, and your wife's got her *work* to do.
[*Laughs.*] That's what she used to call it: her work.
Honest to God. She'd say, "I got to get a little work done
now, Will." Then she'd sit down for a sonofabitchin'
hour, puffing on her cigarettes, writing to good old Alfred
L. Webber, boy wonder. Used to get me jealous. Not
anymore.

ALFRED: You've kept a scrapbook?

MARGARET: Sure. Why not? How many famous people do
I know?

WILL: When are you leaving?

ALFRED: Huh?

WILL: You're living down in the city. Just home for the day?

ALFRED: Oh. I don't know. I'm just looking around. You know.

WILL: [*Smiling*] Funny to see you in the flesh. I think of you as a little picture. You know, it always galls me that somebody like you gets his picture in the paper every five minutes . . . for *what?* Makin' money? Takes no brains ta make money, right?

ALFRED: [*Moves to his suitcase and picks it up. Stands near door.*] Well, I guess I should be going.

MARGARET: Stop it. Will, Alfred's going to stay with us for a while.

ALFRED: Stay? Me?

MARGARET: [*Quickly*] You're not going to the Lord Wakefield! Will?

ALFRED: I really should go.

WILL: No, you don't. Stay.

ALFRED: But I want to go, really.

WILL: [*Really arch, tough, hostile*] No, you don't. Stay. You stay here, like Mag wants. What the hell, you two were sweethearts long before I came into the picture. You're all Mag ever talks about, Alfred. You're her ideal man. I know you better than I know the President. Day doesn't seem to pass without your name comin' up. Alfred this or Alfred that. You're always in the paper. You stay, Alfred. You stay as my guest right here in my house . . . long as you want. Hell, how many celebrities do I get to talk to? None. You're the first. I'm enjoying this already.

MARGARET: [*Chatty; takes* ALFRED'S *suitcase.*] We have a nice quiet room upstairs. . . . Or you could have Will, Jr.'s room. [*Realizes.*] It's your old room! Use that one! That's not as quiet, but it's bright. And it's on the front. There's a lot of traffic . . . [*She laughs. Goes upstairs.*] . . . not a lot of traffic by *your* standards. Five or six cars a day. You remember. You could stay way upstairs and have two rooms adjoining: it's like a private apartment. . . .

WILL: [*Cuts in, abruptly.*] Will you for Chrissakes shut your mouth? You're makin' a goddam fool of yourself! [*To* ALFRED, *coolly; calmly*] Alfred, you'll stay in your old

room. It's my boy's room now. He's away at college.
You can have the whole room to yourself. It'll be good
for you . . . to be back in there. It'll help you to remember what things were like around here. . . . The good
old days, right? [*Smiles.*] I know the room's not big. I
mean, I know it's not what you're accustomed to, but
it's the best I've got. You know what I mean? [*He starts
to exit the room, thinks better of it, stops, returns to
ALFRED.*] Oh, yuh. Only thing I ask is that you not make
too much noise after ten. I work long days. [*Starts to exit
room again, thinks better of it again, stops again, returns
to ALFRED again.*] Oh, yuh. Alfred? One other thing. You
touch my wife, I'll break your head. I don't care who
you are. Okay? Night. [WILL *exits.*

ALFRED *is blank-faced. He opens cigarette box on coffee
table, extracts cigarette, which he places in his mouth.
He extracts matches from the same box, lights cigarette,
drags deeply, coughs deeply, coughs again.*]

ALFRED: [*Brightly*] He's very nice: Will. I like him.
[*The lights black out.*]

END OF SCENE 1

Scene 2

Later.

Stage in darkness.

Three sharp knocks are heard.

First words of scene—WILL's—are heard.

WILL: You ashamed of your ears?
[*Lights to full, suddenly.*
ALFRED, *on sofa, newspaper section on lap. He faces
front.*

WILL, *in chair, remainder of newspaper in his hands. He is staring across at* ALFRED.

ALFRED *has been doing crossword puzzle. He wears a silk paisley robe; pencil is between his teeth.*

WILL *wears white cotton undershirt; has small terry-cloth towel over his neck as scarf.* WILL'*s section of newspaper is open to television page.*]

ALFRED: [*Face turns slowly to* WILL. *He removes pencil from mouth; smiles directly to* WILL.] Hmmm?

WILL: Are you ashamed of your ears?

ALFRED: [*Sustaining the smile*] I don't understand?

WILL: Your hair . . .

ALFRED: [*Pretending to "just get it"*] Oh, my hair! Over my ears. . . . I didn't get it. That's pretty good. "Are you ashamed of your ears?" . . .

WILL: [*Angrily*] Don't bullshit me. It's not that funny. I saw it on television. Watch a lot of television around here. I don't suppose you do. I read in the paper that you think television is the wasteland. 'Sthat true?

ALFRED: Huh?

WILL: [*Prophetically*] . . . Television is the wasteland.

ALFRED: [*Matching* WILL'*s tone, mimicry*] April is the cruelest month.

WILL: Huh?

ALFRED: Sometimes things get into newspapers that aren't exactly true.

WILL: Yuh. You said *that* in the same interview. Where do *you* get off being interviewed? Is that what papers have come to? Coverin' any bullshit that comes down the pike?

ALFRED: I think it's funny.

WILL: Oh, really?

ALFRED: Oh, really.

WILL: [*Quickly, he yells.*] Too bad you don't have a wife who cuts out every goddam word *I* say and pastes it into a goddam scrapbook. Too bad. Then you'd see how *oh-really-funny* you really are. [*Silence.*] What did you do today?

[*Silence.*]

ALFRED: Mrs. Fuller's dead.

WILL: Dead?

ALFRED: [*Displays newspaper to* WILL.] It's in the *Item*. . . .

WILL: Couldn't say "dead." *Item* hasn't printed the word "dead" in thirty years. . . .

ALFRED: [*Looks at newspaper*] Does so. Right here. Look: The headline. "Francine Fuller Passes On."

WILL: Oh, well, right: *passes on.* "Passes on" is a hell of a lot different from "dead."

[ALFRED *looks at* WILL, *silently.*

WILL *laughs.*

A moment passes.

Note: Following section through the silence should play rapidly, reflexively.]

ALFRED: Sold her store quick enough. . . .

WILL: [*Overlapping*] No point in waiting. . . .

ALFRED: [*Quickly*] Who bought?

WILL: Dunno. . . .

ALFRED: Nice old lady. . . .

WILL: She was all right. . . .

ALFRED: *Very* nice, I'd say. . . .

WILL: She was all right. . . .

ALFRED: Never had children. . . .

WILL: Never wanted any. . . .

ALFRED: Nice old lady. . . .

WILL: She was all right. . . .

ALFRED: Ninety-one, they say. . . .

WILL: Nice old lady. . . .

ALFRED: [*Smiles.*] She was all right.

[*A short silence.* ALFRED *smiles at* WILL.]

WILL: [*Without looking up from his newspaper*] It's all changed. Kids don't have to study Latin anymore.

ALFRED: I beg your pardon?

WILL: [*Looks up at* ALFRED *now.*] Saw the coach. Said kids don't have to study Latin anymore. I took Latin all four years. Flunked it twice. Flunked it cold. *Omnia Gallia est divisit in tres partes.* [*Sic.*] I'll never forget that. Never forget that till the day I die. *Omnia Gallia est divisit in tres partes.* [*Sic.*] Oh, yeah. Course, I don't go dropping knowledge like that around, like some people I know. . . .

ALFRED: Sorry, Will. . . .

WILL: [*Redux.*] Now . . . Well, now it's all changed. Kids

ain't gonna get the education. It's all modern. Nobody
has to know nothing anymore. Kids are so stupid I
wanna puke.

ALFRED: What year were you?

WILL: Same as you.

ALFRED: Same year? Well . . . I'm surprised.

WILL: Why? You think you're younger? I got bad news for
you: I'm four months younger than you. I checked it
against the newspaper this morning. You know you're
in the newspaper?

ALFRED: Really?

WILL: Oh, you didn't know?

ALFRED: No, I didn't.

WILL: Really?

ALFRED: Really. Will, I don't understand why you're so . . .

WILL: That's funny. . . .

ALFRED: What's funny?

WILL: Funny you didn't know you were in the paper.

ALFRED: Well, I fail to see where that's so unusual. . . .

WILL: Oh, but it is. . . .

ALFRED: Oh, but it isn't! I'm in the news a lot, dammit!
It's no big deal in *my* life, believe-you-me. . . .

WILL: Then how come you called the paper?

ALFRED: Huh?

WILL: "Huh? Huh?" How come you called the paper? I
heard you on the phone last night. Called the paper from
right here. Couldn't even wait till the paper opened.

ALFRED: I don't . . .

WILL: *Come off the bullshit!* I listened in from my room.
[*Pause.*] I thought it was funny. [*Pause.*] I don't blame
you, Alfred. Hell, if I could get *me* in the paper . . .
what the hell? . . . If you don't push yourself, who's
gonna? I don't blame you, Alfred.

ALFRED: The editor of the *Item*'s an old friend.

WILL: I said, "I don't blame you."

ALFRED: She's an old friend.

WILL: That's rich.

ALFRED: That happens to be the truth!

WILL: Suit yourself.

ALFRED: I don't like the implications. . . .

WILL: *Neither do I!*

ALFRED: She is an old friend.

WILL: And you're news, Alfred. You're news.

ALFRED: [*Stands, moves to stairs.*] Terrific! Look, I'll pack my stuff and clear out. . . .

WILL: [*Yells.*] Alfred! You stay, goddammit! Goddammit! [*Pauses;* ALFRED *stops, looks at* WILL, *who speaks softly now.*]

WILL: I work hard, Alfred. Goddam hard. Eight-to-eight's when I'm there. Got to get there. Up at six. Maggie's always sleeping. Doctor said it was nerves. I used to worry about it, but lately . . . well, I don't much care whether she gets up or whether she sleeps. Barren women get boring after a while. Don't much care if she sleeps or if she gets up: don't seem much different. [*Silence.*] How are *you* doing?

ALFRED: [*A reasonable attempt at contact*] Oh, okay. Okay. I'm a little tired, Will. Can't seem to get my eyes closed . . . at night . . . sleeping. Difficult. Can't seem to get my eyes closed.

WILL: Force them.

ALFRED: I do. I will. It's odd.

WILL: Must be.

ALFRED: The town, I mean. I keep seeing fat grownups with little kids trapped inside. You know what I mean?

WILL: [*Staring at* ALFRED] No.

ALFRED: All the kids I knew became their parents. Like us, I suppose.

WILL: Us? Like our parents? Really? What is that: a joke?

ALFRED: There's a French joke that always makes me smile: *Je pense, donc je fuis.* You ever hear that one, Will?

WILL: [*Humiliated; angrily*] Great. I love jokes.

ALFRED: Sorry, Will. [*Pauses.*] Will?

[WILL *looks at* ALFRED.]

ALFRED: I know exactly why I've come back, Will. I know exactly why I'm in this house, in this town. I know exactly why.

[*There is a short silence.* WILL *stares at* ALFRED. *They hold eye contact.* WILL *breaks the silence.*]

WILL: It's not the same, is it? You come back to a place after years and years of bein' away, and it's smaller, dirtier, it's not so friendly as you remember. . . .

ALFRED: Oh, I don't know about that. . . .

WILL: I went back, too. To Stoneham.

ALFRED: [*Laughs.*] To Stoneham?

WILL: Som'pin' funny? What's funny?

ALFRED: Stoneham's only two miles away. Right up the top of Prospect Street. . . .

WILL: Still my home, isn't it? I've got some real memories goin' there. Nothin' like this garbage heap. . . .

ALFRED: [*Overlapping*] Stoneham's a pretty town. One of the prettiest. . . .

WILL: *Was* a pretty town. Now it's all hot-dog stands. . . .

ALFRED: How many hot-dog stands?

WILL: [*Straight to* ALFRED, *without a pause*] Fifty, sixty. . . .

ALFRED: What?

WILL: [*Exploding*] You really think you're something special, don't you? I listen to you spouting off some foreign goddam words and now I'm supposed to shut up. . . . I'm supposed to tell you how many hot-dog stands got put up in Stoneham??? . . . You really think you're something. . . .

ALFRED: I'm sorry, Will. . . .

WILL: [*Furiously*] I know *who* you are and *what* you are and what you come from, Alfred. I know *plenty, plenty!* You can't pull your highfalutin goddam hoity-toity goddam *airs* around *me*, ya know! So just don't you try, *okay?*

ALFRED: I'm . . . uh . . . I'm sorry, Will.

WILL: [*Imitates* ALFRED's *apology.*] You're . . . uh . . . you're what, Alfred?

ALFRED: I'm sorry, Will. That's what I said: I'm sorry. I apologize. . . .

WILL: Just 'cause I was brought from a foundling home makes me no less of a native son.

ALFRED: It certainly doesn't.

WILL: They put a hot-dog stand where my house used to be. Take-out crap. That's enough, huh? I mean when that happens, it's as though the whole goddam world just became a goddam . . . well . . . you know . . . a goddam . . . well . . . uh . . .

ALFRED: Hot-dog stand?

WILL: Hot-dog stand.

ALFRED: They tore your house down?

WILL: [*Embarrassed*] It fell down.

ALFRED: Really?

WILL: It wasn't much of a house. You may recall that it wasn't much to speak about.

ALFRED: I never saw your house.

[*Silence.* WILL *smiles at* ALFRED.]

WILL: I like having you here. I even hurried home from work tonight. Can't remember hurrying back to this garbage dump in fifteen years. I even told my boss you were staying with me. Showed him the paper. He was very impressed. We don't get much in the way of celebrities around here. You read it yourself in the paper: "luminary." That's what you are in this town, pal. A goddam luminary. [WILL *slaps* ALFRED'*s back and laughs.*] Just like our parents, huh? When are you planning on seeing your father? You better get in a good night's sleep before *that* little *tête-en-tête*, huh?

ALFRED: [*Quietly*] He's dead, Will.

WILL: Who's "dead, Will"?

ALFRED: My father. He's dead.

WILL: Oh, well, your way's fine with me, Alfred: Mr. Luminary. Just fine. Any way you want to play it. [*Silence.*]

ALFRED: Kinda quiet around here.

WILL: Your father hated livin' down here, Mr. Luminary. Hated every minute. Hated the town, hated the people . . . hated the church, hated the steeple. [*He laughs.*]

ALFRED: He loved it. Told me Wakefield, Massachusetts, was the best place on the face of the earth. The very best place. Wakefield . . . Massachusetts . . . U.S.A. . . . North America . . . Western Hemisphere . . . Earth . . . Universe . . . Infinity . . . [ALFRED *smiles.*] . . . New England.

WILL: Musta been drunk . . .

ALFRED: I believe him now. . . .

WILL: . . . or crazy?

ALFRED: Watch it, Will.

WILL: Okay. Okay. Fine. Any way you want. [*He points to coffee table.*] The cigarettes are in the box. That one. Right.

ALFRED: I don't smoke.

WILL: Bring me one.

ALFRED: Huh?

WILL: The matches are in the box, too. Never used to be. *Mahhh*-gret thinks it's classy. Goddam cigarettes and matches together in a goddam wood box on the goddam wood coffee table . . . gettin' stale together. Hurry up.

ALFRED: [*Rather surprised and amused*] You want me to light it?

WILL: Why? You got a cold?

ALFRED: Cold? Oh. No. No, it's just that I don't smoke.

WILL: Light it.

[ALFRED *takes a cigarette, a match, lights it, hands it to* WILL, *who leans back in his chair, drags deeply, smiles.*]

WILL: *Omnia Gallia est divisit in tres partes.* [*Sic.*] That's a pretty sound, isn't it? I dunno. Things just always *sound* better in Latin. I'll never forget it, as long as I live. Ah, some things can't be talked about: they just are.

[MARGARET *enters down stairs, smiling until she hears* WILL's *next line. She winces. Glances disapprovingly at* WILL *as she passes him.*]

WILL: Kids make me want to puke.

[MARGARET *to sofa. Smiles at* ALFRED, *deeply. She wears a lacy nightgown and a capelike robe. She smiles.* ALFRED *stands. She sits on the sofa.* ALFRED *sits opposite* WILL.]

MARGARET: Cigarette?

WILL: [*Quickly*] He don't.

ALFRED: [*As quickly*] I stopped.

MARGARET: [*As quickly*] I forgot. [*Silence.*] I read the article in the paper today. It was lovely. Did you see it?

ALFRED: No.

[WILL *laughs.*]

ALFRED: I think I'll go to bed. I have to be up early. . . . [*Stands, starts an exit.*]

MARGARET: Couldn't we all talk awhile?

WILL: Sit.

ALFRED: I'm a bit sleepy.

WILL: You can sleep late.

ALFRED: I have an early appointment.

WILL: Bullshit.

MARGARET: [*Embarrassed*] Will!

WILL: Just saw it in the paper: in Alfred's *Item* interview. Here . . . [*Reads from newspaper.*] "The Twentieth-Century concept of raised consciousness is all bullshit."

MARGARET: Will!

WILL: He doesn't like TV, either. Says that's bullshit, too.

MARGARET: Will!

WILL: Maggie doesn't like me to say "bullshit."

MARGARET: It's true. I really don't.

ALFRED: It's just a word.

WILL: Bullshit.

ALFRED: Doesn't mean anything.

WILL: Bullshit.

ALFRED: You're acting childish, Will.

WILL: *I* am?

ALFRED: I do remember your being obstreperous . . . your throat . . . infected. . . . I think you had them out. . . . [WILL *is angry; returns to reading his newspaper.* ALFRED *returns to reading his newspaper, as well.* MARGARET *waits a moment in silence, then looks from* WILL *to* ALFRED, *settles a smile on him; speaks.*]

MARGARET: I always look forward to a talk in the evening. [ALFRED *looks up from his newspaper. He and* MARGARET *smile at each other.* WILL *looks up from his newspaper, sees them smiling, watches awhile; speaks.*]

WILL: I would like to see an entrance exam for junior high school. We pay a lot of tax to support a school that doesn't teach nothing anymore. There should be a stiff exam. If a kid flunks, no junior high school. Let 'em work. Like me and Alfred. We worked for what we got. A stiff exam. That's what.
[*Silence.*]

MARGARET: It's very nice.

ALFRED: Huh?

MARGARET: Your robe.

ALFRED: It's Italian.

MARGARET: It's *still* very nice.

ALFRED: Yours is very nice, too.

WILL: For Jesus Christ's sakes . . . I could just leave the room!

MARGARET: I just told him his robe was pretty. It is. *You* wouldn't wear a robe like that. I bought you a robe in

Filene's that was *gorgeous*: absolutely gorgeous. He wouldn't wear it, Alfred. It was much nicer than yours. Yours is lovely, but his was *gorgeous*. Never said "Thank you." Never even acted like I bought him a gift. I think men look just wonderful in evening robes.

WILL: Her *stepfather* wore a bathrobe.

MARGARET: My stepfather wore a *robe*.

WILL: Day and night. You'd think you were in a goddam hospital!

MARGARET: He had a day robe and a night robe. He was a very elegant man.

ALFRED: I remember your stepfather. Sam. Right. I remember him. . . .

WILL: What's to forget? He was here every goddam day! He practically *lived* here for ten years. He no sooner went through the front door of the asylum when he snuck right out the back—right back down here again. Like I said: day and night.

ALFRED: [*Quietly*] When did you . . . lose him?

MARGARET: Lose him?

WILL: Lose him?

ALFRED: Lose him? When did you?

MARGARET: It's complicated.

WILL: He ran away.

ALFRED: He *what*?

WILL: Ran away.

ALFRED: From here?

WILL: Yup. One day he packed up his *day* goddam robe and his *night* goddam robe and he was gone. He didn't even leave a note.

MARGARET: It was awful. His mind weakened.

WILL: Bullshit.

MARGARET: It did. I could see it coming.

WILL: He hooked himself up with Anderson's widow.

MARGARET: His mind was slipping. It was an awful thing to watch. Awful thing to watch. . . .

WILL: Seventy-three and he could still get it up like a kid.

MARGARET: It was an awful thing to watch.

WILL: [*Laughs.*] Isn't that somepin'? Robe or no robe, I gotta hand it to the old son of a bitch: he could still get it up like a kid. The old widow Anderson didn't know what hit her. [*Leans in now; loudly*] Sam and Andy's widow were carryin' on like two cocker goddam spaniels. It was *un-be-lievable!* The speed with which that man could operate! I think he nailed her first right down at Pottle's Funeral Parlor! It's true! It wasn't six days after the burial before she was hanging around here every night. I caught 'em right where you sit: she was leanin' over and he was taking her from behind. I couldn't believe my goddam eyes. It was unbelievable. I hadda ask 'em to leave the house. It's degenerate. You can't come home to a show like that every night.

MARGARET: His mind snapped. It was an awful thing to watch.

WILL: I'm gonna take a shower. You two . . . talk. [*He stands and walks up staircase. Exits.*]

ALFRED: I don't really remember your stepfather well.

MARGARET: He was not terribly tall, muscular, with reddish hair?

ALFRED: Vaguely.

MARGARET: Very short, thin, with brownish-reddish hair.

ALFRED: I think so.

MARGARET: A tiny, little man. Wiry, with thick glasses. Bald with a scraggly fringe. . . .

ALFRED: Oh, yes. I remember him and I do think that I remember your stepmother . . . Roxy, right? Woman of wonderful spirit. Wonderful zest for life. If I remember correctly, she loved a good laugh.

MARGARET: Oh, she did love a laugh. She never had many good ones herself, poor thing, what with her life riddled by scandal and all. . . . But, listen, health is the important thing, really. Don't you think?

ALFRED: Is she still . . . ?

MARGARET: Oh, very much, very much. She's right up there in the home . . . with all of them . . . all of her friends. Nazareth Academy's a home now. . . . [*Smiles.*] Why am I telling *you* this? You certainly know about it. . . .

ALFRED: No, I don't know. And how about Sam? Is he there as well?

MARGARET: [*Totally changed attitude here; suddenly*] I don't understand what the hell you're doing, Alfred!

ALFRED: I'm sorry?

MARGARET: You know he is!

[*Pauses; they hold a stare between them.*]

ALFRED: Who puts the flowers on my brother's grave, Margaret? Quite an extravagant gesture after fifteen years, I should say. . . .

MARGARET: [*Turns away; pauses. Turns back; smiles.*] I could see his mind sliding. Every day he grew worse and worse. . . .

ALFRED: Every day . . . worse and worse? . . .

MARGARET: I hope it never happens to you, Alfred. . . . I hope you're spared.

ALFRED: Spared?

MARGARET: No, Alfred, not me. I've never even *seen* your brother's grave. Not me.

ALFRED: I'm sorry it's so difficult, Margaret, but it is. I'd like nothing more than to be here . . . home . . . with you, relaxed, in my old house, with you, alone, making love. . . .

MARGARET: [*Shocked, somehow*] Alfred L. Webber!

ALFRED: I don't seem to be able to relax anymore. Never. . . . Not even while I was kissing you. . . .

MARGARET: How did it feel?

ALFRED: Huh?

MARGARET: To kiss me: how did it feel?

ALFRED: How did it feel to kiss you?

MARGARET: After all these years: how did it?

ALFRED: Oh . . . well . . . exciting. Kissing you excited me. Stimulating . . . sexually. [*He laughs. Imitates child performing "Ali Baba."*] . . . Made me feel . . . open. . . . Open . . . sexually.
[ALFRED *laughs;* MARGARET *suddenly slaps his face.*]

MARGARET: You haven't changed a bit. Dirty mind. Always a dirty mind.

ALFRED: [*Throwing her on the sofa; roughly*] You're forty! We're forty! What can be dirty when you're forty???

MARGARET: I'm frightened of you.
[*All in one supremely graceful move,* ALFRED *to* MARGARET: *they kiss.* WILL *reenters and sees.* EMILY, ALFRED's *wife, enters through the front door.*
It all must occur in one move.
ALFRED *is the first to sense what's happened.*]

ALFRED: Will, this is my wife, Emily. Emily, this is Margaret's husband, Will. Margaret, this is my wife, Emily. I'm Alfred.

WILL: [*Angrily; incredulously*] What the hell is going on?

ALFRED: Will, calm down. Calm down, Will. This is really quite funny, if you think about it: comic.

[WILL *circles the room.*]

WILL: What the hell is going on?

ALFRED: [*His composure cracking*] Will you calm down?? Margaret and I were kissing. Just kidding around! Two grade-school sweethearts reminiscing and kissing. There is absolutely nothing to worry about. Absolutely nothing. Emily, take your coat off and sit down.

[EMILY *doesn't move.*]

WILL: What the hell is going on?

ALFRED: [*Waxing hysterical*] Will, you're hysterical. Nothing is going on. Emily, take your coat off and sit down. You're staring.

[EMILY *doesn't move.*]

WILL: Margaret. Say something.

MARGARET: [*Catatonic, near-arrest*] I . . . I . . .

ALFRED: Will, there is absolutely nothing to be concerned about.

WILL: I heard every word.

MARGARET: [*Simply, an explanation*] He does that a lot. He listens in on the telephone.

ALFRED: I know.

MARGARET: He heard me talking to my mother.

ALFRED: He heard me talking to the paper.

MARGARET: Who???

ALFRED: The paper! The paper!

WILL: I heard every word. You gonna marry her?

ALFRED: [*Shaken*] Are you crazy?

WILL: Sounded pretty much like that to me. Course, maybe you were both just kidding. Maybe you knew I was listening in from the kitchen and you wanted to give me a good laugh.

MARGARET: I want to go to bed. This is dis*gust*ing!

[WILL *walks to her and slaps her face.*]

WILL: [*After a pause, dryly*] That's because you said "disgusting." You wanna hear *disgusting?* I'll give you *disgusting!* [*To* ALFRED] I almost killed a man because of her.

MARGARET: *Will, for God's sakes!*

WILL: It's true, Alfred. He was from Woburn. The paper

man's helper. The paper man buys our paper. Still does.
Old newspapers, tied in bundles. Fifteen cents a hundred
pounds. Ain't much, but we don't have much. Maybe
you noticed, huh?

ALFRED: I . . . uh . . . I didn't notice anything out of the
ordinary, Will.

MARGARET: *Will, please . . .*

WILL: Can't take it, huh? Why didn'tcha think of that before, huh? All's I'm doin' is playing back what's true, ya
know, *Maahhr*garet. She has no shame. No shame!

MARGARET: Stop, Will. . . .

WILL: Yuh, sure I'll stop, sister. Same as you! [*To* ALFRED]
I go over her house for an afternoon visit, you know.
I was just a kid. I'm having wet dreams in the afternoon
. . . hoping *Maahhr*garet here'll let me have a feel, maybe. [*Pauses.*] I go into the house and it seems like no
one's home, you know? I listen for noises. I'm just about
ready to call out her name and I hear 'em . . . down
below. In the cellar. I go over to the stairs and look down.
There they are. Honest ta Christ! No shame! She's right
the Christ outa her blouse and brassiere and then the
skirt and the underpants and there they are . . . doin' it.
Doin' it!

MARGARET: Oh, my dear sweet God. . . . [*She moans.*]

WILL: [*He moves to the weeping* MARGARET.] Lucky I happened in, huh? Big guy. A real lummox . . . from Woburn. A big stud type. A lummox. [*To* ALFRED] You get
the picture?

MARGARET: Please . . .

WILL: No shame. No shame. I coulda killed him easy. I
didn't. What the hell? He had kids. No reason they
should carry the burden, right? It wouldn'ta taken much
for me to kill him . . . if I had gone on. You follow my
message?

ALFRED: You . . . uh . . . think about it much?

WILL: No. I don't . . . *uh* . . . think about it much.

ALFRED: Well, that's quite a story to swallow, Will. . . .
Really gets the imagination cooking. . . .

WILL: I'll cook your ass.

ALFRED: I beg your pardon, Will.

WILL: Shut up.

ALFRED: Will?

WILL: Shut up!

ALFRED: Calm down, now, Will. . . .

WILL: [*A command.*] *Shut the fuck up!!*

MARGARET: [*Sobbing*] Please . . .

WILL: The light down there's dim . . . dark . . . but I could
see them. Still can. I swear to God, I still can. [*Pauses.*]
We weren't married then. We were falling in love.

[MARGARET *runs from the room; exits up staircase.*]

WILL: [*Softly, almost weeping*] Nice to meet you, Emily.
Heard a lot about you from Alfred here. He's a regular
blabbermouth when it comes to his wife. [WILL *walks to
the door. He yells upstairs.*] I'm takin' a walk round the
lake!

[WILL *opens door. Exits.*]

EMILY *has been staring silently throughout scene.*

ALFRED *crosses and sits in* WILL's *chair.*

[*He holds his back to* EMILY; *does not face her as he
speaks.*]

ALFRED: I told you not to follow me here.

[*The lights fade to black.*]

END OF ACT I

ACT II
Scene 1

Later.

Stage in darkness.

Three sharp knocks are heard.

Church bells in distance, two chimes.

*The first word of the act—*ALFRED'S—*is heard.*

ALFRED: Don't.
  [*Lights to full, suddenly.*
  EMILY, *on sofa, under oversized patchwork quilt. She wears a long night robe.*
  EMILY *faces into back of sofa, upstage. There is a small paring knife in her hand, unseen by audience.*
  ALFRED *stands downstage of her. He speaks to her again, loudly.*]
ALFRED: I said "Don't!" [*Pauses.*] Give it to me. [*No result.*] Hand it over. [*No result.*] I'll just have to take it, then. . . . [*He walks to sofa, in silence, his hand extended. Forces knife away from her.*] That's better. [*He carries an apple, which he cuts into with knife. Eats a slice. Moves to chair. Sits.*] It's a pretty town, isn't it? You'd never guess. Never. I remember when we were little, bunch of us tied a kid named Georgie Landry to a big elm tree. Set a fire. Burned his legs. Crippled him. We

were playing cowboys and Indians. You'd never guess,
would you? [*Pauses.*] Pretty town, isn't it? Try to get
some rest.

[EMILY *sobs.*]

ALFRED: Don't.

MARGARET: [*From top of stairs*] Is she sleeping?

ALFRED: No.

MARGARET: [*Downstairs*] Poor child.

ALFRED: She'll be fine.

MARGARET: [*In room now*] Poor child.

ALFRED: She's fine. Really. Really, she's fine.

MARGARET: [*Very hostile*] Poor child.

ALFRED: Stop it.

MARGARET: Hmmm?

ALFRED: What do you want?

MARGARET: Here?

ALFRED: Here.

MARGARET: Here? In this room?

ALFRED: Here. In this room.

MARGARET: [*Aggressively*] That's a funny question coming
from you.

ALFRED: We'll leave as soon as Emily can travel. She's . . .
overwrought.

MARGARET: There's no need to leave, Alfred. It's quite nice
having you here. *Both* of you. Will is enjoying himself.
He told me this morning. He told me he was enjoying
himself. [*Pauses.*] Will hasn't enjoyed himself in fifteen
years.

ALFRED: Was that true . . . what Will said? Did he really
nearly kill someone . . . like he said? Was that true?

MARGARET: That was the last real pleasure Will had.
[*Silence.*] How was your day?

ALFRED: Pleasant enough. Poked around the house a bit
with Emily. . . . Showed her all my old hiding places. . . .

MARGARET: Yes. I saw you.

ALFRED: We took a walk . . . down by the lake. . . . A bit
of shopping on Albion Street. . . . Pleasant enough.

MARGARET: How's your father? Been up there yet?

ALFRED: My father?

MARGARET: Your father. How is he?

ALFRED: Dead.

MARGARET: Still?

ALFRED: Is he still dead? Is that what you're asking me? Is my father still dead?

MARGARET: Why are you still pretending, Alfred? What are you trying to prove? Can't you see it's difficult enough for me having you back here . . . having you in the house with Will and all . . . without your acting weird like this . . . without this little charade?

ALFRED: Margaret, please believe me, but I really don't know what you're talking about. My father's dead. My father, my mother, my brother . . . they're all gone: all dead. There's just me now.

MARGARET: I don't know why you're acting this way . . . like you forget. . . . I don't know why on earth you're doing what you're doing. I agree that most things are best left swept under the rug, but . . . Oh, God, Alfred, *what do you want from us??*

ALFRED: I don't like jokes like this, Margaret. I suppose it's funny . . . to Wakefield people . . . to play spooky little jokes . . . but my father, Tommy Webber, is dead. Margaret. Dead. I've been in the cemetery and I've seen the headstone. . . .

MARGARET: Your father, Tommy Webber, is in the asylum on the hill . . . just where you put him. I'm sure you have your reasons. [*Exits into kitchen.*]

ALFRED: Margaret? . . . [*Calls to* EMILY.] Sit up. [*He calls to* EMILY *again.*] Sit up. [*She doesn't move.*] Sit up. [*No response; he crosses to her.*] Sit up!!
[*He pulls her arm, hoisting her into a sitting position, just as* WILL *enters from kitchen.*]

WILL: You lovebirds at it again?
[EMILY *drops back to the flat of the sofa.*
ALFRED *drops* EMILY's *arm, turns away from her.*]

WILL: Hey, listen, you wanna kill her, kill her. It's a free country.
[WILL *takes a baseball cap out of his pocket. He places it on his head.*
ALFRED *stares at it; really quite startled.*]

WILL: [*Strutting*] Like it?

ALFRED: [*Shocked; stunned*] Where did you . . . Where? . . . Where did . . .

WILL: You're stuttering.

ALFRED: That cap is . . .

WILL: Vet's Field . . . church league . . .

ALFRED: My . . .

WILL: Very racy. Like it.

ALFRED: His . . .

WILL: Cost me an arm and a leg.

ALFRED: [*Laughs nervously.*] That's my father's cap.

WILL: Couldn't be. It's mine.

ALFRED: That's my father's. I know that cap. My father's
. . . Hey, Will?

[ALFRED *stands and walks up to* WILL. *He reaches for
the cap, but* WILL *pulls it back from him.
The action should much resemble a child's prank.*]

ALFRED: Hey, let's see it, Will?

WILL: How could it be your father's cap, Alfred? I thought
your father was dead? Isn't he, Alfred?

ALFRED: That's true. It couldn't be. Couldn't be his.
[ALFRED *sits, smiling at* WILL.] Seen today's paper?

WILL: Nope.

[ALFRED *pretends to get interested in newspaper.* WILL
struts in front of ALFRED *now, cap on his head.*
WILL *laughs.*]

WILL: Don't know what you're talking about. [*He laughs
again.*] Alfred? [*Pauses.*] Don't you know, Alfred? You
act like you don't know. . . . [*Pauses.*] Look at me,
Alfred.

ALFRED: Give me the cap, Will.

WILL: [*To* EMILY] He's crazy, your Alfred. I heard that all
celebrities were crazy. Always heard that. Now I know
for sure.

ALFRED: Give it to me, Will.

WILL: Don't think so. Not until you open your eyes.

ALFRED: You're going to pay for this.

WILL: Already did. Six bucks.

ALFRED: Okay, Will. We'll play it your way.

WILL: [*Flips cap back onto his head. He walks to the door,
laughing.*] You know something, Alfred? I'm glad you
came home. I figured it would get piggy, you know. Lot
of screaming and yelling. Really obstreperous bullshit.
Ya know what I mean? But you've got real style, Alfred.
Real style. [*Smiles.*] You really spruce up the old place.
You add a little spice. [WILL *opens the door.*] I do, however, think it's kinda weird . . . the way you're tryin' ta

kinda remain . . . well . . . *blind* to certain matters, huh? You really ought to open your eyes. [*Exits.*]

ALFRED: [*Sits in chair. He seems stricken.*] Emily? [*No reply.*] Fine. Don't look at me. [*Pauses.*] Emily, I . . . very frightened. [*Pauses.*] I'm . . . I'm sorry I left the way I did. I don't pretend to understand why I did, I just did. I . . . I felt I had to. I was frightened. . . . [*Pauses.*] Emily? [*Pauses.*] There's something wrong with my mind, Emily. My memory . . . My mind. I seem to have forgotten . . . things. [*Pauses.*] My knees are wet. My entire body is perspiring. This is simply atrocious. Look at me. . . . No. Don't. . . . [*Pauses.*] Emily, I need your help. I believe that my brother was murdered and that Will . . . well . . . did it. [*Pauses.*] I'm going to need your help. I know it's odd for me to be asking . . . asking you . . . for help . . . but I must. I must push on through this . . . be certain . . . what happened. [*Pauses.*] They're listening in, Emily, so I'm going to have to yell now. [*Pauses; then he yells loudly, sobbing.*] Em-i-leeee!

[ALFRED *places his head on his knees.*
EMILY *sits up, faces forward; smiles.*
Tableau.
The lights fade to black.]

END OF SCENE 1

Scene 2

Later.

Stage in darkness.

Three sharp knocks are heard.

*First words of scene—*EMILY'S*—are heard.*

EMILY: It's just an old thing I picked up somewhere. [*Lights to full, suddenly.*

WILL, *in chair, staring at* EMILY, *who sits center-stage, on sofa.*

EMILY *wears long, straight-lined dress, no shoes. Quilt is gone.*

Note: EMILY *should sit in precise position, smiling, as end of prior scene; as though freeze frame in which only dress and companion have changed. All else the same.*]

EMILY: It's really old. Fifteen years. It's really old.

WILL: I think it's . . . sophisticated. That's what it is: sophisticated. You look very sophisticated in that dress, Emily.

EMILY: Thank you, Will. You're kind to say that.

WILL: It's true. You must have been quite a looker in your day. . . .

EMILY: Mmmm. You're kind to say that, too.

WILL: Not that you're not okay now. You are: okay now. But I can tell that you really must have been something. Something special, I mean. Margaret and I never have talks like this, ya know that? We almost never talk at all. [*Pauses; shrugs.*] Oh, sure . . . in the beginning, we musta . . . Maybe not. In the beginning, there's plenty a' other things occupying your mind, right? [*Smiles.*] I'm really enjoying this. You?

EMILY: Yes.

WILL: Where did you first hook up with Alfred?

EMILY: I believe that Alfred and I first hooked together in Magnolia. At a weekend at Magnolia Manor. We spent our first date watching the Greasy Pole Contest in Gloucester. [*She smiles at* WILL.] Have you ever seen it?

WILL: Yuh, seems to me I did. I forget.

EMILY: A long hard stiff pole sticks straight out from a wharf. Men walk it. I found the contest to be quite stimulating.

WILL: Sounds great.

EMILY: Alfred never had a girl before me. I was his first. Can you imagine?

WILL: Now I gotcha. . . .

EMILY: Sorry?

WILL: [*Thinks he's back in a world of reason.*] Margaret.

EMILY: Margaret?

WILL: He had Margaret. Had her in the eleventh grade.

EMILY: [*She laughs.*] Nooooo.

WILL: He did so.

[EMILY *laughs again.*]

WILL: Alfred got Margaret in trouble, during the summer of the eleventh grade.

EMILY: Trouble?

WILL: Family way. She was in it.

EMILY: I see.

WILL: Little girl. They gave it away.

EMILY: They gave it away? Like a gift? That sort of thing?

WILL: To a home, up over the line in New Hampshire. They do those sort of things up there.

EMILY: I don't follow.

WILL: Alfred and Margaret had a little girl together and they gave it away . . . to some home . . . for adoption . . . in New Hampshire. What's so hard to follow?

EMILY: [*Quietly*] It's not hard to follow. It's hard to . . . accept.

WILL: Alfred was the father all right. He ruined her. Margaret: ruined. Did something to her mind. Made her barren. Alfred ruined her.

EMILY: Are you certain, Will?

WILL: I saw it with my own eyes . . . Margaret. . . . Saw her stomach. Everybody in town saw it, too. I myself had my own trouble. . . .

EMILY: In what way?

WILL: Family, same as Margaret. I got a Wakefield cheerleader in trouble. F. . . .

EMILY: F?

WILL: F.

EMILY: And you gave the child away?

WILL: *Are you crazy??*

EMILY: What is this? A pop quiz, Will?

WILL: I would *never* do a thing like that!

EMILY: Nor would I.

WILL: I would cut off a finger before I would give a baby up for adoption. . . .

EMILY: As would I.

WILL: It isn't manly.

EMILY: That's not *my* reason, exactly, Will, but I do understand.

WILL: My son, Will, Jr. . . . I made sure he was born and

I made sure he was raised with the best money could
buy. . . .

EMILY: Your *son?* Where is he?

WILL: My son. Beautiful kid. He's off in college now.
Imagine that? I'm forty and I've got a kid twenty-
one. . . .

EMILY: You must be proud?

WILL: Proud? Proud? I'm *more* than proud! Best thing I
ever did was to insist that Will, Jr., be brought up right.

EMILY: And you never wanted more?

WILL: Kids? Sure I did.

EMILY: But you didn't?

WILL: It wasn't me: it's her. Barren. I told you. Alfred saw
to that. Why do you think I hate him so much?

EMILY: I'd wondered why.

WILL: Now you know.

EMILY: Margaret's been tested?

WILL: A million times. There's no doubt. . . .

[EMILY *just stares at* WILL *silently.*]

WILL: What're you starin' at? There's no doubt. I talked
to the doctor myself. Psychological barrenness. . . .

EMILY: Really?

WILL: What are you getting at?

EMILY: Margaret's clever.

WILL: What are you? . . . Kidding me? . . . Or what?
Margaret? Clever?

EMILY: I could have saved myself a lot of, well, trouble,
Will . . . if I had known what Margaret learned in high
school. . . .

WILL: And what's that?

EMILY: To stop trying.

WILL: I don't follow.

EMILY: No, you don't. You certainly don't.

[*Silence.*

WILL *doesn't move.*]

WILL: I guess you couldn't get interested in a townie like
me. Ah, I know. Alfred's got all those city ways down
pat. That kind of round-shouldered bullshit. [*Pauses,
changes tone.*] I got dirt under my fingernails. Alfred
probably bites his. I used to know a joke about fingernails . . . I forgot it.

EMILY: He *did*.

WILL: Huh?

EMILY: He quit. He quit biting his fingernails when he quit smoking. He gave up all forms of sucking.

WILL: [*Honestly embarrassed*] Heyyy, watch your talk, okay?

EMILY: You're sweet, Will. [*She smiles at* WILL.] You're living in another century.

[WILL *moves to* EMILY; *stops. Momentarily loses courage.*]

EMILY: I do find you attractive, Will. I really do. Kiss me. [*As they kiss,* ALFRED *enters.*]

ALFRED: Nice. Really nice.

[*They pull apart.*]

ALFRED: Sorry. I'm not being discreet. I should have knocked.

WILL: There's nothing going on, Alfred—really.

ALFRED: Oh. I thought you two were . . . you know.

WILL: Naw. . . .

EMILY: Alfred?

ALFRED: Forget it. Forget it. Sorry I asked. [*He exits.*]

WILL: Hey! Alfred!!! Where the hell's he going??? He just left us alone.

EMILY: [*Quietly*] Balls!

WILL: What?

EMILY: Balls?

WILL: [*Disgusted*] That's what I thought you said. God-dam! [*Clenches eyes closed, three times. Sits.*] I'm getting a headache.

[*Three knocks at the door.*]

WILL: Yeah?

[ALFRED *enters.*]

ALFRED: It's lonely in the kitchen. Mind if I sit in here with you?

WILL: [*A gentleman*] Come in. Sit down. I don't mind. It's fine with me.

[ALFRED *sits.*]

WILL: Cigarette?

ALFRED: [*Smiling*] Quit.

EMILY: Fingernail?

ALFRED: [*Without changing his smile*] Why don't you try stuffing it where the sun never shines?

WILL: Jesus. Nice talk. Really piggy. You know what I mean? [*Squints.*] My head feels like a broken arm.

EMILY: I was just telling Will about Magnolia.

ALFRED: I know. I heard. You only watched Margaret get *laid*, Wilbur. I had the pleasure of watching *Emily* get beaten up.

WILL: Hmmm?

ALFRED: The Magnolia locals didn't take really well to Emily's . . . to Emily's *kind*. [*Smiles.*] The word is that they chased Emily's . . . How would you say it? . . . They chased Emily's *party* right out of town. On *foot*, too. Straight up the old route one-twenty-seven into Manchester Center and then on through to Gloucester Harbor. It must have been a hell of a run for an old man. . . . [*Pauses.*] The Greasy Pole Contest was on that day and their departure caused quite a sensation, I'm sure. A youngish woman, naked, a craggy old man, also naked, and a gaggle of locals chasing after.

WILL: [*To* EMILY, *who is looking away*] What's he talking about?

ALFRED: They say the Greasy Pole contender . . . a B. J. something . . . was so disconcerted, he walked right off the end of the pole, forgetting to lift the red flag. . . .

WILL: [*To* ALFRED] What craggy old man?

ALFRED: [*Smiles.*] Oh, *that!* Emily's always had a certain active curiosity about craggy old men. . . . At the time Emily and I first hooked up together, she was seeing a very wealthy, very craggy, very old fellow—from Yugoslavia, I believe.

WILL: Yugoslavia?

ALFRED: Silk robes are nothing, Will. Nothing. Emily's Slav wore the real stuff.

[EMILY *slaps* ALFRED's *face. A clean, loud single slap, with her left hand.* ALFRED *stands firm; continues, apparently unbothered.*]

ALFRED: . . . garter belts . . .

[EMILY *slaps him again: right-handed.*]

ALFRED: . . . dark-seamed tinted nylons . . .

[EMILY *slaps him again: left-handed.*]

ALFRED: . . . fake-fun-fur coats . . .

[EMILY *slaps* ALFRED *again: right-handed.*

He stops talking, smiles. He walks to the door: stops.
He walks to EMILY.]

ALFRED: That was unpleasant. Not unattractive. But unpleasant. [*Pauses. He then returns to the door.*] Night.
[ALFRED *exits.*

WILL *stares wide-eyed, disbelieving.*
There is a pause. WILL *exhales a great deal of breath:*
sits.]

WILL: I don't understand.

EMILY: [*To* WILL; *cruelly direct*] No, you don't! You certainly don't! [*Pauses; inhales, exhales.*] My mother was a
virgin when she married him. [*Pauses.*] She was a virgin
when she died. [*Pauses.*] My father was a sainted man.
[*She lights a cigarette.*] I wish I'd met him. [*She coughs.*]
Alfred's right. I really must quit. [*Pauses.*] Just shut up,
Will. [*Pauses.*] *I LOATHE NOISE! I CAN'T THINK!*

WILL: Are you all right?

EMILY: I'm all right.

WILL: You sure?

EMILY: I have never in my entire life met another woman
who was even one half as unhappy as I am.

WILL: What are you looking for here, Emily?

EMILY: [*After a pause*] There are times I look in the mirror
and there's no one there.

WILL: I'll bet you look great in the mirror.

EMILY: Sometimes, instead of me, it's Alfred in there . . .
in the space reserved for my reflection.

WILL: Sneaking up? That kind of thing?

EMILY: Yuh.

WILL: Sometimes, a man just sneaks. He doesn't want to.
He just does.

EMILY: I spent my first ten years in an orphanage. The next
ten in California, in a boarding school for the very gifted.
I was very gifted, Will.

WILL: Not me. Not even at Christmastime. [*He laughs.*]
That was a good one. [*Smiles.*] The best ones just sneak
out, don't they?

EMILY: Is Alfred's father still alive, Will?

WILL: Course he is.

EMILY: Where?

WILL: Up on the hill. Nuthouse, with all the rest of 'em.

. . . How come he's pretending his father's dead, huh?
What's all that about, anyway?

EMILY: I don't know. I *will* know. I just don't . . . yet.
[*Smiles.*] We do have a lot in common, Will.

WILL: Now that you mention it, I guess we do. Yuh . . .
Hey, listen, I gotta tell you, Emily: around these parts,
growin' up 'n' all, Alfred was known as a real jerk, ya
know? Eighteen years old and he makes a clear million
sellin' a swamp. Who woulda guessed, huh? I mean, who
the Christ woulda ever guessed? But, so far as *I'm* concerned, million or not, interviews or not, boy wonder or
not, Alfred L. Webber was, is, and will be a first-class
jerk. I gotta tell ya that.

EMILY: Thanks, Will. That certainly clears things up.

WILL: You're playin' with me. I don't like it, okay?

EMILY: Can you prove that Alfred's father's alive, Will?

WILL: Easy. Have a look? [*He takes a baseball cap from
his pocket and places it on his head.*]

EMILY: Is that Alfred's father's cap?

WILL: Yup. You like it? His father just gave it to me.

EMILY: Alfred told me his father died . . . fifteen years
ago. . . . Alfred came up here for the funeral. I remember
consoling him.

WILL: That was his brother.

EMILY: His what?

WILL: His brother. Alfred had a crazy brother . . . Bruce.
. . . A real jerk. It's all through Alfred's family. Bruce,
his name was. Big. He grew up in Woburn.

EMILY: But Alfred grew up *here* . . . in Wakefield.

WILL: Half brother. Different mothers. Alfred's father
moved around a lot. You get what I mean?

EMILY: Not exactly.

WILL: This is a small town, Emily. Things maybe . . . well
. . . *pass* in a town like this that might not pass elsewhere.

EMILY: I don't understand.

WILL: [*Suddenly turns to* EMILY, *cap on head. He mimics
her cruel epithet, precisely.*] No, you don't. You certainly
don't. [*He smiles. He settles back into chair. A pause.*]
They built a hot-dog stand where my house used to be,
Margaret. They really did.

EMILY: Margaret. You called me "Margaret."

WILL: I'll tell you somepin': if I had the courage, I would run myself a nice hot tub, climb in, close my eyes, and slide.

EMILY: [*Pauses, then softly*] You called me "Margaret." Will? [*Pauses.*] Will?

WILL: [*A forlorn statement; a fact.*] She's the only woman I'll ever love.

EMILY: Margaret?

WILL: Margaret.

EMILY: Perfect.

WILL: She is the only woman I have ever met who really pays attention.

EMILY: Have you ever told her this? Margaret.

WILL: She wouldn't listen.

EMILY: You ever try?

WILL: She doesn't listen.

EMILY: I'm confused.

WILL: I had a chance . . .

EMILY: To what?

WILL: . . . get out of here. I had a chance to get out of here. Fifteen years ago. Her boyfriend . . . I should have left then.

EMILY: Her *what?*

WILL: Boyfriend. The guy in the cellar. From Woburn. That was her boyfriend. . . .

EMILY: The one you strangled? . . .

WILL: The one I *what?*

EMILY: Strangled. You said you strangled the man from Woburn.

WILL: [*Stares absently at the sofa.*] Re-covered.

EMILY: Who?

WILL: The sofa. [*He pauses; speaks softly now.*] Used to be a nice dark blue. She changed it to that stuff that's on there now. . . . I liked the dark blue better. . . .

EMILY: How do you feel about red, Will?

WILL: Red?

EMILY: Red roses, specifically?

WILL: I like them. I like them very much, but I don't like your questions. [*Silence.*] Alfred's come a long way.

EMILY: He works hard. . . .

WILL: I work hard. . . .

EMILY: [*Sits on the arm of* WILL's *chair.*] Not the same.

WILL: [*Jumps up and moves away.*] Another article in the paper today. About a scholarship. Is that true?

EMILY: Didn't see it.

WILL: Alfred's set up a big scholarship in the old man's name.

EMILY: Will, I . . . yes. Yes, he did.

WILL: [*Counts to himself, in whispers.*] Nine, carry two . . .

EMILY: What are you counting, Will?

WILL: I'll *never* see that much money, ya know. . . . Not in my life . . . not in one lump sum. [*Looks up.*] Betcha wonderin' how I came to own this house, huh? Betcha wonderin' where I got the money. . . . His old house, too.

EMILY: How?

WILL: Back taxes. Ten thousand dollars . . . a thousand down, nine ta carry . . . fifteen years. Almost *free*, as house prices go, and I could barely swing it. I had ta work weekends first five years or so . . . just ta make ends meet. . . . And that jerk gives a goddam scholarship at the high school that'd buy ten of these rattraps! Ten of 'em! Ain't that just the last laugh on all of us, huh? On *me*, especially! He grows up right here, goes away at eighteen—a millionaire—comes back a trillionaire, probably—and here's good old Wilbur M. Lynch, pushing the truck every mornin', trying to pay off the taxes he left behind. Livin' in the *box* Alfred's champagne bottle came in.

EMILY: It's only money. Alfred is unhappy.

WILL: What am I: a laugh a minute?

EMILY: [*Crosses to* WILL'*s chair and leans over him.*] Alfred's impotent.

WILL: In what way?

EMILY: Alfred's impotent. . . . He can't . . .

WILL: Get it up?

EMILY: Get it up.

WILL: [*Amazed and delighted*] You're crazy.

EMILY: That may be, but it does not in any way alter the fact that Alfred cannot . . .

WILL: [*Laughing*] Get it up?

EMILY: Get it up.

WILL: He got it up last night.

EMILY: What?

WILL: He got it up last night. I saw them.

EMILY: Margaret . . .

WILL: . . . and Alfred.

EMILY: You saw Margaret and Alfred . . .

WILL: . . . doing it.

EMILY: Will you FOR CHRISSAKES let me finish a sentence??

WILL: Sorry.

EMILY: Where?

WILL: Same as always. In the living room . . . here. . . .

EMILY: . . . On the sofa?

WILL: Same as always. . . .

EMILY: You watched?

WILL: Well . . . yuh . . . yuh . . . I did . . . I watched.

EMILY: For how long?

WILL: Thirty-five minutes.

EMILY: What? You watched for thirty-five minutes?

WILL: That's *nothing*. I can go an hour.

EMILY: Say that again.

WILL: I can go an hour.

EMILY: You want to prove it?

WILL: I wouldn't . . . I wouldn't mind. We have to find a place. . . .

EMILY: Sofa's fine with me. . . .

WILL: They're in the house.

EMILY: So?

WILL: So I think we should find a place.

EMILY: You care if they catch us?

WILL: No. You're right.

[*Pause.*

EMILY *turns off light and begins unbuttoning* WILL's *shirt. She stands behind chair, leaning over him. Both face front.*]

EMILY: You think about it much?

WILL: No.

EMILY: What do you think of, when you see them?

WILL: See them?

EMILY: In your mind?

WILL: How pretty they are.

EMILY: Really?

WILL: Maggie's pink, the slipcover was a nice deep dark blue. Like deep water. He was all suntanned from being outside. She was pink. Pushing and pulling at each other.

I thought he was killing her . . . with all the pushing and pulling and the noises she was making. . . . She never made those kind of noises for me. [*Pause.*] Then I saw her face. [*Pause.*] He wasn't killing her. [*Pause.*] Around here, people understand.

EMILY: You've still got a pretty good figure . . . physique. [*Moving in now*] . . . Very nice to the touch.

WILL: [*Seriously considers what* EMILY *has said.*] Naw, I'm way outa shape. Soft. You shoulda looked me up twenty years ago. . . . Used to be really something. Something special. [*Pauses.*] Too much drink, too much TV, too much sittin' around. . . . [*Pauses.*] Course, I could join the Y an' work out a little. Maybe get some development back, huh? [*Pauses.*] Would you like that?

EMILY: That's a terribly exciting idea, Will.

WILL: You gonna keep your things on?

EMILY: No. Uh uh . . . [*She unbuttons front of dress.*]

WILL: You're really beautiful.

[WILL *stands and moves to* EMILY, *who moves back from him.*
She is against the sofa. He follows: hugs her.]

WILL: We never get women like you around here, Emily, not even in the summertime. Never. . . . Tell me what to do. . . .

EMILY: Will, listen. . . .

WILL: What?

[EMILY *is bent backwards against the arm of the sofa.* WILL, *in front, trying to press her down.*]

EMILY: The man on the sofa was Alfred's brother, right? You killed Alfred's brother, right, Will???

WILL: What are you talking about???

EMILY: That was his brother, right? Will, I've got to know. Please, Will. The man from Woburn . . . in the cellar . . . and the man on the sofa? That was the same man: Alfred's brother. Right, Will? Will, please? . . .

WILL: You must think I'm stupid. You must think I'm a dope!

[WILL *rises with clothes and moves to stairs, trips.*
ALFRED *appears at top of stairs.*]

ALFRED: You okay?

EMILY: Nothing is certain.

ALFRED: What did he tell you?

EMILY: Nothing is certain.

ALFRED: *What did he tell you???*

WILL: What the hell gives here?

ALFRED: Strip him.

EMILY: Alfred, don't be ridiculous. . . .

ALFRED: I'm tired of waiting. *Strip . . . him.* [*Yells.*] *Move!*
[WILL *has fallen on the stairs and has, until this point,
remained frozen in one spot, listening.*
He now crawls up the staircase, two steps. Stops.
ALFRED *moves down the staircase, two steps. Stops.*
EMILY *moves across room to bottom stair. Stops.*
WILL *raises his head and stares wordlessly, first to* EMILY,
then to ALFRED.
They each move one additional step toward WILL, *as the
lights fade to black.*]

END OF ACT II

ACT III

Later.

Stage in darkness.

Three sharp knocks are heard.

Church bells in distance, two chimes.

First words of the act—ALFRED's—are heard.

ALFRED: How do you like it so far?
  [*Lights to full, suddenly.*
  ALFRED *stands on landing on top of staircase behind*
  WILL, *who is stripped to his underpants and socks,*
  bound, and gagged.
  WILL's *legs and arms are poked through staircase railing*
  and tied around spindles.
  The gag in his mouth is his white cotton undershirt.
  EMILY *and* MARGARET *sit on sofa, as far apart as possible.*]
ALFRED: I think that Will looks rather well in rope, don't
  you? [ALFRED *leans down into room, smiling.*] Don't you
  think he does, Margaret?
MARGARET: Please, Alfred?
ALFRED: Please, *what*, Margaret?
MARGARET: Let me take the gag out of his mouth.
ALFRED: But if I were to do that, Will could talk. . . . I
  prefer holding the old status quo, for a while. . . . [*To*
  WILL] You don't mind holding the old status quo, do
  you, Will?
WILL: [*Struggling*] Argghh. . . .

105

ALFRED: Right! Will has a great affinity for things Latin. Status quo is Latin, Will: the tongue of the Church. . . .

WILL: Ughhh. . . .

ALFRED: I would have to say that Will actually has a proclivity for things Latin.

WILL: Uggghhhhhhhh!

ALFRED: Now you've gone too far, Will. I'm afraid I'll have to put my finger to your proclivity, so to speak. [*Twists gag tighter.*]

WILL: Arggghhhh!

[ALFRED *twists gag considerably tighter.* WILL *winces.*]

ALFRED: I should have said so not to speak. [*Pauses.*] Better. Much better.

MARGARET: I think the gag may be hurting his mouth.

ALFRED: Yes. I think so. Emily, I want a cold drink. Ginger ale.

[EMILY *stands and exits. All watch.*]

ALFRED: Emily's been a good wife.

MARGARET: You must be very happy. You two seem like you were made for each other.

ALFRED: She should not have followed me here. She was told to stay home. Not like Emily at all. Not at all. . . .

MARGARET: What do you want?

ALFRED: Want?

MARGARET: Want.

ALFRED: Now?

MARGARET: Now.

ALFRED: Ginger ale.

[EMILY *enters, gives* ALFRED *a glass of ginger ale.*]

ALFRED: Thank you. [*Pause.*] Here's to you. [*Tips his glass to* WILL.] Nice. Really nice. [*Pauses.*] Emily? [EMILY *smiles, stands, walks to* WILL.]

EMILY: The thing is, Will, we think you murdered Alfred's brother.

MARGARET: What?

ALFRED: Shhh. This is the good part.

EMILY: When you walked in that day, Will . . . when Margaret here was being indiscreet . . . that's when you strangled him, right?

MARGARET: What is she talking about?

EMILY: The man in the cellar and/or on the sofa: the man

who was monkeying with you in the cellar and/or on
the sofa. That was Alfred's brother. . . . Right?

MARGARET: I'm leaving the room. I see no reason why I
should be made to sit through such a disgusting display
of . . . of . . .

EMILY: Of what?

MARGARET: In my own home.

EMILY: [*Smiles.*] I appreciate your obligatory false exit,
Margaret. Sit down.

[MARGARET *does.*]

EMILY: Better. If there is one thing on the face of this
earth I understand, I understand the reason a woman—
any woman—moves from point A to point B. Any
woman. Even a Wakefield woman. Alfred?

ALFRED: Huh?

EMILY: It's your ball game.

ALFRED: Right. Now then, Will . . . Margaret . . . when I
first came back to town . . . to Wakefield . . . to the old
turf, I didn't actually have an inkling why. I've had
increased difficulty . . . with my memory. I don't remember easily. . . .

WILL: [*Yells through his gag.*] Yoooaww rememmmm. . . .

ALFRED: Was that a low-flying plane? [*Smiles.*] Well, now.
Almost as soon as my foot touched down in Wakefield,
on Albion Street, precisely . . . I knew why . . . why I'd
come back . . . what I had to do. Will? Margaret?

MARGARET: What?

ALFRED: My brother was murdered. I'd tried for years to
put it out of my mind . . . not get involved. But now I'm
home. The murder of my brother needs avenging. His
murderer must confess and . . . well . . . be punished.

WILL: [*Trying to yell through gag.*] Yooo awrrr craazzzziii
. . . !!

ALFRED: I beg your pardon?

MARGARET: How dare you . . . of *all* people . . . carry on
like this?

ALFRED: Me, of all people?

EMILY: Him, of all people?

MARGARET: Yuh. *Him* of all people. Yuh.

EMILY: What exactly do you mean, Margaret? I'd like to
know.

ALFRED: I wouldn't mind knowing myself, Margaret.

MARGARET: Alfred, for the love of God! [*Sudden anger.*] Not in front of *her*, Alfred!

EMILY: Me?

MARGARET: You! Right, you! There are certain matters that don't concern outsiders like you. . . . [*Pauses.*] Just what I said: not in front of you.

EMILY: I'll turn my back. . . .

MARGARET: [*Yells; suddenly.*] *We . . . don't . . . talk . . . about it!*

ALFRED: About what? [*Pauses.*] About what?

EMILY: About what?

ALFRED: About what?

MARGARET: I'm sure you have your reasons, Alfred. I'm sure you do.

ALFRED: Rest assured. Rest assured. I talked to a lot of people downtown, before I came here to the house. Wakefield people love to talk, don't they? [*Smiles.*] It seems that quite a lot of people knew that you and my brother were quite close. . . .

MARGARET: We were . . .

ALFRED: Lovers.

MARGARET: That's not true!

ALFRED: Do you solemnly swear?

MARGARET: I've never had a lover!

WILL: Arggghhh!

MARGARET: Never!

WILL: ARGGGHHHH!

ALFRED: Just one. My brother.

MARGARET: That's not true.

ALFRED: Seems my brother used to come here just about every day . . . while Will was working.

MARGARET: Who told you that?

ALFRED: Will.

MARGARET: Will?

WILL: Arggghhhh!

ALFRED: See?

MARGARET: Why would Will say anything like that?

EMILY: Will's an unusual man.

ALFRED: We'll see. [ALFRED *runs upstairs to* WILL.] Okay, Will. [ALFRED *removes* WILL'*s gag.*] Shut up, Will. Margaret?

MARGARET: What?

ALFRED: Don't you miss him?

MARGARET: Not in front of Will . . .

ALFRED: Don't you?

MARGARET: No.

ALFRED: He loved you.

MARGARET: I know.

ALFRED: He used to write to me about you.

MARGARET: He did?

WILL: He didn't, ya dumb bitch! [*Yells down to* ALFRED *now.*] Knock it off, Alfred! You're really wearing out your welcome, you know that, pal?

[*They are, all three, sitting now on the sofa:* ALFRED *and* EMILY *on the ends,* MARGARET *sandwiched in the middle.* WILL *breaks the silence.*]

WILL: I never did. I couldn't . . . This is really crazy!

EMILY: Why is Alfred's concern for his brother crazy, Will? [*No reply.* EMILY *yells.*] Why?

WILL: Alfred's brother, Bruce B. Webber, was a prime, first-class *jerk*, that's why! You know what we use'ta call him? I'll tell you what: *Cootie!* That's what Bruce B. Webber was known as in this town: Cootie Webber. . . .

MARGARET: Wilbur Lynch, that is not true!

WILL: May God strike me down deader than a doornail if it's not true!

MARGARET: In fifth grade! In fifth grade, yes . . . Cootie. . . .

WILL: On accounta his monkey. . . .

EMILY: I beg your pardon?

WILL: On account of his monkey. That's why we called him Cootie . . . because all the kids figured he caught cooties . . . from his pet monkey. Bruce B. Webber had a pet monkey . . . on his *shoulder!* Some normal fella, huh?

MARGARET: In fifth grade, for God's sakes! Bruce B. Webber had a pet monkey in fifth grade!

WILL: That doesn't make him any less of a joke around here. That's exactly what your brother was, Alfred, and you know it: the town joke. You were so ashamed of him, you didn't hardly acknowledge he was even alive. Everybody knew that to be true. *Everybody!*

ALFRED: My brother was valedictorian of his class here, Emily . . . voted the most likely to succeed. . . .

WILL: Cooties . . . all over his shoulders. . . .

ALFRED: Right. You got it, Will. . . . Now I see why you had to murder him: a man with cooties can't be allowed to walk a Wakefield street. The town's just not big enough. . . .

MARGARET: Why the good Lord ever *ever* stuck me in a house for all these years with Wilbur Lynch is something I will never understand . . . if I live to be a hundred and eighty! *What . . . did . . . I . . . do???*

WILL: You want me to answer that question, sister? Want me to?

[MARGARET *looks away from* WILL'*s stare.* WILL *laughs.*]

WILL: All right. Suurrrrre . . . [WILL *looks at* EMILY.] I've got plenty to say about Mr. Bruce B. Webber. Plenty!

EMILY: I'm all ears, Will.

WILL: Straight A's at Wakefield High and where did it get him? Think about *that*, huh? He goes off to college, starts drinkin' and highfalutin politics and bullshit . . . next thing we know he's back here in town, a layabout, a good-for-nothin', a Guinea-wino. . . .

MARGARET: Wilbur Lynch!

WILL: Wilbur Lynch my ass! Bruce B. Webber was a falling-down wino and that's a *fact*. A *fact!*

MARGARET: Bruce B. Webber was a fine, understanding man who made me feel clean and beautiful and, for once in my life, not dumb . . . and that's a fact. *That* is a fact. . . . [*Quickly, to* ALFRED] He was never as special as you, Alfred . . . never as exciting to me . . . never as funny or clever as you. . . . But he was fine, Alfred. . . . Emily . . . it's true. Bruce B. Webber—drinker, or not; skinny, or not; oddball, or not—was a fine, understanding man, who made me feel clean and made me feel beautiful and let me be what I am.

WILL: And what's that?

MARGARET: What's what?

WILL: What you are? What's that?

MARGARET: Not dumb.

WILL: You were dumb enough to fall for Bruce B. Webber's bullshit . . . and Alfred L. Webber's bullshit . . . and Tommy Webber's bullshit . . . and if there had been a Webber dog, you woulda fallen for Doggy Webber's bullshit, too!

EMILY: Tommy?

ALFRED: You're stooping, Will. . . .

EMILY: Will?

MARGARET: Stop it!

WILL: Bullshit, I'll stop it. Everybody's looking at me here
like I'm the crazy one, right? Well, I've got a real piece
of craziness to straighten out here: Tommy Webber is
alive. Alive. Alive and the same sex maniac he was sixty
years ago. And that's a fact. They use ta say if somebody would hold a rattlesnake's mouth open long enough,
Tommy Webber would—

ALFRED: God damn it, this is really enough! I will not have
my father's memory dragged through this mudwrestle
of yours, Will—

WILL: Memory?

MARGARET: Memory?

ALFRED: Memory. My father's life was hardly perfect, but
it was hardly what Wilbur Lynch's filthy little mind would
have it be. Now God damn it. God damn it! [*Pauses.*]
My brother was murdered and I will have a confession
now, please. Now, please! [*Pauses.*] I feel cold!

MARGARET: Will . . . please don't. . . . [*She sobs.*]

WILL: Cry your ass off! See if I care. I've played dumb
long enough. . . .

[ALFRED *places his head in his lap and sobs.*]

WILL: Great. Two of you cryers . . . perfect, huh? You
wouldn't catch me crying. It ain't manly.

[EMILY *walks to* ALFRED *and strokes his cheek.* WILL
watches a moment.]

ALFRED: Enough!

[ALFRED *stands, eyes clenched closed. He crosses to the
chair, feeling his way as a blind man. He knocks against
the chair, causing the pedestal ashtray to fall over. He
sits, smiling into the others' astonished silence.* ALFRED
faces forward, smiling broadly now.]

EMILY: What are you doing?

ALFRED: That's better. It's okay now, Will . . . I'm okay.
Talk, Will. I'm still listening.

EMILY: You closed your eyes. What are you doing?

MARGARET: You've closed your eyes. [*To* WILL] Alfred's
closed his eyes.

ALFRED: Talk, Will. Will? Will? *Will!*

MARGARET: Alfred, please . . .

WILL: It's been fifteen years . . .

MARGARET: Alfred . . .

WILL: C'mon. Alfred . . . what's the point?

ALFRED: My brother . . . that's the point. My brother.

MARGARET: Stop acting like this, Alfred. Emily, make him stop. . . . Please, Emily. . . .

ALFRED: Yes, Emily, make me stop.

EMILY: That's enough, Alfred.

ALFRED: What's enough?

EMILY: Open your eyes.

ALFRED: And why?

EMILY: I said, "Open your eyes."

ALFRED: And if I don't?

EMILY: Think.

ALFRED: About what?

EMILY: Think.

ALFRED: Don't try to run me, Emily! I won't have it!

EMILY: *THINK!!!*

ALFRED: Don't talk to me like that.

EMILY: Like what?

ALFRED: Like I'm a fool.

EMILY: But you are.

ALFRED: I despise you.

EMILY: I own you.

ALFRED: Stop it.

EMILY: Say it!

ALFRED: I despise you.

EMILY: Say it.

ALFRED: [*Quietly*] You own me.

EMILY: Much better.

[ALFRED *has shrunk in the chair. He is very frightened indeed.*]

EMILY: Sit up now, Alfred. Don't embarrass me. [*Pause.*] I said, "Sit up!"

[*He does*]

EMILY: Better. Now open your eyes.

ALFRED: [*He slumps back down in chair.*] Nope.

MARGARET: Why are you acting this way?

ALFRED: [*Slowly at first; then with moderate speed*] Why am I acting this way? Why am I acting this way? [*Pauses.*] I had one brother, just one. He was very spe-

cial to me. I don't have to explain to anyone why he
was: he just was. I come home. I discover that what I've
thought to be true was: was true. That my brother was
murdered . . . by him: Will. A man who claims my
brother had, of all things, a monkey; and my brother
was with you at the time of his death, Margaret. That
you were hanky and he was panky. *All that! All that!*
I am slightly more than forty years of age. That's not
a toddler, forty. I'm sure you'll agree. And here I
am, sitting in a room with my dead brother's mistress,
her husband the killer, my wife Emily, who has been
unfaithful to me in ways known only to scholars of
ancient tribal unfaithfulness. I am told that my late,
great, dead father is not only alive, but is, by reputation,
the most promising pervert of this town. And I, his only
remaining son, like most middle-aged men of my height,
have but one father: him. I am sleepy. I am confused.
I am frightened. I am unhappy. And last but not least,
I am impotent. Why am I acting *which* way, Margaret?
I don't know what you mean.

MARGARET: [*After a long pause*] Like you hate me.

ALFRED: Oh, my Margaret. You *have* grown dumb.

MARGARET: [*Head bows; sobs.*] Oh, Alfred. . . .

ALFRED: I am a very successful young man, I really am,
Will. Spent my life . . . watching: eyes wide open.
[*Pauses: hears* MARGARET'S *sobs.*] Why is she crying?

EMILY: I think the word you used was "dumb."

ALFRED: I used a dumb word, or the word "dumb." That
was a syntactically ambiguous sentence, Emily. I'm surprised.

MARGARET: *Dumb.* You called me *dumb.*

ALFRED: Sorry. Come here, Margaret, we'll kiss and make
up.

WILL: Go on. Couldn't care less.

ALFRED: [*To* MARGARET] Well? Well? Will you?

MARGARET: Doesn't frighten me, not at all.

ALFRED: [*A sudden pause.*] Oh . . . yes.

EMILY: Oh . . . yes, what?

ALFRED: My mind . . . [*Pauses.*] My late brother, he did
have a monkey. I'd forgotten. . . .

WILL: See? Some normal fella, huh? A monkey.

EMILY: He really owned a monkey? I loathe monkeys. . . .

They pick salt from their hairy little bodies and they masturbate.

WILL: Nice talk.

ALFRED: My brother Bruce did in fact have a monkey. He was, as Will said, a very quirky fellow—not the monkey: Bruce. The monkey was, as monkeys go, quite average. . . . [*Pauses.*] I believe his name was either Peru or Argentina. . . .

MARGARET: Peru.

ALFRED: Peru . . . right. Peru used to pee on our rug. Sad, but true. Peru'd just walk straight into the living room here and pee on the rug. Bruce used to slap the monkey's behind three times and then take him to the window out there in the front hall and throw him out the window. Not to hurt him. It's only four feet down to the ground. Bruce used to throw Peru out the window to train him . . . so he wouldn't continue to come in here and pee on the rug. Well . . . after about three months of such goings-on, the monkey still used to pee on the rug, but after he finished, he'd whack his own ass three times, run out into the front hall, and jump out the window.

WILL: I never liked monkeys either. They make me nervous.

MARGARET: I like monkeys. I think they're cute.

[ALFRED *smiles into space, in* EMILY's *direction.*

MARGARET *is pleased by what she imagines to be forgiveness in the air.*]

MARGARET: I think it's good that we can all sit down and talk this way. It isn't everyone that can be . . . you know . . . *friendly*, the way we are.

ALFRED: I beg your pardon?

MARGARET: Don't you think?

ALFRED: [*Fiercely; abrupt change in tone.*] Don't I *think*? Is that the question? Don't I *think*?

MARGARET: [*She is angry now, too.*] Don't you think that it's wonderful that we're so friendly? Under the circumstances.

EMILY: [*Crosses to* ALFRED *and begins rubbing his shoulders.*] Margaret thinks it's wonderful that we're so friendly. Do you ever wish you'd married Margaret instead of me? Do you, Alfred?

ALFRED: Margaret? Margaret *who?*

EMILY: You've forgotten so quickly! I thought you'd remember . . . *everything.* [*She laughs, looks at* WILL.]

MARGARET: I remember everything, Alfred. *My* mind's just fine.

ALFRED: Then what went on in the cellar, Margaret? I know that "cellar" and "door" combine to form the finest sound the English language can produce, "cellar door," but what's the truth of it, eh? You and Bruce? Was it you and my brother Bruce? Bollicky? Bare-assed? Starkers? Will caught you, doing it? Didn't he?

MARGARET: It was Will and me. Our first time.

WILL: Margaret!

MARGARET: I never wanted to. He forced me. In the cellar. On the old tied-up papers. He thought I did it too easily. We waited nearly two and a half years. He pawed me for two and a half years, but it was still too soon. . . .

WILL: She *enjoyed* it, for Christ's sakes! You ever hear of a woman, first time, who enjoyed it?

WILL: [*To* EMILY, *who is smiling*] You should have seen her, after that. Couldn't get it enough. Scared me. She did. Scared the hell out of me. One day she was perfectly normal, the next day: like an animal. I couldn't believe it. I think she's a nympho.

[ALFRED *laughs.* WILL *yells to* ALFRED.]

WILL: She is! You think it's a picnic living with one of them? You try it, pal. Every time you walk through the door, she's wearing another silk goddam bathrobe. The place stank of perfume all the time. The French perfumes weren't good enough. Not for *her* kind.

EMILY: Indian, right?

WILL: [*Looking down to* EMILY] Huh?

EMILY: Indian.

WILL: Right, she moved on to them Indian smells: patchouli. You can die from that stuff there. Couldn't get her to get dressed for more'n three years. She just kept changing from one bathrobe to another. On and off, on and off. It was embarrassing. Think about it, Alfred. Nice little house . . . looks normal enough, right. But right behind the door, in a bathrobe, there's a *machine* waiting! She's never had it enough. Never satisfied. It was wicked awful. Can you imagine working twelve hours, then coming home to *that?*

[ALFRED *laughs.* EMILY *laughs as well.* ALFRED *raises his hand and shushes* EMILY. WILL *looks to him again.*]

WILL: You think it's funny, huh? I shoulda left the rotten two of you on the sofa. Maybe you don't believe it, Emily, but I saw 'em with my own eyes. Your wonderful Alfred was in the house no more'n a half hour and they were *right there* . . . right on the sofa.

MARGARET: That is a terrible lie.

WILL: Same place. I bought that sofa with the first money I ever earned after I married the bitch.

MARGARET: That is a terrible lie, Wilbur Lynch. That is a terrible lie.

WILL: I saw you. That sofa means nothing to her. The rotten bitch! It means nothin' to her. That sofa has been *sacred* to me. That's right: sacred! Means nothin' to either one of them. She would flop every man in Wakefield on my sofa if I didn't stop her.

ALFRED: You're really something, Will. [*Laughing again*] Will was . . . watching. Will's a watcher, Emily. A keyholer.

MARGARET: I never know what he's talking about. I never do. The man has the most unthinkable, most unspeakable ideas. . . . Dirty mind, Alfred. Filthy, dirty mind. . . .

WILL: I got eyes, sister! I know what I saw!

MARGARET: It was fifteen years ago. He had no business sneaking in like that after all that time gone. He didn't come home to sleep for nearly six months. I didn't have any married life with Will at all. You know what I mean? None. I wasn't married to you, Will. Not now, not then. It's all in your mind.

EMILY: I haven't heard anybody say "married life" for years.

MARGARET: It's true!

EMILY: I'd certainly like to think you've cured him, Margaret. I hate to think of taking him home . . . not cured.

MARGARET: Taking *who* home?

EMILY: Alfred. He's been suffering for years now. Alfred isn't excitable. He doesn't . . . get excited. That's why he had to see you, Margaret: you're Alfred's stiffest memory.

e flesh, *saw* her . . . doin' it . . . I got real
I never wanted to love her as much as I
ch as I do. I do. I do.
Wakefield is truly wonderful. Quaint. New
akes me want to eat a lobster.
shut up! You shut your mouth! You don't
You don't belong here! *You don't belong*
RET *is weeping.*]
was quite successful once. Came back here
field . . . for truth and beauty. You're the
's the truth. [*Pauses.*] You two certainly
problem: never saw his lids so low, so long.
ll . . . there it is, Alfred: the confession. I've
l of the bargain. . . . Alfred: I've helped.
have to do is punish the criminal and we can
ot that I haven't learned to love it here. I—
.] What is it, Alfred? Alfred?
ather? He's really alive, isn't he? He's really
he?
e tried to tell you. We didn't know you
. . . . I mean, we thought you were kidding
ald you not remember?
in pain? [*Rubs his eyes again; squints.*]
Vorse. The worst: he's silly. How could you
ber? He's been up there for years. . . . Him,
. . . Your father is old, Alfred. He's failing.
[*Pauses.*] Silly. Perfect. I put him there,
d that. . . . [*Pauses; stands. He looks at* WILL.]
to forget . . . somehow. I did. [*Pauses. Rising;*
Vill? Can't seem to get it up, eh, Will? Just
to have the courage, eh, Will?
know why. There's nothing to just staying
his. Nothing! I've been waiting for you, Alfred.
long time. Waiting for you to come home
. punish me. I tried myself . . . to kill myself
a gun in the night table . . . ever since. . .
t do it. . . . I'm . . . afraid.
home, Will. I've come home.
n?
en what, Will?
got to be punished. Alfred's got to punis

ALFRED: I think that'll be about enough.

EMILY: He's been successful in every other way.

ALFRED: I said that's enough!

EMILY: It never seemed to worry Alfred as much as it worried me. [*Pauses.*] I felt . . . guilty. Alfred has a special talent for that: making other people feel guilty. [*Pauses.*] It's quite a treat for me to see you this way, Alfred. Eyes closed, huddled, small. I wonder what it was I thought you were.

ALFRED: Emily had a virgin birth. [*Pauses.*] The day she was born she was a virgin. [*Pauses.*] That was it for Emily. One day. [*Pauses.*] Emily thinks a chaste woman is a moving target. [*Pauses.*] Emily was a child molester.

EMILY: Too bad you grew up.

WILL: We had one of them right here in Wakefield.

ALFRED: A virgin or a grownup?

WILL: A child molester. Looked a lot like you, Alfred. . . . Same slanty eyes, same hunched back.

ALFRED: It's hard for me to sit still for your rapid-fire slashing wit, Will.

MARGARET: Little girl. Gave her away at birth. Up in New Hampshire. Gave her away. Probably better. [*Pauses.*] She doesn't have to grow up with the shame. [*Pauses.*] That's the worst, don't you think? [*Pauses.*] The shame.

EMILY: *Your* daughter, right, Alfred? Had to be, right. Your . . . little girl.

ALFRED: I was just a kid. High school. Will and Margaret had broken up. Will was off with my friend Richard's sister, Ruby. . . . She was a cheerleader, Emily.

EMILY: F.

ALFRED: By God, Emily, you are really something.

EMILY: Jeez!

ALFRED: Margaret got pregnant. Mine. I got frightened. I ran. [*Pauses.*] I heard they'd married . . . these two . . . Will and Margaret. They were married by the time the little girl was born. I heard they put the child up for adoption . . . in New Hampshire. [*Pauses: to* MARGARET] Did he know? Did you tell him she was mine?

MARGARET: *He knew! He knew!* He couldn't *stand* it. *Couldn't stand it!* He promised it would be all right . . . when I married him. He promised me! . . . [*To* WILL]

You promised me, Will. You did! [*To* ALFRED] He couldn't stand knowing she wasn't his . . . his own. He made me give her away, up in New Hampshire, near Keene . . . there's a home up there for that sorta thing. . . . I didn't want to. He made me. . . .

WILL: I thought . . . with my own son living with his mother and all . . . never seeing me . . . I thought I could . . . [*Sobs.*] I couldn't. I couldn't stand having her in the same house with me. . . .

MARGARET: I always forgave you, Alfred, for running . . . away . . . from me and all. You had your right to try to become somebody and you did and I'm proud of you. . . . I understood. . . .

WILL: [*Sobbing*] Oh, God help me. . . .

ALFRED: You open your mouth, Will! You open your mouth and you tell me the words that make this all straight and make this all clear, once and for all . . . *Will!*

WILL: [*Monotone; absolutely clear.*] I . . . am . . . so . . . unhappy.

EMILY: What was the little girl's name, Margaret? [*No response.*] Margaret? [*No response.*] Margaret?

MARGARET: I named her Elsa, but I called her Lorali. I wanted to keep her, but he wouldn't let me. . . .

WILL: [*Whispered*] Margaret . . .

MARGARET: He didn't think it was manly to raise somebody else's child. He wanted his own . . . wanted me to give him his own children. We tried. . . .

WILL: [*Weeping*] Margaret . . .

MARGARET: We couldn't. We tried, but we couldn't. . . . His own son, Will, Jr., he never ever came around . . . visited. . . . He hated Will. We kept a room for him, but he never slept in it. Not one night. Never. . . .

WILL: [*Whispers.*] Margaret . . .

MARGARET: I never thought in my entire life I would ever speak about this again. . . . [*Pauses.*] Will and I have blood between us. . . . Brother and sister, husband and wife. We didn't find out for sure until after we were married . . . after we tried . . . [*Pauses.*] Blood tests, specialists, Mass. General Hospital, the best, spared no expense, the best money could buy, but it didn't matter. . . . [*Pauses.*] Brother and sister, husband and wife

. . . Everybody i[n] why you're preten[d] your reasons. . . . I called her Lora[li] should have a sp[gave her away . . . New Hampshire. . to grow up with t[Don't you think? T[[*Silence.*

ALFRED's *head is bo[* WILL's *head bows d[* EMILY *moves to* MA[MARGARET *pulls bac[*

MARGARET: Don't. [*Pa[* that. . . . Not now. *sofa: sits.*] Tell them,

WILL: I didn't, goddam[you. [*Pauses.*] I didn't[brother.

EMILY: Finally. . . . [*Pa[*

ALFRED: Yes.

WILL: I had to. You w[Alfred. Anyone would [your brother. I, Wilbu[r Bruce B. Webber. Righ[the sofa. I didn't mean[or nothin'. It just happe[did he and Margaret st[I put my hands on his [[*Pauses.*] It happened so [head and he started pulli[and all. He had a heart at[I pull my hands away . .[in the air. No noise eith[fault. . . . My fault. It wa[talked about it. I promise[couldn't help myself. . . . have somebody. I mean, d[thought that she should h[nun or something. . . . I [

actually, in th[crazy, Alfred.[did . . . as m[

EMILY: Love in[Englandy. M[

MARGARET: You[belong here! *here!* [MARGA[

EMILY: Alfred [. . . to Wak[beauty, Will[cured his old[[*Pauses.*] We[kept my en[Now all we [go home. N[[*Sees* ALFRE[

ALFRED: My [not dead, is[

MARGARET: W[didn't know[us. How co[

ALFRED: Is h[

MARGARET: [not remem[all of them[

ALFRED: Yes.[Emily. I di[I managed [*to* WILL] [don't seem[

WILL: Don't[alive like t[Waiting a[Alfred . .[I've kept [I . . . can[

ALFRED: I'[

WILL: Whe[

EMILY: Wh[

WILL: I've [me. . [

EMILY: Oh, right. It's untidy, eh, Will? We've got to tidy things up. . . . [*Sees* ALFRED, *whose head is bowed again.*] Alfred? Will's waiting.

MARGARET: Alfred, please! It's got to stop. . . .

EMILY: Are you protecting Will, Margaret? Why? What the hell do you want with him? You hate Will. Now, please think, Margaret. There has been a crime and there has to be a punishment. That's the way things are. Somebody's got to feel responsible here. This man wants to die. This man *deserves* to die!

WILL: It's true. I do. I really do.

EMILY: I think the decision should be yours, really, Margaret. After all, Alfred and I are . . . outsiders. . . . This thing between you and Will is a family matter. . . .

MARGARET: Please . . .

EMILY: Should Alfred punish Will?

WILL: Yes.

MARGARET: I don't know.

EMILY: Think. . . .

MARGARET: Please . . .

EMILY: Think. . . .

MARGARET: DO IT! Just leave me alone! Leave me out of it!

ALFRED: [*Looking up, staring at* MARGARET] Perfect.

MARGARET: Please, Alfred . . .

EMILY: You make a statement, Margaret. You can't be left out of it. You're in it!

MARGARET: I can't.

ALFRED: YOU OPEN YOUR MOUTH AND YOU TALK, YOU DUMB COW!!!

MARGARET: [*Stops; turns.*] ALL RIGHT!

ALFRED: What, Margaret?

MARGARET: I want Will to die.
     [WILL *laughs.*]

MARGARET: I do. I really do. [*To* WILL, *with deep hatred; yells.*] It's what you said you wanted, Will! [*To* ALFRED] I do. I really do. [*To* WILL, *with deep love; softly*] I believe you now, Will. I do. I really do. [*She stops beside* WILL: MARGARET *on the floor below; her face next to* WILL, *who is tied above, on the landing.*] I really do.

ALFRED: [*Rubbing his eyes against the sting of the brightly lit room*] Yes. I thought so. [*Looks at* WILL.] Been waiting

a long time, haven't you, Will? I should have come home
years ago . . . settled all this.

WILL: When?

ALFRED: When what, Will?

WILL: You've got to kill me, Alfred. You promised.

ALFRED: I what?

WILL: Promised. You said you'd punish the killer.

ALFRED: I said that? I said I'd "punish the killer"? I doubt
it, Will. That doesn't sound like me at all. Not my
style. . . .

WILL: I have to be punished, Alfred. You have to kill me.

EMILY: But you just were, Will. Margaret just killed you.

MARGARET: What are you saying?

EMILY: It was a stunning show of grace, Margaret. Of
strength and grace . . . and of love.

WILL: I have to be punished, Alfred. . . .

ALFRED: Punishing you would be like taking a book from
a blind man. You, Wilbur Lynch, are not only a blind
man, you're also a dead horse, and never let it be said
that I, Alfred L. Webber, ever beat such a beast as you.

WILL: When, Alfred?

ALFRED: My mind. Guess I'll have to visit my pa now. It's
time for that. Better late than never.

WILL: When, Alfred?

ALFRED: When *what*, Will? You just won't *quit*, will you?

WILL: I have to be punished, Alfred.

MARGARET: Will?

[WILL *stares at* MARGARET *a moment. She takes his face
in her hands.*]

MARGARET: I forgive you, Will. I do. I believe you now.
I believe you and I forgive you. I do.

[*She kisses* WILL *on the lips and runs up the staircase
past him, into the bedroom, exiting the room.*

WILL *looks after her a moment, faces front, bows his
head.*]

ALFRED: It's Pa's turn now, Emily. My pa. . . . [*Pauses.*]
I'm going to have to visit him. . . . [*Pauses.*] He's failing.
My father's failing. He's an old man, Emily: mine.

[*A gunshot sounds offstage, upstairs.* WILL *is dead.*

MARGARET'S *scream, offstage. There is a silence.*

A second gunshot.

ALFRED: I think that'll be about enough.

EMILY: He's been successful in every other way.

ALFRED: I said that's enough!

EMILY: It never seemed to worry Alfred as much as it worried me. [*Pauses.*] I felt . . . guilty. Alfred has a special talent for that: making other people feel guilty. [*Pauses.*] It's quite a treat for me to see you this way, Alfred. Eyes closed, huddled, small. I wonder what it was I thought you were.

ALFRED: Emily had a virgin birth. [*Pauses.*] The day she was born she was a virgin. [*Pauses.*] That was it for Emily. One day. [*Pauses.*] Emily thinks a chaste woman is a moving target. [*Pauses.*] Emily was a child molester.

EMILY: Too bad you grew up.

WILL: We had one of them right here in Wakefield.

ALFRED: A virgin or a grownup?

WILL: A child molester. Looked a lot like you, Alfred. . . . Same slanty eyes, same hunched back.

ALFRED: It's hard for me to sit still for your rapid-fire slashing wit, Will.

MARGARET: Little girl. Gave her away at birth. Up in New Hampshire. Gave her away. Probably better. [*Pauses.*] She doesn't have to grow up with the shame. [*Pauses.*] That's the worst, don't you think? [*Pauses.*] The shame.

EMILY: *Your* daughter, right, Alfred? Had to be, right. Your . . . little girl.

ALFRED: I was just a kid. High school. Will and Margaret had broken up. Will was off with my friend Richard's sister, Ruby. . . . She was a cheerleader, Emily.

EMILY: F.

ALFRED: By God, Emily, you are really something.

EMILY: Jeez!

ALFRED: Margaret got pregnant. Mine. I got frightened. I ran. [*Pauses.*] I heard they'd married . . . these two . . . Will and Margaret. They were married by the time the little girl was born. I heard they put the child up for adoption . . . in New Hampshire. [*Pauses: to* MARGARET] Did he know? Did you tell him she was mine?

MARGARET: *He knew! He knew!* He couldn't *stand* it. *Couldn't stand it!* He promised it would be all right . . . when I married him. He promised me! . . . [*To* WILL]

You promised me, Will. You did! [*To* ALFRED] He
couldn't stand knowing she wasn't his . . . his own. He
made me give her away, up in New Hampshire, near
Keene . . . there's a home up there for that sorta thing.
. . . I didn't want to. He made me. . . .

WILL: I thought . . . with my own son living with his
mother and all . . . never seeing me . . . I thought I could
. . . [*Sobs.*] I couldn't. I couldn't stand having her in the
same house with me. . . .

MARGARET: I always forgave you, Alfred, for running . . .
away . . . from me and all. You had your right to try
to become somebody and you did and I'm proud of you.
. . . I understood. . . .

WILL: [*Sobbing*] Oh, God help me. . . .

ALFRED: You open your mouth, Will! You open your mouth
and you tell me the words that make this all straight and
make this all clear, once and for all . . . *Will!*

WILL: [*Monotone; absolutely clear.*] I . . . am . . . so . . .
unhappy.

EMILY: What was the little girl's name, Margaret? [*No
response.*] Margaret? [*No response.*] Margaret?

MARGARET: I named her Elsa, but I called her Lorali. I
wanted to keep her, but he wouldn't let me. . . .

WILL: [*Whispered*] Margaret . . .

MARGARET: He didn't think it was manly to raise somebody
else's child. He wanted his own . . . wanted me to give
him his own children. We tried. . . .

WILL: [*Weeping*] Margaret . . .

MARGARET: We couldn't. We tried, but we couldn't. . . .
His own son, Will, Jr., he never ever came around . . .
visited. . . . He hated Will. We kept a room for him, but
he never slept in it. Not one night. Never. . . .

WILL: [*Whispers.*] Margaret . . .

MARGARET: I never thought in my entire life I would ever
speak about this again. . . . [*Pauses.*] Will and I have
blood between us. . . . Brother and sister, husband and
wife. We didn't find out for sure until after we were
married . . . after we tried . . . [*Pauses.*] Blood tests,
specialists, Mass. General Hospital, the best, spared no
expense, the best money could buy, but it didn't matter. . . . [*Pauses.*] Brother and sister, husband and wife

. . . Everybody in town's known for years. I don't know why you're pretending not to, Alfred. I'm sure you have your reasons. . . . [*Pauses.*] Alfred's little girl, Elsa . . . I called her Lorali because I think a special little girl should have a special-sounding name, don't you? We gave her away . . . up the Newburyport Turnpike, up in New Hampshire. . . . Probably better. She doesn't have to grow up with the shame. [*Pauses.*] That's the worst. Don't you think? The shame. [*Pauses.*] Lucky.
[*Silence.*
ALFRED's *head is bowed now. He may be weeping.*
WILL's *head bows during* MARGARET's *small litany.*
EMILY *moves to* MARGARET *and touches her shoulders.*
MARGARET *pulls back from her.*]
MARGARET: Don't. [*Pauses; straight at* EMILY] I don't need that. . . . Not now. [*Pauses.*] Not anymore. [*Moves to sofa: sits.*] Tell them, Will. [*No response.*] Will?
WILL: I didn't, goddammit, I didn't! [*Pauses.*] I swear to you. [*Pauses.*] I didn't. [*Head drops.*] I did. I killed your brother.
EMILY: Finally. . . . [*Pauses.*] Alfred?
ALFRED: Yes.
WILL: I had to. You would have done the same thing, Alfred. Anyone would have. I had to. I did it. I killed your brother. I, Wilbur M. Lynch, strangled and killed Bruce B. Webber. Right there where you're sitting. By the sofa. I didn't mean to . . . I mean, I didn't plan it or nothin'. It just happened. I started screaming and so did he and Margaret started pissing and moaning and I put my hands on his throat and started squeezing. [*Pauses.*] It happened so *fast!* His eyes rolled up into his head and he started pullin' at his own chest and gasping and all. He had a heart attack, Alfred. It was some scene. I pull my hands away . . . he falls on his back, chest up in the air. No noise either. He's dead and it's all my fault. . . . My fault. It wasn't that she didn't tell me. We talked about it. I promised I wouldn't butt in . . . I just couldn't help myself. . . . I promised her that she could have somebody. I mean, deep down, I never ever really thought that she should have to live like some kind of nun or something. . . . I did promise . . . but when I

actually, in the flesh, *saw* her . . . doin' it . . . I got real crazy, Alfred. I never wanted to love her as much as I did . . . as much as I do. I do. I do.

EMILY: Love in Wakefield is truly wonderful. Quaint. New Englandy. Makes me want to eat a lobster.

MARGARET: You shut up! You shut your mouth! You don't belong here! You don't belong here! *You don't belong here!* [MARGARET *is weeping.*]

EMILY: Alfred was quite successful once. Came back here . . . to Wakefield . . . for truth and beauty. You're the beauty, Will's the truth. [*Pauses.*] You two certainly cured his old problem: never saw his lids so low, so long. [*Pauses.*] Well . . . there it is, Alfred: the confession. I've kept my end of the bargain. . . . Alfred: I've helped. Now all we have to do is punish the criminal and we can go home. Not that I haven't learned to love it here. I— [*Sees* ALFRED.] What is it, Alfred? Alfred?

ALFRED: My father? He's really alive, isn't he? He's really not dead, is he?

MARGARET: We tried to tell you. We didn't know you didn't know. . . . I mean, we thought you were kidding us. How could you not remember?

ALFRED: Is he in pain? [*Rubs his eyes again; squints.*]

MARGARET: Worse. The worst: he's silly. How could you not remember? He's been up there for years. . . . Him, all of them. . . . Your father is old, Alfred. He's failing.

ALFRED: Yes. [*Pauses.*] Silly. Perfect. I put him there, Emily. I did that. . . . [*Pauses; stands. He looks at* WILL.] I managed to forget . . . somehow. I did. [*Pauses. Rising; to* WILL] Will? Can't seem to get it up, eh, Will? Just don't seem to have the courage, eh, Will?

WILL: Don't know why. There's nothing to just staying alive like this. Nothing! I've been waiting for you, Alfred. Waiting a long time. Waiting for you to come home, Alfred . . . punish me. I tried myself . . . to kill myself. I've kept a gun in the night table . . . ever since. . . . I . . . can't do it. . . . I'm . . . afraid.

ALFRED: I'm home, Will. I've come home.

WILL: When?

EMILY: When what, Will?

WILL: I've got to be punished. Alfred's got to punish me. . . .

EMILY: Oh, right. It's untidy, eh, Will? We've got to tidy things up. . . . [*Sees* ALFRED, *whose head is bowed again.*] Alfred? Will's waiting.

MARGARET: Alfred, please! It's got to stop. . . .

EMILY: Are you protecting Will, Margaret? Why? What the hell do you want with him? You hate Will. Now, please think, Margaret. There has been a crime and there has to be a punishment. That's the way things are. Somebody's got to feel responsible here. This man wants to die. This man *deserves* to die!

WILL: It's true. I do. I really do.

EMILY: I think the decision should be yours, really, Margaret. After all, Alfred and I are . . . outsiders. . . . This thing between you and Will is a family matter. . . .

MARGARET: Please . . .

EMILY: Should Alfred punish Will?

WILL: Yes.

MARGARET: I don't know.

EMILY: Think. . . .

MARGARET: Please . . .

EMILY: Think. . . .

MARGARET: DO IT! Just leave me alone! Leave me out of it!

ALFRED: [*Looking up, staring at* MARGARET] Perfect.

MARGARET: Please, Alfred . . .

EMILY: You make a statement, Margaret. You can't be left out of it. You're in it!

MARGARET: I can't.

ALFRED: YOU OPEN YOUR MOUTH AND YOU TALK, YOU DUMB COW!!!

MARGARET: [*Stops; turns.*] ALL RIGHT!

ALFRED: What, Margaret?

MARGARET: I want Will to die.
   [WILL *laughs.*]

MARGARET: I do. I really do. [*To* WILL, *with deep hatred; yells.*] It's what you said you wanted, Will! [*To* ALFRED] I do. I really do. [*To* WILL, *with deep love; softly*] I believe you now, Will. I do. I really do. [*She stops beside* WILL: MARGARET *on the floor below; her face next to* WILL, *who is tied above, on the landing.*] I really do.

ALFRED: [*Rubbing his eyes against the sting of the brightly lit room*] Yes. I thought so. [*Looks at* WILL.] Been waiting

a long time, haven't you, Will? I should have come home
years ago . . . settled all this.

WILL: When?

ALFRED: When what, Will?

WILL: You've got to kill me, Alfred. You promised.

ALFRED: I what?

WILL: Promised. You said you'd punish the killer.

ALFRED: I said that? I said I'd "punish the killer"? I doubt
it, Will. That doesn't sound like me at all. Not my
style. . . .

WILL: I have to be punished, Alfred. You have to kill me.

EMILY: But you just were, Will. Margaret just killed you.

MARGARET: What are you saying?

EMILY: It was a stunning show of grace, Margaret. Of
strength and grace . . . and of love.

WILL: I have to be punished, Alfred. . . .

ALFRED: Punishing you would be like taking a book from
a blind man. You, Wilbur Lynch, are not only a blind
man, you're also a dead horse, and never let it be said
that I, Alfred L. Webber, ever beat such a beast as you.

WILL: When, Alfred?

ALFRED: My mind. Guess I'll have to visit my pa now. It's
time for that. Better late than never.

WILL: When, Alfred?

ALFRED: When *what*, Will? You just won't *quit*, will you?

WILL: I have to be punished, Alfred.

MARGARET: Will?

[WILL *stares at* MARGARET *a moment. She takes his face
in her hands.*]

MARGARET: I forgive you, Will. I do. I believe you now.
I believe you and I forgive you. I do.

[*She kisses* WILL *on the lips and runs up the staircase
past him, into the bedroom, exiting the room.*

WILL *looks after her a moment, faces front, bows his
head.*]

ALFRED: It's Pa's turn now, Emily. My pa. . . . [*Pauses.*]
I'm going to have to visit him. . . . [*Pauses.*] He's failing.
My father's failing. He's an old man, Emily: mine.

[*A gunshot sounds offstage, upstairs.* WILL *is dead.*

MARGARET'*s scream, offstage. There is a silence.
A second gunshot.*

The sound of MARGARET's *body on the floor, offstage.*
MARGARET *is dead.*]

EMILY: Oh . . . my . . . God. . . .

ALFRED: Oh . . . my . . . dear . . . sweet . . . God. My
God. . . .

[EMILY's *and* ALFRED's *eyes meet.*]

ALFRED: [*He walks backwards to wall; back against it, he
speaks.*] My . . . fault.

[*He is silent.*
Tableau.
The lights fade to black.]

THE PLAY IS OVER.

Paris, Waterford, Providence, Pittsburgh, New
York City, Gloucester—1971–1978

The Wakefield Plays, Part IV

OUR FATHER'S FAILING
A Play in Three Acts

For Jean-Paul Delamotte.

The People of the Play

SAM: Ancient, white-haired, thin.
PA: Ancient, white-haired, thin.
ALFRED: Forties, thin, receding elegance.
EMILY: Forties, thin, receding elegance.

The Place of the Play

Alternating between the porch and backyard of the asylum, and the living room of the Wakefield, Massachusetts, house.

The Time of the Play

End of fall.

Our jealousy on seeing children appear and enjoy life, when we are about to part with life, makes us all the more grudging and strict with them. We resent their stepping on our heels as if to urge us to be gone. And if we are made afraid because, truthfully, it is in the order of things that children can exist and can live, only at the expending of our existences and our lives, then we really should not get mixed up in this business of being fathers.

—Montaigne

ACT I
Scene 1

Asylum. Sunday, dawn.

Stage in darkness.

Three sharp knocks are heard. Same sound will precede each scene of play.

*First words of play—*SAM's—*are heard.*

SAM: Relax! It's not like you're starting fresh. Just pickin' up where you left off. Relax!
[*Lights to full, suddenly.*
Two ancient men, PA *and* SAM, *seated on asylum porch, on rocking chairs.*
Screen door visible behind them, also partly boarded window. Possible to see figures hiding behind screen or window. Building oversized. Top and side edge not visible on stage.
But for essential shrubs, porch, chairs and broken-off flagpole, sense of infinite space all around.
SAM *and* PA *dressed in woolen robes against chill.*]

SAM: Are you relaxed?

PA: Your tellin' me to relax is gettin' me nervous, Sam. We've gotta find out why Alfred's coming here, Sam. We've gotta have a plan.

SAM: Dangerous for a man your years to get excited. Think about pulmonary strangulation, heart attack, and stroke. Think about spontaneous pneumothorax.

PA: Well, now . . . that calms me right down. Thinking
about pulmonary strangulation is the most calmin' thing
I've thought about all day! I've gotta admit that now that
I'm thinkin' about heart attack and stroke, I'm . . . well
. . . almost tranquil. [*Pauses.*] You're so dumb, you don't
know how stupid you are! Sometimes your ignorance
astounds me!

SAM: Nothin' astounds *me* anymore. I've seen it all.
[*Pauses; looks around.*] Where's the crow? Where's the
goddam crow???

PA: Where's the what?

SAM: The crow! The crow! [*Looks around for crow and
then to* PA] Sure didn't take your Alfred long ta cause
trouble, huh? Haven't heard buzzin' around Wakefield
like this since the time the hornets got into the mollusk
conch.

PA: What mollusk conch?

SAM: The one I use'ta hold up ta my ear ta hear the ocean.

PA: Buzzing?

SAM: Hornets.

PA: Hornets don't buzz. Bees buzz.

SAM: Hornets buzz. Believe you me, hornets buzz. [*Pauses.*]
You see the *Item*?

PA: What for?

SAM: [*Reading*] Says here "Alfred L. Webber"—your son
—is givin' out ". . . a yearly scholarship to the top
graduating Wakefield High senior—male or female—
who intends to enter the field of real estate." [*Pauses.*]
A thousand a year. Imagine that.
[*Note: from time to time, it will be possible to see* ALFRED
*behind either the screen of the screen door or the glass
of the window, peering out from the inside, eavesdrop-
ping on* PA *and* SAM. *This might be a possible point in
the play to introduce the image. Caution must be employed. The image must be extremely subtle. In this
first instance, the audience should not be able to discern
who it is they are seeing, just that* someone *is present
in the house and is spying.*]

PA: Male or female?

SAM: It's gotta be one or the other, right?

PA: That a statement or a question?

sam: I'll let that one slide, too. [*Reads.*] "This year's prize was awarded to Arthur Goldberg." Goldberg? Must be newcomers.

pa: Enter the field of real estate?

sam: That's what it says here.

pa: Lemme see that! [*Grabs paper; reads date.*] This paper's three weeks old!

sam: [*Takes paper again; reads.*] News is news.

pa: A field of real estate. I get it. A humorous coded message.

sam: He personally bestowed the award to Goldberg. Wellll, look at that: the award's in your name.

pa: I can read.

sam: But you're not dead yet.

pa: Huh?

sam: Awards haveta be named for dead people. Like the Nobel, or the Pulitzer, or the Oscar, or the Emmy. . . .

pa: Emmy who?

sam: *Nobel* who? *Pulitzer* who? *Oscar* who? Who really knows? They were people . . . they had major money . . . and they passed on.

pa: "Field of real estate" is a joke. Can't you see? Alfred planted a joke in the *Item* to let us know he's finally comin' up here . . . that he's in touch. That's a joke, ya jerk!

sam: What's a joke?

pa: Field of real estate.

sam: That's a joke?

pa: Like a jam of raspberries. A drawing of curtains.

sam: Those are jokes?

pa: If he's planning to open up that certain can of beans, we're screwed. Sam, we need a plan.

sam: Peas.

pa: Huh?

sam: Can of peas. You said beans.

pa: And if I wanted to say "peas," I woulda *said* "peas"! You've got the brains of a peanut butter and marshmallow fluff sandwich. [*Pauses.*] I'm hungry. What time is it?

sam: I was just pointing out that Alfred's causing quite a commotion for a boy his age.

PA: He's no boy anymore.

SAM: He have an operation you didn't mention?

PA: Ho, ho, ho. Ho, ho, ha, ha, ho.

SAM: You know what they say: "Lightning never strikes once, but it strikes again."

PA: Who says that?

SAM: Protestants! Protestants say that all the time! If you'd only pay attention sometimes to what people are sayin', you'd hear! You would, ya know!

PA: Why don't you go somewhere?

SAM: Like where?

PA: Like away.

SAM: I will, I certainly will. And when I go, I know how I'm goin', too. Wanna try listening? Out route one-twenty-eight, Lynnfield way. . . .

PA: When I grow a head under my arm is when I'll listen to that one again! Been listenin' to that one sixty-one years now. . . .

SAM: But I never finished!

PA: 'Cause you *can't* finish! 'Cause you ain't got the stuff to finish *with!* You'll *never* finish!

SAM: I think I'll take a little walk . . . a stroll . . . a little promenade . . . a sashay . . . [*Pauses.*] Alone. [*Pauses.*] Some people are unable to do any or all of the above-mentioned.

PA: Ho ho. Some rapid-fire slashing wit. Ho ho ho.

SAM: Anything you might want from me before I shoot on up ahead?

PA: Yuh. There is. One thing.

SAM: What?

PA: A question.

SAM: Fire away. [*Smiles.*] This'll be rich. [*Pauses.*] I'm ready.

PA: What crow?

SAM: Hmmm?

PA: What crow?

SAM: The crow. The crow.

PA: I don't remember any crow around here.

SAM: He crows every mornin'. . . .

PA: You're outa your mind. . . .

SAM: That's beside the point.

PA: There ain't no crow.

SAM: He gets woken up by a crow every mornin' and he don't know it. And he's callin' *me* dumb and stupid.

PA: A crow?

SAM: A crow.

PA: What's he sound like?

SAM: You're askin' me what a crow sounds like? That's a question that needs to be answered? [*Pauses.*] Like a crow. Cock-a-doodle-doo.

PA: Cock-a-doodle-doo, huh?

SAM: [*Realizes.*] Awww!

PA: Cock-a-goddam-doodle-doo, eh, Sammy?

SAM: Awwwwwww!

PA: Goddam - cock - a - goddam - doodle - cock - a - doo, eh, Sammy-boy?

SAM: Stop your gloatin'!

PA: I ain't gloatin'. Your loss ain't ever my victory.

SAM: No laughin', either.

PA: I ain't laughin'. Nothing funny about the aged, the miserable, or the pathetic.

SAM: No wonder my mind is crackin'. Trapped in an insane asylum, day in, day out, with a nut like you. [*Pauses.*] You are the worst. The absolute worst.

PA: I know the worst. The absolute worst. He's still blamin' me for his mother, that's what. Still holding it against me.

SAM: He ain't still blamin' you.

PA: He'll remember every detail.

SAM: Not *me*. I don't remember *any* detail.

PA: He'll probably have the police crawling around here . . . probably have us right into court.

SAM: My mind's been foggy for about thirty years now.

PA: That's exactly how long it's been: thirty years.

SAM: Yuh, I must be blockin' it out.

PA: We need an ace of a plan if Alfred's gonna admit why he's here . . . what he's really looking for.

SAM: An ace?

PA: An ace. You got a pencil?

SAM: What for?

PA: Our ace. You'll forget without a pencil. A man your age forgets. You're a hundred.

SAM: I am like hell! I'm only ninety-three.

PA: Get a pencil.

SAM: [*Produces pencil and pad.*] Okay, shoot.

PA: First, you be me. That'll shake him up. Destroy his guard. Make him speak what's really on his mind without a cover-up. You pretend to be me. Okay?

SAM: You mean, "Hiya, Alfred, I'm your pa"? That kind of you-be-me? Yuh. That'll probably work.

PA: That'll never work. I'll go deaf right after that.

SAM: Deaf?

PA: Deaf. Stone deaf.

SAM: Deaf?

PA: [*Feigning deafness*] Eh?

SAM: That's older than Kelsey's nuts. That'll never work. Deaf is a deuce. We need an ace. We need something else.

PA: Then we might hit him with an elm tree. He always loved elm trees.

SAM: We hit him with a *what?*

PA: That's a manner of speaking. The elm trees are dead.

SAM: You know, sometimes I think you're less coherent than I am.

PA: I know. It worries me.

SAM: How about my "Way outa town" puzzle?

PA: Your "Way outa town" puzzle is way out of the question, Sam. . . .

SAM: Give me a break.

PA: Not *that* one. No way.

SAM: The Widow O'Brien Scandal.

PA: The what scandal?

SAM: You tell him you lived with the Widow O'Brien. That you squired her daughter.

PA: You mean "sired," not "squired."

SAM: Whatever. Just tell him.

PA: *Tell* him? That'll work. There's our wild card. Even better than an ace!

SAM: I have my moments. They don't call me "Old Sam the Fox" for nothing.

PA: You mean "Old Sam the Limp" don'tcha?

SAM: Thanks a lot.

PA: You forget that, too?

SAM: Thanks. Really. Thanks.

PA: Crane's Beach. I love a dune.

SAM: Unlimited cruelty . . . [*Pauses.*] Tom? It's been so

many years now, I'm not sure I remember—I'm not really sure what really happened. Or even when. . . .

PA: Her name was Susan. She was a' Congregationalist. Dark eyes. You were on the dunes. Crane's Beach.

SAM: I was in the truck. . . .

PA: [*Suddenly angry*] Don't open the door I think you're opening, Sam.

SAM: I never actually saw . . .

PA: That is a door in history that's long since closed and locked, Sam.

SAM: Well, I gotta crack it open for a peek, Tom. Before Alfred does.

PA: Alfred is never *ever ever* to know for sure, right, Sam? I've got your sacred word, right, Sam?—no talk to Alfred or Emily.

SAM: You've got my sacred word.

PA: Okay. I'll help you remember. You begin. You tell me what you recall.

SAM: Okay. Here's what I remember. I'm in the truck nibbling my cruller. You go into the house to see if the brisket's ready or whether we should hit a couple of more stops first. I'm sittin', kind of in a daydream, when I hear an awful commotion. You run out, white-faced, and you tell me that you found Sophie and Willie-Boy sacked up together in your big bed and that you lost your marbles and went into a terrible crime-of-passion state and that you . . . well . . . used a knife.

PA: Alfred's Boy Scout knife. I killed them.

SAM: Dead.

PA: Dead.

SAM: Jesus! *Then* what'd we do? I hate age. I really do. I used to be able to lie with complete ease. Now look at me. I'm a wreck!

PA: Alfred came in and we gave him the stuff to bury and then we sent him off to play with your nephew . . . Lynchie.

SAM: What stuff?

PA: The knife . . . Alfred's Boy Scout knife.

SAM: Oh, right. The Boy Scout knife. . . .

PA: And his baseball cap and the bedsheets, all stained from the crime and the wiping up. . . .

SAM: [*Weeping*] What a thing.

PA: If you start your weeping again, Sam, I swear to God I will make your life miserable. . . .

SAM: [*Looks up; amazed.*] That's painting both the pot and the kettle black, ain't it?

PA: I'm tired of talkin' on this subject, Sam: pay attention.

SAM: I am.

PA: We burned out the room; and the police and the paper agreed with us that it'd just be better to cover up the clandestine and filthy part of it and let life go on. They all let it pass as though it was the fire that did it . . . punishment was given out all around: they were . . . well . . . dead . . . and we agreed to live up here. . . . And that's it. The facts have been stated, Sam. You remember any of it, or is your brain too eaten away by disease?

SAM: If you were the Liberty Bell and I was Philadelphia, I still wouldn't dignify a crack like that! *I* remember! *I* remember! I only needed refreshing.

PA: Oh, really?

SAM: Oh, really! I remember each and every detail like it was the back of my hand. First the firemen came . . . Lazzaro's oversexed son, Alan . . . and then the new motorcycle cop—what's his name?

PA: Swede MacShane.

SAM: Swede MacShane.

PA: He pitched a great game against Melrose—

SAM: He sure did. Didn't give up a single hit till the top of the eighth. . . .

PA: There's nothing to worry about, Sam. What was done was fair and forgotten. And forgiven. Everybody understood. [*Pauses.*] Sam?

SAM: What?

PA: Imagine if we'd just let them go on with their clandestine and filthy meetings and sex. . . . This isn't Boston, ya know. This is Wakefield.

SAM: I'm just tryin' to get the story straight. No more, no less.

PA: They say Swede's brother, Mouse, used to sleep with his sister?

SAM: Mouse slept with Swede's sister?

PA: With Mouse's sister.

SAM: Are you kidding me? Mouse slept with his own sister?

PA: She was good-lookin'. . . .

SAM: Mouse slept with his own sister? Jesus God! If these old lips could ever talk . . . [*Pauses.*] Wait a minute! Mouse never had any sister! He was adopted. He was an Indian! He never had any sister.

PA: [*After a long pause*] I think you're right. [*Pauses.*] Old age is no picnic, Sam.

SAM: Picnic? You hungry?

PA: I said that aloud, if you'd only listen.

SAM: Fluffernutter?

PA: I *asked* ya for one maybe ten minutes ago!

SAM: [*Starts to exit. Stops. Turns to* PA.] On pumpernickel?

PA: If you'd unwax your ears, you'd understand!

SAM: I hope *you* understand *this*: If I had my choice, I would never live with you . . . waxy ears or not!

PA: If I had my choice of living with a toad or living with you, I would definitely hop for the toad. [*He laughs.*] Hop for the toad! [*He laughs again.*]

SAM: How do I endure your rudeness? [*Exits.*]

PA: Because you're waiting to cash in on my money.

SAM: [*Reenters immediately.*] Me? Money? Me? Ah, well now, sure—there it is—the lurking truth. [*Pauses.*] Alfred, yes. Me, nuts. Alfred is coming for the money. I didn't want to leap to that before, champ, but that is certainly what's been right up there in the back of my mind, Alfredwise! And I'm glad it's out in the open now, too. I really am!

PA: Money is the *last* thing he'd want.

SAM: Course he wants our money. Why else the hell do you think he'd take to troublin' himself to climb up here? To drink a whiskey with us? We don't drink. To smoke a cigar with us? We don't smoke.

PA: Maybe he's lookin' to triple-date.

SAM: Sometimes you ain't funny at all.

PA: First off, it ain't *our* money. It's my money.

SAM: I didn't say anything different.

PA: Oh yes ya did. . . .

SAM: Oh no I didn't. . . .

PA: [*Yells.*] Ya did!

SAM: [*Yells.*] I didn't!

PA: [*Screams.*] Did!

SAM: [*Screams.*] *Didn't!*

[SAM *exits into house, slamming door.* PA *sits alone.* SAM *reenters with fluffernutter sandwich, which* PA *eats in one chomping move.* SAM *sits in rocking chair, silently, as does* PA, *in opposite chair. They stare straight out, rocking back and forth. Each man is furious with the other.* PA *finally breaks the silence after he first stops rocking.*]

PA: Ain't a one of my so-called friends hanging around for anything but my kickin' off, is there? Well, I can promise you one thing, Sam: you ain't seein' a penny of *my* money, so you might as well just knock me down and take whatever coins there are in these old pockets of mine.

SAM: Ain't no coins in your pockets. . . .

PA: That's all you got to say?

SAM: I might add how I feel about that filthy rotten mouth of yours: I don't like it much, I might add that. I might just add how you sometimes break my old heart. . . .

PA: Only thing even come close to breaking *my* heart was your grotesquely ugly brother.

SAM: Which brother?

PA: Willie-Boy.

SAM: We were twins.

PA: You walked right into that one, Sam.

SAM: That supposed to be a joke?

PA: You walked right into it!

SAM: You think that's a joke?

PA: Walked into it, hook, line, and sinker.

SAM: A joke is a sacred thing to me. I have lived my life lookin' for the perfect joke. A joke, for me, is an ideal, a way of life, a religion, a great blind date: a sacred thing. What you just mouthed ain't nothin' *like* a joke. The midget and the monkey: *That's* a joke. . . .

PA: I heard it.

SAM: The raccoon and the chicken farmer's niece: that's a joke.

PA: I heard it, and I didn't get it.

SAM: The mongoose and the Mexican chef's boa constrictor. . . . [SAM *is giddy with laughter.*]

PA: I heard it, I got it, I hated it.

SAM: [*Angrily*] The Polish dancer and the pink whale.

PA: Nothin'.

SAM: The Italian priest and the ice-cream freezer. . . .

PA: Pure smut.

SAM: The swimmer and the loan shark. . . .

PA: C'mon, will ya?

SAM: The molester and the stunted linebacker. . . .

PA: Sad to see . . .

SAM: The groundhog and the skinny man. . . .

PA: [*He quietly chortles.*] Yuh. . . .

[*SAM waits, watches, gurgles laughter. PA laughing.*]

PA: That was a good one.

[*Silence. They rock in their chairs awhile.*]

SAM: You're gonna love Alfred, all right. I can hardly wait to see your face all lit with lovelight.

PA: Save it for a song, will ya?

SAM: Oh, sure, for you it'll be just like lookin' in an old mirror. After all, an apple tree can't fall far from the ground.

PA: That's the truth.

SAM: What's the truth?

PA: Alfred's the only one loves me for what I am.

SAM: And what would that be?

PA: Huh?

SAM: And what would that be that he loves you for? Your warm and friendly smiles? Ain't ever seen one. Your happy, chatty conversations in the mornings? Can't say I seen one of them, either. Your fancy clothes? Would he be lovin' you for your fancy clothes? Maybe it's your breath? . . .

PA: Don't be bitter, Sam.

SAM: [*Building to screams*] Bitter? Bitter? Me, bitter? Not on your rotten life am I bitter! I don't care if you get yourself conned out of your life savin's by your Alfred. I really don't!

PA: He don't want the money, Sam.

SAM: [*Yells.*] *I'll prove to you he does!*

PA: [*Yells.*] *I'll prove to you he don't!*

SAM: [*Screams.*] *You're on!*

PA: [*Screams.*] *You're on!*

[*They sit. Rock awhile.*]

SAM: [*After a silence*] Sorry I yelled. It's just that I hate to see you, you know . . . do it.

PA: Hate to see me do what? This'll be rich. Hate to see me do *what*, Sammy?

SAM: Hate to see you make such a raccoon's ass of yourself.

PA: I ain't gonna get myself engaged in this bickerin'. Not over money. And certainly not over a raccoon.

SAM: In the bushes.

PA: Huh? Animals?

SAM: Don't look now! Wait a minute! Now look. See him? Alfred! [*To* PA] You just shut up, now.

PA: What for?

SAM: Ace number one is about to be dealt! Where's your memory? We have a plan! [*Calls.*] Alfred! Over here! [ALFRED *enters.*]

SAM: Hiya, Alfred.

[ALFRED *looks from one old man to the other, staring at them, silently smiling.*]

SAM: Yup, it's me, your old pa. [*Moving to* ALFRED] Don't you recognize me, Alfred? It's me. It's really me. [*To* ALFRED] You haven't changed a bit, Alfred. Twenty— thirty years older, but that's all. [*Pause.*] How do I look? [ALFRED *stands staring.*]

SAM: Don't say much, do ya, Alfred?

[ALFRED *turns his back to men.*]

ALFRED: [*Without turning to face* PA] Hello, Pa. You look great.

SAM: Musta been a hard climb up. Up the hill, huh?

ALFRED: You're a sight for sore eyes. . . .

SAM: Wicked awful climb, huh? [*Smiles.*] How come it took you thirty years? . . . [*Pauses.*] Good thing we didn't plan supper.

ALFRED: You haven't changed a bit, Sam . . . still full of spunk. [*Faces* SAM; *smiles.*] How's Roxy?

SAM: You knew it was me all along, didn'tcha?

ALFRED: I never forget a mouth, Sam. [*Smiles.*]

SAM: I ain't closin' it just yet, sonnyboy. I got more aces to play. Crap! What's next?

ALFRED: Hello, Pa. You look great. You're a sight for sore eyes. You haven't changed a bit.

PA: [*Pawing the air*] Who's there?

ALFRED: [*To* PA] What're you doin'?

PA: What say?

ALFRED: [*To* SAM] What's the matter with him?

SAM: Deaf.

ALFRED: Deaf?

SAM: Deaf.

PA: Deaf.

SAM: Went deaf just a short time ago. If you had been here earlier, he mighta heard you. [*Pauses.*] It's a pity you're late, Alfred.

ALFRED: How late?

SAM: Thirty years. How's that for late?

ALFRED: [*As if deaf*] What's that?

SAM: [*Loudly*] How's that for late?

ALFRED: You walked right into that one.

PA: [*Laughs.*] You haven't changed *too* much, son.

ALFRED: Not too much, I guess. . . . Been down by the old Elm Street house.

SAM: Seen the . . . [*Loudly*] ELM TREES?

ALFRED: Elm trees are gone. Front of the house. Beetles, prob'ly, huh? Musta finally killed 'em.

SAM: Just as well. Elm trees give off poison gas. Just as well they're gone. You live around elm trees long enough, you die.

[PA *and* SAM *laugh.*]

SAM: Four aces.

ALFRED: Does he mean the singing group?

SAM: I wish you'd seen the beetles, Alfred. Seen 'em at work. . . .

ALFRED: Does he mean John, Paul, George, and Ringo?

SAM: You're in a pickle, Alfred. And I know a way out.

PA: Exactly what card are you playing, Sam?

SAM: I repeat: You're in a pickle, Alfred. And I know a way out.

PA: Uh-uh, Sam.

SAM: C'mon. . . .

PA: He's been tryin' this one-liner on me for sixty-one years now, Alfred. It's the lowest.

SAM: I am not talkin' ta you, ya know. I am talkin' to your son! [*To* ALFRED] If you wanted to end it . . . elsewhere, Alfred, I do happen to know a way out of this pickle. . . . [*Pauses.*] If and when I go, it's the way I want to go. . . . [*Pauses.*] You know what I mean, Alfred? [*Pauses.*] First I'm going to head out one-twenty-eight, Lynnfield way, then up the Newburyport Turnpike: route one.

Then straight up to New Hampshire. [*Pauses.*] You know where to go after that, Alfred?

PA: Close it down, Sam.

SAM: I didn't finish.

PA: Sam . . .

SAM: I almost finished.

PA: Belt it up, Sam. I'm takin' over the deal.

SAM: God damn. [*Pauses.*] God damn . . .

PA: [*To* ALFRED] How old are you now?

SAM: Ninety-three.

PA: [*To* SAM] Not you. [*Points to* ALFRED.] Him. [*To* ALFRED] You. How old?

ALFRED: Forty . . . ish.

SAM: His money ain't gone, ya know. He ain't spent a penny of it. It's all here somewhere.

PA: Sam!

SAM: Whoopsie!

PA: Goddam you, Sam Lynch!

ALFRED: Fascinating.

SAM: Huh?

ALFRED: I think it's fascinating. This place. You two. . . . The way you quibble. Like an old couple. Like a husband and wife.

SAM: What's he sayin'?

PA: What're you sayin'?

ALFRED: Quibble. Quibbling. You two. Like a couple: a husband and wife.

SAM: What the *hell's* he saying?

PA: What the *hell* are you saying?

ALFRED: I do believe our respective needles are stuck in our respective grooves. . . . [*Smiles.*] A husband and wife . . . a couple . . . usually sexually opposed, which is to say a man and a woman . . . married . . . joined . . . hitched . . . one might even say *flying united* . . . [*His attitude suddenly changes.*] I think you two should know that I've forgotten nothing. Every fact, every detail, every shred of the past is at my disposal. . . . *Laissez-moi dire tout d'abord que je ne pardonne à personne . . . personne!* [*Smiles.*] That's French. It means I don't forgive you. . . .

PA: You're not speaking English, Alfred. . . .

SAM: You don't forgive us for not gettin' married? Is that

what you're sayin'? [*To* PA] Is *that* what he's sayin'?
[*To* ALFRED] Is that it? [*To* PA] Jesus! That's it! [*To*
ALFRED] Pardon *my* French, but as far as I'm concerned,
I hope the Boston and Maine Railroad runs over your
legs. And that's the truth.

ALFRED: I don't forgive and I don't forget. There is a very
large debt owed to me . . . There is a very large amount
that wants to be collected . . .

SAM: What's this now? Money, is it?

ALFRED: I don't forgive and I don't forget. You two will
pay . . . like a husband and wife . . . a joint return.

PA: If that ain't the most disgusting thing I've ever heard!
If you think that's a way to talk to a father, you've got
rocks in your head! Play a card, Sam!

SAM: [*Stands: a proclamation.*] *The Widow O'Brien Scandal!*
[SAM *exits into house.* ALFRED *doesn't seem to notice that*
SAM *has yelled what he has yelled. Instead of becoming
anxious,* ALFRED *seems calmed by* SAM's *exit.*]

ALFRED: How ya feeling, Pa?

PA: Huh?
[ALFRED *goes to screen door, looks in.*]

PA: What're you looking for?

ALFRED: Are we really alone?

PA: Looks that way.

ALFRED: [*Closes the solid door behind the screen door.*]
How ya feeling?

PA: You closed the door.

ALFRED: I thought Sam might . . . ya know . . . be listening
in. I'd like to talk.

PA: Did you hear Sam, Alfred? He screamed, "The Widow
O'Brien Scandal," and then he made a sudden exit.

ALFRED: Oh, yes. I noticed that.

PA: The Widow O'Brien Scandal, Alfred. That's supposed
to throw you for a loop. A major ace was played there.
Think about it, Alfred. *The Widow O'Brien Scandal.*

ALFRED: Ahhh, yes. I think I remember. Wasn't she the
Polish dancer with the pink whale? Or was she the
swimmer who got involved with the loan shark?
[*Silence.*]

PA: What the hell did you come back here for???

ALFRED: An old debt, Pa. I told you.

PA: An old what?

ALFRED: [*Pauses; then quietly*] I have to clear up an old debt.

PA: You need money?

ALFRED: [*Laughs.*] Money? Not me. Don't touch the filthy stuff.

PA: Heard you set up a scholarship in my name.

ALFRED: That's a fact.

PA: "Enter the field of real estate."

ALFRED: [*Smiles.*] Yes.

PA: That a city joke, Alfred?

ALFRED: Sir?

PA: I'm too old for this. I'll have to play another ace now. . . .

ALFRED: I beg your pardon.

PA: How's what's'ername?

ALFRED: Who?

PA: What's'ername.

ALFRED: I don't know. . . .

PA: How she is?

ALFRED: *Who* she is?

PA: What the hell is her name? She's medium height . . .

ALFRED: You're gonna have to give me a better clue.

PA: She's your wife.

ALFRED: Emily? Why did you bring her up?

PA: Yuh. That's her: Emily. Emily O'Brien, isn't it? How is she?

ALFRED: She's gone.

PA: Gone?

ALFRED: Gone.

PA: How come?

ALFRED: She threw a clock radio at me.

PA: She did?

ALFRED: Didn't reach me. [*Pauses.*] It was plugged in.

PA: Good thing it wasn't a portable.

ALFRED: She must have tiptoed . . . into the room. [*Pauses.*] I have trouble sleeping. I don't blink.

PA: O'Brien is an ace of a name. You don't what?

ALFRED: Didn't you notice? I don't even blink.

PA: No wonder you have trouble sleeping. Isn't there risk of your eyes drying out or something?

ALFRED: I use drops.

PA: I would try to blink, if I were you. I really would.

ALFRED: I haven't blinked in thirty years. Not since my mother . . . passed away. Doctors say I must have been traumatized.

PA: It was rough on all of us.

ALFRED: Yuh. Rough.

PA: I heard you're stayin' back down at the old house. 'Sthat so?

ALFRED: Yup. I'm sleeping in the upstairs room. Same as ever.

PA: I haven't been down there, even for a visit. Not since your brother Bruce . . . passed away. Musta traumatized me, too. Huh?

ALFRED: Musta. It was rough on all of us.

PA: Sam's family . . . what's'isname and his wife what's-'ername . . . they still livin' down there?

ALFRED: Will and Margaret? They . . . moved.

PA: I'd love ta have a look at the old place. . . . Wonderful memories.

ALFRED: Pretty weird.

PA: Who?

ALFRED: Bein' in my old room. I should feel bigger in it, now that I'm . . . you know . . . grown. But I don't. Opposite.

PA: I'm shrinkin', myself: 'bout four inches shorter already. Age. Hope I don't grow much shorter. Hate to end up . . . you know . . . *tiny*.

ALFRED: If that's your idea of small talk, let's drop it, okay?

PA: But I didn't start it. You started it. Lemme just ask you straight, Alfred: Why'd you come back up here, really?

ALFRED: I don't forgive you. That's exactly why I'm back here right now . . . 'cause I don't forgive you.

PA: *You* forgive *me*? That's a switch, ain't it?

ALFRED: How so?

PA: Don't you kinda have it switched around? Aren't *I* the one who's s'pose'ta be forgiving *you*?

ALFRED: For what?

PA: Are you kidding me? What the hell are you playing here?

ALFRED: I'm not playing anything.

PÀ: Wait a minute! Just wait a minute. Are you trying to tell me you're not grateful?

ALFRED: For what?

PA: *For goddam protecting you!* That's what!

ALFRED: You're not making a lot of sense, Pa.

PA: Your mother.

ALFRED: My mother's dead, Pa. She's still dead.

PA: You don't remember, do you? Is that how you're playing it? [*Pauses; yells.*] Look at me!

ALFRED: [*Screams.*] *I'm looking at you!*
[*Silence.*]

PA: You really don't remember, do you?

ALFRED: Remember what? Remember what?

PA: [*Calls to screen door.*] Sam!
[SAM *enters through door.*]

PA: We're done with our personal family talk now, Sam.

ALFRED: Remember what?

SAM: [*Hands* PA *a plate and a glass.*] Fried chicken and a beer.
[SAM *offers a pencil and a pad of paper to* ALFRED.]

SAM: You oughtta write this down. A man your age forgets. [*Pauses.*] Fried chicken and a beer. Twice a day. Never misses. [*Pauses.*] Keeps him fit.
[ALFRED *doesn't accept paper.* SAM *shrugs. Smiles.*]

SAM: How's what's'ername? [*To* PA] Her name? What's her name? Irish, isn't it?

ALFRED: Emily? What's Emily's name? You want to know what Emily's name is?

PA: That's sort of a *city* way of bein' angry, huh, Alfred?

SAM: Alfred's picked up a lot of city ways. [*Pauses.*] No dirt under his nails. [*Pauses.*] Probably bites 'em. [*Pauses.*] Probably files 'em. [*Pauses.*] I don't file mine. I just throw 'em away. [*Laughs.*] You picked up a lot of city ways, Alfred.

ALFRED: Remember what, Pa? Remember what?
[SAM *exits into house.* SAM *reenters through screen door, carrying food tray. Hands bowl to* PA.]

SAM: Here's dessert. [*To* ALFRED] One scoop vanilla, one scoop strawberry, one tablespoon hot Indian pudding, and thick hot fudge over the whole heap. [*Pauses.*] Twice a day, also. [*To* ALFRED] Keeps him fit.

[SAM *pauses. Offers paper and pencil.* ALFRED *refuses them.*]

SAM: Well, Jesus, Alfred, if you're gonna' be takin' care of him 'stead of me, you gotta learn the ins and the outs. [*Pauses; angrily*] Well, who the hell did ya' think's been gettin' the food in 'im all these years? Greta Garbo? Mary Pickford? Eric von Stroheim?

PA: Is she pretty.

ALFRED: Who?

SAM: What's'ername?

PA: Does she . . . satisfy you? Was it a . . . smart move . . . to marry her?

SAM: You can speak your piece here, Alfred. [*Pauses.*] We're . . . family.

PA: Did ya hear that, Alfred? [*To* SAM] Jesus, Sam, if you're not the pathetic one. [*Pauses.*] You ain't family, Sam. Just get that crazy thought out of your head. Alfred's family, I'm family: you ain't family.

SAM: I crouch like a toad inside there for ten minutes waiting for an ace to work, and now I have to listen to this? The two of you make me sick. [*Pauses.*] The *three* of you make me sick. . . .

PA: Shut up, Sam.

ALFRED: What three?

PA: Sam! God damn you . . .

ALFRED: What three, Sam?

SAM: You, your old man, your nervous wife: all in it together. Three thumbs in the pudding, three short-order cooks in the broth, three coins in the fountain . . .

PA: You're dealing too many cards, Sam!

ALFRED: She's been here all along, huh, Pop?

PA: Sam, I never shoulda started with the likes a' you. I shoulda seen your colors sixty-one years ago! No more cards! This is a mixed deal!

ALFRED: I want an answer!

SAM: You try hanging around with the likes of yourself for sixty-one years. See how you like those particular colors! [*To* ALFRED] It's been hell, Alfred. . . .

ALFRED: [*Sits; folded arms.*] I'm sitting and I'm waiting . . . Sam . . . Pa . . . [*Stares at them.*] I said I'm sitting and I'm waiting. Let's hear it. . . .

[PA *looks at* SAM; SAM *looks at* PA; *speaks.*]

SAM: [*To* ALFRED] Oh, I'd love to tell you. Oversexed and foul-mouthed: those are your father's main qualities. I hate to be the one to tell you, Alfred. I really do. But it's the God's honest truth. Foul-mouthed and oversexed. He doesn't just *think* he's had 'em all; he's actually had 'em all. I know. Believe me, I know. Who do you think they run to—poor old things—after he's . . . used them? To me. To Sam. Safe Old Sam: that's what they call me. [*Pauses.*] Now I'll bet you're wondering why they would call me such a thing. Why they would ever come running to old Sam. You deserve an explanation. I'm gonna tell you why. [*Pauses.*] I'm impotent, Alfred. Been impotent for sixty-one years now. [*Pauses.*] I can still actually remember the moment it hit. . . . Laying on the beach in Ipswich. Crane's Beach.

ALFRED: When? How long has she been here?

PA: Sam? Answer Alfred.

ALFRED: [*To* SAM] When?

SAM: Around midnight on a Tuesday. Susan . . .

ALFRED: [*To* SAM] The subject is Emily. . . .

SAM: I said "Susan." Her name was Susan. Little dark-and-darting-eyed Congregationalist. Slim and very wealthy. Just got ourselves ready . . . Just mounted her . . . when the biggest fuckin' wave you ever seen . . . washed right over us . . .

ALFRED: I said the subject was Emily! Where's Emily? Now you open your mouth and speak, Pa.

SAM: . . . like a ton of wet bricks. . . .

PA: Don't worry yourself about it, Alfred. . . .

SAM: . . . Drug me right off of her. You might even say that it washed us asunder. . . .

ALFRED: *Don't worry about it?* My wife moves in with my father and I'm not supposed to worry about it?

SAM: Hoisted me up and catapulted me more'n a hundred yards. Slammed me right down on the beach, like a clean but crazed human bomb, bareassed, right beside a nun. . . . She was, at that point, just minding her own business, cooking weenies on an open fire. . . .

PA: You've got to learn to face things, Alfred. . . . Open your eyes.

SAM: Landed almost on top of her. Knocked the poor sonofabitchin' nun face down in the sand. . . . Goddam full moon, too. . . .

PA: It's going to be painful, Son.

SAM: Painful? I haven't had a hard-on in sixty-one years.

ALFRED: [*To* SAM] I really think you should stop. Emily's here, right? How long? When? Answer me, goddammit!

SAM: June it was. Black June. [*Stepping in between* PA *and* ALFRED] Gonna be sixty-one years this spring. [*Pauses.*] I must hold some kind of Guinness record. [*Pauses; smiles.*] Maybe I should have a party and celebrate.

ALFRED: I have never actually punched a hundred-year-old man before. . . .

SAM: I'm ninety-three. . . .

PA: [*Calls off.*] Okay, Emily, c'mon out!

SAM: Are you crazy? He's going to get violent. He threatened me. Didn't you hear him?

PA: [*Calling again*] Emily!

SAM: Pay no attention to your father, Alfred. The man's mind is gone. Been gone for years. Now, then: she started throwing weenies at me. Flinging them wildly, out of control. There wasn't much I could do but run.

PA: Emily?

SAM: The Fourteenth Annual Sacred Blood Beach Party was a mere ten yards away. They must have thought I was just someone come to help with the weenies. Until the moon broke through the clouds. Pay attention, Alfred.

PA: Emily! Get out here!

SAM: Sixty nuns, thirty priests and two hundred deeply religious children. [*Pauses.*] Doubt if I'll ever actually have a hard-on again.

[EMILY *enters from inside the house. She wears an old woolen winter coat, collar up, unbuttoned. She hugs the coat closed.*

ALFRED *stares at her, backing away as she continues forward.*]

SAM: Saw dozens of doctors. Even some specialists. But there's nothing you can do once it's planted in your mind. [*Pauses.*] Every time I see a decent-looking woman, I . . . well . . . feel a little urge, you might say. . . . But

then . . . right away . . . I feel the thud of weenies
against my chest. . . . [*Pauses.*] Ten or twelve thuds and
I'm finished. [*Pauses.*] Might as well kill all the women,
far as I'm concerned. [*Pauses; sees* EMILY.] Hi, Emily.
How's it going? [*Crosses to door; pauses.*] That's how it
happened.

[SAM *exits.* EMILY *stands facing* ALFRED.]

EMILY: Hello, Alfred. [*No response*] Aren't you going to
talk to me? [*No response*] It's not what you're thinking.
Don't look so wounded. [*Pauses.*] I haven't betrayed you.
[ALFRED *looks down.*] Alfred?

PA: Look at her, Alfred.

[ALFRED *turns away.*]

PA: You cryin', Alfred? [PA *tries to stand; cannot. Calls
to screen door.*] Sam!

SAM: [*Enters immediately.*] What's'a madder?

PA: Is he crying?

SAM: [*Crosses to* ALFRED *and looks.*] Looks that way.

PA: God damn it. Goddammit.

[ALFRED *bolts from the stage.*
Silence.
PA *looks after* ALFRED.
EMILY *bows head.*
PA *looks at* EMILY.
SAM *looks at* EMILY.
PA *and* SAM *turn their faces to each other.*
Tableau.
The lights fade to black.]

END OF ACT I

ACT II

Scene 1

Asylum.

Night, later.

Stage in darkness. Three sharp knocks are heard.

*First words of the scene—*EMILY's*—are heard.*

EMILY: Open your mouth, *God damn it!* You can't just sit there, staring! *Say something!*
[*Lights to full, suddenly. Two chairs—one a wheelchair; table with plate of cookies upon it.* EMILY, *on pathway at trellis.*
Wheelchair has been turned upstage, so occupant of wheelchair faces EMILY, *back of chair to audience.*
Man in wheelchair's identity disguised from audience at this point.]

EMILY: You can't just smile and stare. Who the hell do you think you are? Buddha? [*Pauses.*]
[*There is no reply.*
EMILY *walks downstage. As she does, chair swivels with her.*
Man in wheelchair is now revealed as SAM.]

EMILY: [*Sits on other chair.*] Nothing drives me bananas faster than smiling, staring, and silence. Will you *for Christ's sake* say something?

SAM: [*Looks up, quietly.*] Did I tell you the one about the elephant who became an Iowa University co-ed and the field of corn?

EMILY: [*After a long pause*] The hell of it is that I actually *asked* you to speak.

SAM: You heard it?

EMILY: Yuh.

SAM: How about the Canadian pole vaulter and the nymphomaniac?

EMILY: Heard it. Hated it.

SAM: How about the fast turtle and the slow Arab?

EMILY: Adolescent ravings.

SAM: I told you already?

EMILY: Mmmm. You did. Sorry.

SAM: How about the six Polacks and their American light bulb joke?

EMILY: [*Mimes changing an electric light bulb, one hand.*] You mean "Only one American is used to change a bulb: like this?" [*Looks at her own hand.*] Oh, my God! Now you've got *me* doing it! I think you should stop all jokes, Sam, before some people get their feelings hurt.

SAM: How about the Polish war bride and the exploding python?

EMILY: Vile. And please skip the ten-foot Pole, okay?

SAM: How about the bald soprano and the Polish Mime Opera?

EMILY: My grandmother was Polish.

SAM: You should never wait to tell a man like me a fact like that. I could've said something embarrassing.

EMILY: [*She offers* SAM *a cookie.*] What do you really want, Sam?

SAM: [*Eats cookie.*] Outta this mess. And I know how I'm gettin' out, too. . . . [*Pauses; slyly.*] First I'm heading out route one-twenty-eight, Lynnfield way, and then up the Newburyport Turnpike into New Hampshire . . .

EMILY: [*Screams.*] Sam!!!

SAM: I've got to find out why Alfred came back . . . what he wants from us.

EMILY: I'd be the last one to know what he wants from anyone.

SAM: You're his wife.

EMILY: That's what I said: I'd be the last to know.

SAM: Don't play it so smart, Eileen.

EMILY: Emily.

SAM: Yuh. Don't play it so smart, Emily. He's planning to take him back, isn't he?

EMILY: Who's planning to take whom back?

SAM: Alfred. Tommy: his father. Alfred's gonna take him back with him, isn't he? To the city. That's Alfred's plan, isn't it?

EMILY: Oh, I don't think you have to worry about *that*, Sam. [*She offers him another cookie.*]

SAM: Pardon my French, but the way I see it, *merde* has to be the word that springs to mind. [*He eats cookie in a gulp.*]

EMILY: Let me slip a fact your way, Sam. Alfred is definitely not planning to take his father away from Wakefield . . . not to the city, nor any place else. That's a fact.

SAM: Take him! Couldn't care less, believe you me! He don't represent nothin' more ta me than sixty-one years of hard luck and bad times. No more, no less.

EMILY: I don't know . . . from where I'm standing, it seems to me you two get on real well . . . a kind of *team*. . . .

SAM: Sure, from where *you're* standin'! [*Ironic laugh*] Don't you believe it, dolly! That's only the top layer you're lookin' at! Underneath all those smiles and backpats, there's an *iceberg* lurking! And you know what they all say: underneath that iceberg, there's *fire!*

EMILY: I never looked at it quite that way.

SAM: Well, I'm sorry ta haveta' be the one ta open your eyes, but there it is.

EMILY: Uhh, there *what* is?

SAM: The sorry truth. I wouldn't spend five minutes more in this rattrap, if I didn't gotta.

EMILY: You don't "gotta," nobody's "gotta" . . .

SAM: Oh, no. I'm not here for my health! Of course I gotta!

EMILY: Why? How come? How come you gotta, Sam? How come you gotta stay here . . . in Wakefield . . . cooped up with Pa? It's like you're in prison together, isn't it?

SAM: That's about it. Yuh. You sure love snoopin', don'tcha'?

EMILY: Are you?

SAM: Am I what?

EMILY: In prison?

SAM: That's for me to know and you to find out, cookie. . . .

EMILY: Are you waiting to inherit some money? Is that it?

SAM: What money? I don't think I like your insinuendos, sweetheart!

EMILY: Ah, that's it, huh? Cash.

SAM: I wouldn't touch his rotten money if I were on my hands and knees in the Sahara and he had the only spare change for a Coke in the whole desert. . . . I'd rather parch and pass out . . . maybe even away.

EMILY: Your just *saying* it doesn't make it so. Not enough for me.

SAM: There's *more* than enough, cupcake!

EMILY: Money?

SAM: Money.

EMILY: To go around?

SAM: You bet your sweet little derrière-ie.

EMILY: It amazes me that in practically no time I've learned to follow your thoughts. You've brought out a talent in me I didn't even know I had. . . .

SAM: That's what they all say.

EMILY: You're quite a guy, cookie-pally-sweetheart-dolly-baby-cupcake . . .

SAM: So they tell me.

EMILY: You make an offer, Sam?

SAM: Sex?

EMILY: Money.

SAM: Sex for money or money for sex?

EMILY: What's the difference?

SAM: *What's the difference?* You've got to be kidding! One way, you pay me: the other . . .

EMILY: . . . you pay me. [*Smiles.*] What I had in mind was neither. I meant an offer of money for me to . . . well . . . leave.

SAM: The yard?

EMILY: The town. To stop my snooping. [*Smiles.*] What's your offer? [*There's a long pause.*] Sam?

SAM: No deals.

EMILY: Really?

SAM: No deals.

EMILY: It seems to me that something terrible is going to happen here.

SAM: I know. No deals.

EMILY: I'm sorry you're caught up in it. You're a charming fellow.

SAM: Yuh. Charm is my secret. Got me where I am today. No deals.

EMILY: [*Change of attitude*] Okay, Sam. Let me just get right down to it. What's keeping you here? [*No reply*] Answer me!

SAM: [*Matches her attitude.*] How about you answerin' me, Suzie! What's keepin' *you* here? Yankee hospitality? Cheap lobsters? How about you answerin' *me* for a change, huh? I wouldn't mind a fact or two.

EMILY: Want to trade off?

SAM: How so?

EMILY: Fact for fact.

SAM: I don't follow.

EMILY: We trade facts. I give you a fact . . . a nice big juicy one. Then you pay me back: fact for fact. Seems fair, doesn't it?

SAM: Depends on your nice big juicy one.

EMILY: Okay, let's see. . . . [*Suddenly angry*] Pay attention!

[SAM *stares at her.*]

EMILY: Once upon a time, there was a very young and very beautiful young woman, of Irish persuasion, named Emily Marie O'Brien, who shall remain nameless. She was born to unknown parents; reared, as they say, in a foundling home in Boston; sent to California for ten years to a very special boarding school for very special *gifted* children. There, she was first told her full name by a visiting Eastern nun, who claimed to know young Miss O'Brien's natural mother, who was said to have been a nun as well. [*Pauses.*] Mine was a deeply religious family: *all nuns*, it seems. In my mind's eye, I see them all lined up for a family portrait: two hundred penguins at a buck a head. . . . The scene is a banquet . . . cafeteria style. [*Smiles.*] I have just winked the lid over my mind's eye.

[SAM *looks up.*]

EMILY: Just shut up, Sam.

SAM: I didn't say a word.

EMILY: Now then. In Magnolia, Massachusetts, just up route one-twenty-eight, out Lynnfield way . . .

SAM: You think I don't know that?

EMILY: I said "Shut up," Sam. . . .

[SAM *sneers.*]

EMILY: In Magnolia, Massachusetts, Miss E. M. O'Brien, the very special and very beautiful young woman, was vacationing for the summer . . . also working as a chambermaid. At the hotel, she met one Alfred L. Webber, Boy Wonder. Young Mister Webber was called "Boy Wonder" because he had made his first million by the age of eighteen. He sold a swamp in Wakefield, Massachusetts, due south of Magnolia, just down route one-twenty-eight . . . [*Puts her finger to her lips; looks at Sam.*] Shhh . . . [*Smiles.*] At the age of eighteen, Alfred L. Webber, buyer and seller of vast parcels of land, was already outstanding in his field . . . real estate.

SAM: Yuh. Sure. Out, standing in his field of real estate. Heard it. Hated it.

EMILY: *Pay attention!*

SAM: Okay.

EMILY: They met and married. They honeymooned at the very hotel at which they met. He bought it for their honeymoon: all cash. He sold it just after their honeymoon, realizing a considerable profit: all cash. [*Pauses.*] The next twenty years passed quietly, without incident. There were four children, all born dead.

SAM: I'm sorry.

EMILY: *You're* sorry? *You're* sorry? How the hell do you think *she* felt???

SAM: Wicked awful.

EMILY: Ah Bartleby! [*She looks up at* SAM *and smiles.*] One day the husband, who was to that instant the hardest-working and most energetic man the wife had ever even *heard* of, he . . . the husband . . . woke up and turned to her . . . the wife . . . and you know what he said to her?

SAM: How many guesses?

EMILY: "I'm giving it away."

SAM: He . . . the husband . . . said, "I'm giving it away"?

EMILY: Precisely.

SAM: Sounds like the start of an off-color joke to me.

EMILY: I loathe jokes, Sam. A joke to me is the lowest thing

I know. I rate joking right down at the bottom of the list with pushing and shoving.

SAM: You musta been a great date in your day, Emily.

EMILY: He, the husband, gave it all away. Every penny they had. [*Pauses.*] Can you imagine?

SAM: Certainly, I can imagine.

EMILY: Their car, their other car, their house, their other house, their boat, their other boat, even his, umm . . . autographed baseball cards and pictures from show-business personalities: all of it. [*Pauses.*] Lucky thing they were spared having children.

SAM: Me, too.

EMILY: Four stillbirths. They all died in their seventh month, but she carried them . . . the whole route. Four of the great mystifying freaks of medical history, those four kiddoes. Every specialist was called in, but nothing could be done. Baby after baby, born dead. Can you imagine?

SAM: I can imagine.

EMILY: Just about everyone and everything near them suffered. Even their flowering rhododendron bush . . . it withered and wilted and . . . well . . . passed on. [*Pauses.*] What a depressing couple they were, those two.

SAM: Four.

EMILY: Huh?

SAM: I thought you said *four*. Kids.

EMILY: The mother and the father. She is speaking now of the mother and the father: Emily and Alfred.

SAM: Oh.

EMILY: The father gave up hope, finally. He never again put himself in a position in which he might again be . . . disappointed. They had an unwritten agreement. . . . [*Pauses.*] He stopped touching her and she stopped talking to him. They stayed together in that state . . . for years. Very crazy, huh? Can you imagine?

SAM: How come you keep asking me that, over and over?

EMILY: Asking you what?

SAM: If I can imagine. Of course, I can imagine. I've been livin' right beside the real source of crazy, sixty-one years now. You don't own suffering, you know.

EMILY: It's Alfred I own.

SAM: Huh?

EMILY: I own him, Sam. Where my life began is a mystery
. . . and where it ends . . . that's a mystery, too. But
right now, in the middle of it all . . . I intend for day
after day of perfect clarity. Alfred L. Webber, Boy
Wonder, tied himself up with me and I intend to keep
the knot just where it is. And if anybody interferes,
Sam . . . you or anybody else . . . [*Pauses.*] . . . they have
me to contend with. We have a lot in common, Sam. . . .

SAM: I know. . . .

EMILY: I should think you do. . . . [*Pauses.*] I have no
more intention of giving Alfred up than you have of
giving Tommy up.

SAM: The money? Is that it?

EMILY: Money is simply a detail that will have to be dealt
with, no more, no less. Such is life. Although money is,
however, one of the buttons that I push to get Alfred's
dander, as they say, up. Whenever you hear me mention
money, Sam, you'll know that I am pushing Alfred's
button. It's way beyond money, Sam. Way beyond. It's
his soul. Just now I don't seem to have one of my own.
Until I do, Alfred is not free. He's owned. [*She stands,
walks behind chair; lights cigarette, sits; exhales.*] I have
never in my entire life met another woman who was
even one half as unhappy as I am. . . .

[SAM *offers her a cookie. There is silence.*]

EMILY: Here we go, Sam. I intend to keep my promise to
Alfred. I've promised him that I would help uncover
certain information—juicy facts. Alfred has a memory
problem . . . a serious memory problem. There's a great
deal I have to help him remember. And when he does,
we go home. Life passes "go," collects two hundred
dollars, and goes home. [*She produces a baseball cap,
which she shows to* SAM.] This is a baseball cap that is
supposed to shock and amaze you. Fami*lia*r or fami*lial*?

SAM: Where . . . where . . . where'd you get that?

EMILY: Whose is this?

SAM: Where'd you get that? Who gave you that cap?
Where'd you get that? *Answer me!*

EMILY: Why are you so upset?

SAM: Did Alfred give you that? [*Quietly*] You better tell
me.

EMILY: It's just something I . . . well . . . something I dug up. To show you. Talk, Sam.

SAM: About what?

EMILY: Sam?

SAM: We used to wear hats like that. Years ago.

EMILY: And?

SAM: [*After a long pause*] It's just a cap.

EMILY: Whose?

SAM: Ours. We used to wear 'em, years ago, when we were together.

EMILY: We? You and Alfred?

SAM: Me and Tommy.

EMILY: Did you play on a team?

SAM: When we were in business together: the paper business.

EMILY: Manufacturing?

SAM: Delivering. We had the biggest route on the North Shore. Covered maybe ten or twelve towns. . . .
[SAM *reaches for the cap, when* EMILY *withdraws. There is a pause. They look at each other silently.*]

SAM: It's true!

EMILY: [*Suddenly*] Don't you fucking tell me what's true and what isn't!

SAM: [*Whistles.*] Boy, what a mouth on you . . .

EMILY: Why are there so many old people in Wakefield, Sam? I've never in my life *seen* so many people so incredibly old! Do they move here? Were they born here? Who are they all? [*Pauses.*] What the hell did you *do???*

SAM: [*Stands.*] I can't talk anymore.

EMILY: You're gonna have to!

SAM: I'm . . . going in the house. Tommy must be hungry now. [*Moves to door.*] Sorry ta haveta just run like this. . . .

EMILY: What is going on in this town, Sam? What are you hiding? What terrible thing have you all done??? *Talk! TALK!!!!*

SAM: Back off, tootsie. . . .

EMILY: [*Moves between* SAM *and door.*] I spent a week watching Alfred badger a man into confessing to a murder. You know what? I don't believe that man committed that murder at all. You know who I'm talking about, Sam Lynch . . . your niece and nephew, Sam Lynch:

Will and Margaret. I watched Alfred settle in at the home of his old high school girlfriend, Margaret, and her husband, Will. I discovered that Alfred's brother was murdered. That Alfred's one tiny shred of sanity focused itself on finding his brother's killer. . . . [*Pauses.*] Lo and behold . . . Lo and behold. . . . [*Pauses.*]

SAM: You're snooping way outa line! Now *back off!*

EMILY: I don't think Alfred's brother was killed by Will. I think Alfred killed his own brother. I think Alfred killed his own brother and you're all hiding it . . . protecting him.

SAM: *Back off!*

EMILY: I've got a right to know the truth, Sam. Is that what Alfred's unable to remember? Is that the crime here? Is that what Alfred's unable to remember? Is that the crime that drew him back to this horrid little scene? He did, didn't he? Alfred killed his brother, didn't he? *Didn't he???* See? I know who dunnit! Alfred dunnit. But, *what*, God damn it! *Alfred dun what???*

SAM: [*Summoning his strength, he pushes* EMILY.] Back . . . the fuck . . . off!

EMILY: It's really anxiety-producing, isn't it, Sam? Whatever it is you're all hiding—you're all protecting Alfred from—it's really quite anxiety-producing. It makes you all quite nervous, doesn't it, Sam? [*Quietly*] Sam?

SAM: [*Composure reasonably regained, but winded*] I'm really sorry I hit you, Emily. I try never to hit women and I hate like hell to make an exception out of a girl like you. You gotta understand something: I've made promises here. When you've made a promise and kept it for thirty years . . . well . . . it ain't too easily breakable, is it? [*Pauses.*] I'm sorry I struck you . . . physically and all . . . but you're milking some very sacred cows around here. I can't be party to such goin's-on. My advice to you is simple: get out while you still can. All this mess is strictly family: his, not yours. [*Reaches out.*] Gimme the cap. I'll take it in to Tommy. It's his.

EMILY: Does Alfred know about it?

SAM: About *what?*

EMILY: Okay. The cap. Does Alfred know about the cap?

SAM: Course he does. He buried them, didn't he? Didn't Alfred give that cap to you?

EMILY: Alfred buried *who*, Sam?

SAM: "*Who?*" Alfred buried the caps . . . the stuff. I've said too much. I'm goin' in! [*Moves again to door to leave.*]

EMILY: Sam, this is an awful thing to say to a man of your good looks and pride, but here it comes. . . . Sam, I'm a lot stronger than you are and, if it comes to it, I could hurt you. . . . I wouldn't want to . . . but I see what's needed here.

[*The back door suddenly swings open.*

ALFRED *enters.*

He smiles to EMILY.]

ALFRED: Very kinky goin's-on . . .

SAM: He musta heard everything! What a goddam family!

ALFRED: Excuse me for not knocking. I was listening in from behind the door. [*Nods to* SAM.] Sam.

[*He smiles to* EMILY; *sits.* EMILY *hides the cap.*]

ALFRED: Do you really, Emily? [*Pauses.*] Do you really "*see what's needed here*"?!! [*Pauses.*] That's quite a prospect: your really seeing what's needed *here.* [*Smiles, to* SAM.] Get inside, Sam.

SAM: It's nothin' like you think! Nothin' went on between us. I swear to God, Alfred, we were just talking. [*Pauses; frantically, to* EMILY.] Tell him, Emily.

ALFRED: Out!

EMILY: Alfred?

[ALFRED *smiles.*]

EMILY: I'll destroy you, Alfred.

[ALFRED *laughs.*]

EMILY: Alfred? [*No response*] Answer me, Alfred.

SAM: I'm gonna leave you two lovebugs alone, okay?

[ALFRED *now stands directly in front of* SAM.]

SAM: I'm goin' in. . . . [*Pauses.*] I'm gonna tell him what I've seen, Alfred. How weird you're behavin'. . . . [*Pauses.*] He ain't gonna' be too proud.

ALFRED: Good night, Sam. . . .

SAM: I'm goin' in, don'tcha worry about *that.* . . . [*Pauses; looks at* EMILY.] I'm goin' in now. [*Smiles.*] Good seein' ya again, Emily. [*Nods.*] Nice little wife ya got here, Alfred. [*Door opens.*] 'Night all! [*Exits.*]

ALFRED: [*After a pause*] I'm really shocked and amazed that you've missed what you've missed. All this time in

town and you don't know. [*Shakes his head.*] You're
slowing down, Emmy. [*Smiles.*] All those golden old-
timers are Wakefieldians. [*Pauses.*] That's what they like
to call themselves: Wakefieldians. [*Pauses.*] Status quo
set in. About thirty years ago. Around the time my
mother passed away. . . . [*Pauses.*] "Passed away" is a
euphemism. "Status quo" is, of course, Latin: the tongue
of the church. [*Pauses.*] You might say that Wakefield
is the ultimate town experience: no one's been born
and no one's died in thirty years now. Everyone here's
stayed put . . . so to speak. It's been a real curse.
[*Pauses.*] I'd forgotten. My father *had* to be alive, didn't
he? They all are. It's a Wakefield tradition: a real status
quo.

[ALFRED, *sitting in rocking chair smiling across to* EMILY.
EMILY, *sitting on porch railing.*
She bows her head.
Tableau.
The lights fade to black.]

END OF SCENE 1

Scene 2

Asylum. Dawn.

Stage in darkness.

Three sharp knocks are heard.

*Church bells in distance, four chimes. Repeat. Rooster
crows twice.*

Silence.

*First words of scene—*SAM's—*are heard in darkness.*

SAM: How about the Englishman and the trained kipper? How about the pig with the poker game? How about the Czechoslovakian whore with the French tennis racquet? [*Pauses.*] How *about* the Czechoslovakian whore with the French tennis racquet?

[*Lights to full, suddenly.*

PA, *on porch alone, in rocker. He is silently staring at* SAM, *who stands hiding from* PA, *head bowed, at corner of house.*

SAM *raises his head a bit; nearly weeping. He is frightened.*]

SAM: How about the magician's trained snake and the Scotch brand Magic tape?

PA: You come out here on a high-level mission and I don't even get a report? What kinda joke is this?

SAM: There was a two-horned toad and a unicorn . . .

PA: Nobody ever comes out here to *fail*, Sam!

SAM: Maybe it wasn't a unicorn? . . .

PA: Where the hell have you *been?*

SAM: Maybe it wasn't even a two-horned toad! . . .

PA: You're not gonna even try, huh? No explanations: just babble? Just more goddam *babble?*

SAM: Maybe it was the sailor and the trained cod. . . . They all start to blend together at my age. . . . Poor old me.

PA: Did you tell her? [*Pauses.*] Sam? [*Pauses; no reply.*] I'm talkin' to you, Sam. . . . [*No reply*] Did you tell Emily? [*No reply*] Sam? [*No reply*] Did you . . . betray me? [*No reply.* PA *screams.*] SAM!

SAM: [*Quickly*] No, dammit! Course not! [*Pauses; turns, looks at* PA.] I . . .

PA: Easy enough to find out, ya know. [*Points his finger at* SAM.] You got your last chance right now. [*No reply.*] She's still here, ya know.

[SAM *looks up, surprised.*]

PA: Emily!

[EMILY *enters through screen door. She carries tray, laden with food. Walks to* PA.]

EMILY: Here. The usual.

PA: You know my friend Sam, don't you, Emily? Sam, this is my friend Emily. Emily, this is my friend Sam.

[*Pauses.*] Always pleases me when I can get friends together: when I can get worlds to, you know, collide.

EMILY: [*Smiles to* SAM; *turns to* PA, *smiles.*] BLT on toast
and a mocha frappe. Hope you like it. [*Looks at* SAM;
smiles sweetly.] Hello, Sam.

PA: Aren't you ever gonna say hello, Sam? [*After a pause;
to* EMILY] He's kinda rude for his years. Grew that way.
Didn't used to be. [*To* SAM] You didn't used ta be rude,
did you?

[EMILY *exits through screen door, with tray. Men are
suddenly animated; rapid-fire exchange.*]

SAM: You are the looney-bird of all time! What the hell
did you tell her?

PA: *Me??? Me??? You're* asking *me???*

SAM: Well, *I* certainly didn't tell her anything!

PA: You think *I* did? You're a major-league dodo, Sam!

SAM: And you're a gorilla's ass!

PA: What'd you call me?

SAM: Looney-bird?

PA: Gorilla's ass.

SAM: That's right . . .

PA: *I'm* not the one's be'n spillin' the wax beans. . . .

SAM: Well, it ain't me, pally-pal. Not a bean—not a *pea*—
has slipped through these sealed lips. . . . I am a bank
vault.

PA: You better be tellin' the truth!

SAM: *You* better be tellin' the truth!

PA: Why don't I believe you somehow? . . .

SAM: Because you've been senile for sixty-one years!

PA: You've been *impotent* for sixty-one years!

SAM: Impotence has no effect on decisions and thinking
the way senility does! Impotence attacks the *body*, not
the mind!

PA: If I could walk, I'd chase you!

SAM: I'll let ya walk: c'mon, walk! Chase me!

[PA *strains to stand. Cannot.*]

SAM: *Hah! hah! hah! HAH!* If you aren't the most foolish-
lookin' turd I've ever seen! [SAM *now fakes deep laughter,
as* PA *strains again to stand.*] Whew! Lookit you! If you
aren't the most ridiculous-lookin' dung ever dumped
around here! Whew! I'm gonna split open from this

uproar of laughter!

[PA *stands.*]

SAM: Whew! [SAM *sees* PA *standing.*] You're standing.

PA: That's right.

SAM: But you can't.

PA: That's right.

SAM: I take it all back. [SAM *rushes to* PA. *Stops. Backs up.*] Sit down. [SAM *takes a rational tone.*] Sit down.

[PA *stares at* SAM.]

SAM: Tommy?

EMILY: [*Calling from behind screen door*] Ready or not, here I come.

[PA *sits.* EMILY *enters.* SAM *stares.* EMILY *is wearing cap.*]

EMILY: Like it?

PA: [*To* SAM. PA *beams at* EMILY.] It's nice to have the touch of a young woman again. [*Pauses.*] Such a touch has been missing around here for quite a while.

SAM: She has the cap. [*Pauses.*] It's on her head.

PA: [*Looks at* EMILY.] I think you're looking prettier every day, Emily.

SAM: Oh my God. If I drank, I would drink now. If I smoked I would smoke now. If I used drugs, I would drug now. [*Pauses; walks to rail, sits on it.*] I am one shocked and amazed old duffer, that's what I am. [*Feels his chest. Stops; looks up, walks to* PA *and places* PA's *ear to his chest as best he can.*] Listen to my heart!

PA: Put it in a song and sing it.

SAM: [*Raises a clenched fist to* PA.] I'll put this in a song, ya jerk! You see what's on her head?

PA: [*Looks at* EMILY. *Sees hat.*] Where'd you get that? From Alfred?

EMILY: Warm.

PA: Huh?

EMILY: You're getting warm. [*Smiles.*] Want another try?

PA: [*Motions to* SAM; *speaks to* EMILY.] Him?

EMILY: Closer.

PA: Gimme a hint: familiar or familial?

EMILY: I'm going to find out sooner or later, you know. . . .

PA: Sam?

SAM: What?

PA: Buy us some time.

SAM: *What?*

PA: I need to think.

SAM: Huh?

EMILY: Sam?

SAM: What?

EMILY: Aren't you ashamed?

SAM: Did you ever hear the one about the bloodsucker and the scarecrow?

EMILY: [*To* PA] Aren't you ashamed?

SAM: How about the Hollywood starlet and the Santa Monica starfish?

EMILY: [*To* PA] Aren't you humiliated?

SAM: How about the agony and the ecstasy?

EMILY: [*To* PA] It's pathetic to watch. . . .

SAM: How about the old man and the sea?

EMILY: It shames me just to look at the two of you . . .

SAM: The greatest story ever told?

EMILY: . . . to feel . . . connected . . . to feel connected to you. It shames me.

SAM: The butcher, the baker, the candlestick maker . . . [*Pauses.*] Christ! [*Panicked*] I'm running dry! [*To* PA] Will you *for crying out loud* do something!?!

PA: Go on!

SAM: [*Panicked*] Where? [*Pauses; then slyly.*] I know where. [*Smiles.*] Out route one-twenty-eight, Lynnfield way . . .

PA: [*Screams.*] Sam!!! [*After a long pause; quietly*] Alfred's mother.

EMILY: Alfred's mother?

PA: Alfred's mother.

EMILY: What about her?

PA: How she . . . died.

SAM: Here we go. . . .

PA: Nobody even thinks about it anymore. . . . It's a small town, Emily. People understand.

SAM: It was terrible on the boy.

PA: She was all charred.

SAM: Burned to a crisp. Most horrible thing you'd ever want to see.

PA: Just her room . . .

SAM: Only hers . . .

PA: Can you imagine?

SAM: Can you imagine?

PA: Whole house left untouched . . .

SAM: Just her room . . .

PA: Hardly a trace of smoke in the air . . .

SAM: No smell . . .

PA: Just her room . . .

SAM: Awful thing . . .

PA: She certainly was . . .

SAM: Shocked us all . . .

PA: Years to come . . .

SAM: Quite a blow . . .

PA: Dead.

SAM: Burned.

PA: God damned cigarettes!

SAM: Filthy habit.

PA: Begged her to quit.

SAM: Couldn't quit.

PA: Hardly even tried.

SAM: He begged her to.

PA: I begged her to.

SAM: Did no good.

PA: Not a bit . . .

SAM: Once habit takes hold . . .

PA: You're a goner . . .

SAM: Goner.

PA: Done for.

SAM: Absolutely.

PA: Absolutely.

SAM: Alfred!

PA: Huh?

SAM: There! Alfred.

[*In silence,* ALFRED *enters, walks to porch, sits.*
Silence.
ALFRED *stands. Walks downstage toward rose trellis, in*
silence.
Stops near EMILY, *turns to men.*]

SAM: We were just tellin' Emily about the wicked awful
fire.

ALFRED: I came home from school and there was a wicked
awful commotion at the house. [*Pauses; smiles.*] That's
the right word, isn't it, Pa? Commotion? Isn't that what
we called it?

[PA *nods.*]

SAM: Alfred.

ALFRED: What?

SAM: She . . . uh . . . she don't . . . uh . . . she don't exactly . . . *comprendez*.

ALFRED: Well, let's just straighten her right out then, Sam. [*To* EMILY] *Preparez* to *comprendez!* [*Pauses.*] Lynchie and I were playing together. Lynchie was a neighborhood kid. Very *close*, eh, Pop? Lynchie was Sam's nephew. . . . Lynchie was also Margaret's brother and, as it turns out, her husband-and-brother Will's half brother. [*Smiles.*] Family ties are some little buggers to bind, huh, Em? Don't even bother trying. Hardly worth the effort . . . and not central to my tale of woe. [*Pounds his chest with his fist, acting tragedy. He smiles.*] Oh, woe. Oh, woe. [*To* EMILY] Lynchie was beating me up. That's what we did after school most days, Lynchie and me. We'd beat me up. We'd wrestle. He'd win and I'd . . . well . . . lose. . . . [*Smiles.*] There was a fire engine. Red and loud. Rushing up North Avenue, crossing the tracks down at the bottom, near Prospect. We were playing in the patch of grass at the intersection. [*Pauses.*] That is to say, that's where Lynchie was holding me down and choking me. [*Pauses.*] We chased the engine to the house . . . my house. Right to it. [*Pauses.*] They'd brought a resuscitator to try to bring them around. Too late. Both gone.

SAM: Awful thing.

ALFRED: Huh?

SAM: I was just commenting that it was an awful thing. [ALFRED *stares at* SAM.]

SAM: Sorry.

ALFRED: Sam was there first. Pa'd come home early with Sam. Sam found them together in the big bed. [*Pauses.*] Sam was there first. Weren't ya, pally? First to see the dirty deed.

SAM: [*To* PA] What the hell did you tell him? What's goin' on here?

ALFRED: [*To* EMILY] Pa usually brought his business associates home for lunch.

SAM: I demand an explanation!

ALFRED: [*Cutting him off*] Try not to interrupt.

SAM: I was in the truck, waiting. I never saw . . .

PA: Sam!

ALFRED: Ah, yes, the truck. Pa and Sam and Willie-Boy had a purple Chevy. Very pale, pouf-purple—quite an advanced color for Wakefield, now that I think of it. They were in the paper business together. [*Smiles.*] I'm surprised Sam didn't tell you.

EMILY: He did.

ALFRED: I'm not surprised.

EMILY: They delivered.

ALFRED: Wrong.

SAM: I smell a double-cross.

PA: Shut up, Sam.

EMILY: That's what Sam said: delivering.

ALFRED: Nope. Collecting. Door-to-door buying. They bought bundles of old newspaper from people—baled them in sixteen-hundred-pound bales and sold them to the mills up in Bedford and Fitchburg. [*Pauses.*] The West Side Waste Paper Company. [*Smiles.*] Ten. I was ten years old, Emily. And they never even thought to ask me how I felt about it: about my . . . mother. [*To* PA] S'pose you had a lot on your mind then, huh, champ?

EMILY: Who set the fire?

ALFRED: The fire was after the fact, Emily. More of a cremation than a death. The fire just . . . well . . . destroyed the evidence. The evidence being one mother and one mother's friend.

EMILY: Mother's friend?

SAM: I've been lied to for thirty years. Thirty miserable years. [*To* PA] You broke your word. You broke your word. God damn you . . .

ALFRED: Don't bother, Sam. Let's face the facts, okay? Let's remember together. . . . [*To* EMILY] My mother had a boyfriend. Not really the man of *your* dreams, her boyfriend. He drove a bread truck. Bond Bread, to be specific. He brought my folks their morning crullers. They found my mother and her boyfriend together and they . . . did . . . what they did. [*Walks to porch and sits; looks at* SAM.] You see, I really do remember.

SAM: Me too. I remember, too. [*To* PA] You hear me? [*Yells.*] You hear me!?

PA: *Who invited you?* [*Pauses.*] He talked me into it, Emily. I was a worker back then. I wanted to work.

[*Pauses.*] It wasn't even eleven, it was ha'-pahst ten. Who the hell wants lunch at ha'-pahst ten? [*Pauses.*] Insatiable Sam, that's who. Badgered me into it. He did, Emily. He worked me up into it.

SAM: It was done before I ever got into the house, Emily— that's the truth of it. I just helped with the fire.

PA: She hated my guts. I knew she did. For years I did. [*Pauses.*] Did nothin' about it, though. [*Pauses.*] I was a gentleman. [*Pauses.*] Never knew a woman to carry on in her own house, though. Never did. He was there every *day*, Emily. I swear to God, I never knew when to come home . . . never knew when he would be there with her. [*Pauses.*] Finally, I got them to meet in his truck, first thing in the morning. He'd drop off the crullers and she'd go out the back and into his truck and then they'd drive out God knows where together for the rest of the morning. I'd have my coffee and, well, cruller, you know, alone . . . and then I'd go off into a hard day's work. Straight through—nonstop—till dinnertime: noon. [*Pauses.*] Arm in arm in my own room in my own house in my own bed.

EMILY: Is that why there's only one grave? Are they buried together?

PA: Huh?

SAM: The bodies. Only one grave. How come. Tell her how come. [*Screams.*] *Tell her!* She wants to know where my brother's grave is and I'm just gettin' a fuckin' good hunch! *Tell us both!*

PA: There's just one: hers. I wouldn't bury him. I wouldn't have him—you know—near her no more. I had him cremated.

SAM: You lied to me! You said he didn't want burial! You said it would've gone against his will. You said he *wanted* cremation. Wanted his ashes strewn over the lake. Asked for it in his will. I shoulda known you were lying. He always hated the lake. I scattered them: me. From over near the Yacht Club. Some of them blew back on me. His ashes. They got in my eyes, on my sport coat, and even into my T-shirt. [*Pauses; near tears.*] He was my brother.

PA: Willie-Boy. That was his name: Willie-Boy. Sam's

ugly twin. He was supposed to be my friend . . . partner
and friend. Can you imagine?

SAM: He wasn't a bad guy, Emily.

PA: [*Screams.*] *Don't you defend him!*

SAM: I didn't. I stuck by you, didn't I? *Didn't I?*

PA: [*Screams.*] If I had that son of a bitch here right now,
I'd kill him. I would. I really would. You did exactly
the right thing, Alfred.

EMILY: What right thing? [*No reply*] What right thing?

ALFRED: I am a man. I am forty. I am standing in an
insane asylum with my mother's killers; my old pa and
his best friend, Sam, two major-league lunatics. I see that
my charming and python-like wife, Emily, is here, too:
Emily: a devoted wife. [*Smiles.*] Devoted to exactly
what, God only knows. [*Smiles again; moves to side.*]
I could kill you all now, to avenge my mother. It wouldn't
make any difference to me. I can only be punished once.
[*Sternly*] The murder of my mother will be revenged:
absolutely and completely. I stake my life on that fact.
My brother couldn't do it, but I can. I will. I stake my
life on that fact. . . . [*Pauses, smiles.*] I'm going back
down below now . . . to the house. Join me if you want
to, Emily. Or don't. Either way, I actually couldn't care
less. [*Nods to* PA *and* SAM.] Pa. Sam . . . [*Smiles.*] Be
seein' ya.

[ALFRED *exits.*

There is a long pause. EMILY *speaks, coldly.*]

EMILY: Pa, what right thing?

SAM: For the love of Christ, what right thing? What the
hell's goin' on here?

PA: I'm through talkin' on this subject now. [*To* SAM] Get
her out of here. [*To* EMILY] I'm through talkin' on this
subject now.

SAM: I can't believe my own ears anymore. . . . [*Pauses.*]
I never thought I'd live to see the day. . . . [*Pauses.*] I'm
goin' inside. [*To* PA] You're comin' with me. We're going
to talk: just you and me. You stand, and you walk and
you follow me. Now. [*Pauses.*] I know you can. Remember? [*To* EMILY] He can.

EMILY: Sam?

SAM: What?

EMILY: A simple yes or no will do. . . . [*Pauses; then matter-of-factly*] Did Alfred kill his mother?

PA: Sam!

EMILY: Answer me. Sam. Am I right, Sam? Is that what you're all hiding? Did Alfred kill his mother? Sam? Sam? Am I right? Sam?

SAM: I hope you're wrong, girlie. For the sake of somebody's goddam so-called best friend. I hope you're wrong.

PA: *God damn it!* [*Punches arm of chair.*] *God damn it!* [*Turns to* EMILY.] Just what the hell are you lookin' for, huh? HUH?

SAM: What the hell is going on here? [*Screams.*] *WHAT THE HELL IS GOING ON HERE?*

PA: Sam. Go inside! *Go inside!!!* I'll be right in. Go, Sam. Goddammit, go!

SAM: Thirty years, you two-faced lying coot! [*To* EMILY] Thirty years I've been protecting him. [*To* PA] Guilt! *Guilt!* I didn't throw Willie-Boy and Sophie into the sack together, ya know! I didn't ask for him to be my twin, either! Both of those things just happened. [*To* EMILY] He's kept me guilty—kept me protecting him— more'n thirty years now. [*To* PA] Something's fishy here, pally. Something's as fishy as a trout. I've been lied to, right? *RIGHT!* [*To* EMILY] I know I'm crazy. I've never doubted it. First one of my brothers hangs one of his own sons and now look what's happened to my only *other* brother. *All my brothers, for Christ's sake!* Course I'm crazy! Who the hell wouldn't be? [*To* PA] But I'm no dummy, pal! I'm no dope! That's where you made your big mistake. [*He turns away and faces* EMILY. *He will check* PA's *reactions, defiantly, as he speaks to* EMILY.] You asked me why I've been stayin' here, Emily. . . . Now you're gonna know: because I figured I'd get the electric chair if I didn't. . . . Because I was an accomplice to a murder. . . . Because I was an accomplice to the murder of his wife, Sophie, and my brother, Willie-Boy Lynch. . . . [*To* PA] Here we go, pal. [*Pauses.*] *Here . . . we . . . go!* I was in the truck, waiting. Tommy here ran out of the house and told me he'd killed 'em— told me that as straight as a man talking to God. Asked me to help with the fire. It all happened fast. He killed

Sophie and Willie-Boy and I helped light the fire to burn up the evidence—to make it look like an accident. [*Screams; to* PA.] *That's all I did in this:* help. I think they were dead before this one—Tommy Webber—ever got into the house! I think I've been lied to. I think I was an accomplice to nothing more than a lie. I think the best years of my life have been shot protecting a lie. I'll get you for this. I'll get even. I curse you! [*To* EMILY] I think it's time for certain non-family members to join together against certain family members, if you get what I'm driving my point at, so to speak. [*Pauses.*] I think that you and I have more in common than just good looks, Emily. First I want to talk to him and then you. [*To* PA] I'll be waitin' inside, pally. [*Pauses.*] I've got a whole new ace ta deal. A whole new ace.

[SAM *exits into house, slamming door behind him.*
After a long pause, EMILY *speaks.*]

EMILY: He killed her, didn't he?

[PA *looks up at* EMILY.]

EMILY: Alfred killed his mother, didn't he?

PA: *I* killed her. She wasn't just his mother, she was also my wife. A husband has certain rights, when a wife is out of line. [*Pauses.*] And a father has certain obligations . . . to a son. A father has an obligation to protect his son. No matter what. *No matter what.*

[*Silence.*
PA *stares at* EMILY. EMILY *bows her head.*
Tableau.
The lights fade out.]

END OF ACT II

ACT III
Scene 1

Living room, as in Alfred The Great. *Midnight.*

Stage in darkness.

Three sharp knocks are heard.

Church bells commence sounding their midnight: twelve chimes.

*First words of the scene—*SAM's—*heard in darkness.*

SAM: [*Off*] I'm hiding you in the kitchen, Tommy Webber. You're gonna have to know the truth!
  [*Bells complete twelve chimes.*]
SAM: Now you keep your ears open and listen! You hear me?
PA: [*Off*] What?
  [*Lights to full, suddenly.*
  Stage is empty.
  ALFRED *appears on the top of the staircase. He is wearing robe and slippers.*
  He leans over railing, looking into room. He leans back, looking up to foyer on second floor, not visible to audience.
  He leans into room again, calling quietly.]
ALFRED: Who's down there?
SAM: [*Calling from kitchen*] It's me: Sam . . . your father's friend from the hill.

174

[ALFRED *moves down staircase to center section of stairs.*
He waits and watches.
A moment passes.
SAM *enters from kitchen, carrying glass of water. He*
looks around living room; seems confused.]

SAM: Alfred?

[*No response.* ALFRED *is leaning against wall on staircase,*
into shadows.]

SAM: Hello? [*No response*] Alfred?

[SAM *moves into room, looking around.*
He carries water carefully.
SAM *gives a cursory, desultory look to staircase area,*
but turns instead suddenly to look at area near kitchen
door, believing someone is waiting on living-room side.
SAM's *back is now fully turned to* ALFRED, *who leans into*
room and speaks quietly.]

ALFRED: What's in the kitchen?

SAM: [*Whirling around to face* ALFRED] Huh? *There* you
are!

ALFRED: Why were you in the kitchen?

[ALFRED *sits on landing, allowing his legs and feet to fit*
between spindles in staircase railing.
He smiles.
SAM *drinks the glass of water, slowly and deliberately.*]

ALFRED: You drank a glass of something.

SAM: Wakefield water. Nothin' like a glass of Wakefield
water when you're feelin' outa sorts. [*Toasts* ALFRED,
raising glass to him, and then smiles.] Here's lookin'
atcha. . . . [*Drinks remaining drops of water.*] Mmmmm-
mmmm-good. [*Sets glass on table.*] I might as well get
right to the point. [*Looks around room again and then*
speaks in loud, stagy voice.] I kinda got some bad
news. . . .

ALFRED: Why are you yelling?

SAM: [*As loud as before*] I said, "I kinda got some bad
news."

ALFRED: She can hear you perfectly well if you use your
normal voice.

SAM: Who?

ALFRED: Can't you, Emmy? [*No response*] You're gonna
have to take my word for it, Sam. . . .

SAM: Who? Her? [*Laughs.*] That's rich.

ALFRED: What's your news?

SAM: *Bad* news. . . .

ALFRED: What's your *bad* news?

SAM: Your father.

ALFRED: My father?

SAM: [*Stagy too-loud voice again*] He's been threatening it for sixty-one years. . . . [*Pauses.*] Guess he meant it.

ALFRED: Guess he meant *what*?

SAM: He ran away.

ALFRED: [*Smiling; amused*] He what?

SAM: [*Annoyed*] It's no goddam laughin' matter. He ran away. They were beating him, ya know. He was hurt, ya know. [*Pauses.*] He broke free and scooted.

ALFRED: I don't think my father is much of a scooter, Sam. . . .

SAM: There's a lot you don't know about him. [*Looks around the room.*] Where is she?

ALFRED: Emily? [*Pauses.*]

SAM: [*Suddenly worried*] Oh, crap.
[SAM *turns and runs into kitchen.*
ALFRED *stands and walks down staircase slowly, entering room. He goes to sofa, sits; waits.*
SAM *reenters room and goes to staircase.*]

SAM: She ain't in there. . . . [*No response*] Hello?

ALFRED: [*Quietly*] Hello.

SAM: [*Whirls about.*] That supposed ta be cute?

EMILY: [*Quietly, from top of staircase*] Hello, Sam.

ALFRED: Why, look! It's Emily. . . . [*He has imitated* SAM'S *stagy voice.*]

SAM: Coupla goddam hot spooks. . . . Wicked funny, you two—wicked funny.

EMILY: What's the matter, Sam?

SAM: I got some really bad news. [*Pauses.*] The old folks, they came around and beat up Tommy: Alfred's father. [*Pauses.*] While they were hitting him he broke loose and ran away. Sorta fired off, loping, into the fields. . . .

EMILY: What about the money, Sam?

ALFRED: [*To* EMILY] What did you ask him, you?

EMILY: Did he take it with him, Sam?

ALFRED: I find it slightly monstrous . . .

EMILY: Answer me, Sam?

SAM: One at a time!

ALFRED: I find it slightly monstrous of you, Emily, to be mentioning money at this particular time. . . . Please, don't.

EMILY: Okay, *you* ask him.

ALFRED: Not yet.

EMILY: Sam?

SAM: [*Wide-eyed; astonished*] What?

EMILY: Did he take it with him?

SAM: Definitely not. He took nothing with him. [*Shrugs.*] You . . . uh . . . *can't* take it with you.

EMILY: How do you know?

SAM: How do I know *what*?

EMILY: That he didn't.

SAM: I just do. [*Pauses.*] I was there. [*Pauses.*] I . . . uh . . . held his arms.

ALFRED: That certainly fits the category of surprising retorts, Sam. You say you held his what? His arms?

SAM: It was right that it be me who did it. Who held him. [*Pauses.*] It was more like a hug than anything else. I wouldn't have hurt him knowingly. [*Pauses.*] Not physically.

ALFRED: [*Smiling*] What the hell are you talking about?

EMILY: I think you should pay attention, Alfred. You have something to tell Sam and Sam has something to tell *you*.

SAM: I tried to stop it, Alfred! I really did. . . . The old people. They came from all over town. They hated him. Roxy . . . the hag . . . she's hated him for about seventy years now. Hates you, too, Alfred. She figures you're the reason this town's cursed the way it is. Old folks livin' way past their prime, the way we do. Your fault . . .

ALFRED: Roxy? Your Roxy?

SAM: Yuh, my Roxy. My ex. His ex . . . everybody's ex. [*Smiles.*] She's never been one to forgive or forget. She's been especially hateful since she heard what went on with Margaret and Will down below. . . . And when I told her you were takin' all his money . . . well . . . *welllll* . . . that just kinda drove her off her nut, altogether. [*To* EMILY] Roxy was the one who actually broke his arm. She hit him with a shovel. [*Pauses; to* ALFRED.] I was just holding.

ALFRED: Is this somebody's idea of a joke?

SAM: Worst thing I ever saw: all the old folks—they got

like beetles in for a feast: swarming all over him. Their
minds were poisoned. They were scared . . . scared he
was gonna' die finally . . . without, you know . . . sharing.
[*Pauses.*] He broke loose, twistin' and snakin' through the
rotten pack of them. He slithered right and left until he
saw the clear of the field over Winn Street way, near
the Boston and Maine bridge. . . . Then he pranced and
galloped. . . . [*Pauses.*] Ya really gotta hand it to 'im,
Alfred. For a fella his age, he's still quite a spunky
broken-field runner. . . .

EMILY: Where are they now?

SAM: Who?

EMILY: Where are they? The old people . . . everybody?

SAM: Still looking. Still out there . . . hunting.

ALFRED: For my father?

SAM: For the money.

ALFRED: But . . . we've got to . . . we should . . .

EMILY: Go out?

ALFRED: We should. We have to find . . .

EMILY: Your father?

ALFRED: Emily, for God's sakes . . . you've got to let up on
me. . . .

EMILY: Say it, Alfred!

ALFRED: Is any of this true, Sam?

EMILY: Finish your sentence, Alfred. . . . [*Screams.*] *Alfred!*

ALFRED: Will you please just pull back from me?

EMILY: [*Pauses; then angrily*] Alfred, will you for Christ's
sakes finish *something???*

ALFRED: Sure.

EMILY: [*Falsely composed*] Fine. Fine. Now, Alfred, we
have to find *what?* [*Composure ended*] Sam's waiting!
I'm waiting!

ALFRED: Really smug, aren't you? [*Pauses; to* EMILY]
Really getting pleasure from this, aren't you? [*Pauses;
to* SAM] I want the money, Sam. I have a large debt to
pay. [*To* EMILY] You're going to get every speck of what's
coming to you, Emily. Every crumb. Okay?

SAM: [*Loud stagy voice*] *Is that the reason you came back
here?* [*Even louder; more slowly as well*] *To . . . get . . .
your . . . father's . . . money?*

ALFRED: [*To* EMILY] What's the matter with him? [*To*
SAM] What's the matter with you?

SAM: [*Still loud and stagy; projecting his voice into the kitchen, over his shoulder*] I said, "Did you come back here to get your father's money?"

ALFRED: Sam, we're right here in the room with you, re-member? What is this?

SAM: [*Not stagy at all now, but fiercely angry*] I wanna hear it from you once and for all, ya little bastard! [*Moves to* ALFRED.] You go off for years . . . *years!* . . . and you never make any real contact with us. . . . We never know what the hell you're doin' . . . what you're sayin' . . . nothing! [*Close to* ALFRED *now and even more fiercely and seriously spoken*] Now you're here . . . suddenly . . . unannounced and uninvited, too. [*Pauses.*] You really threw my schedule off. [*Suddenly yells.*] What the hell do you want from us? [*Pauses; tone changes.*] If it's his money, just tell me, loud and clear.

ALFRED: I hardly think it's the money, Sam. I hardly think that fits.

EMILY: Alfred!

ALFRED: Money is actually Emily's level of need just now. Money's exactly what it will goddam take to goddam get her goddam once and for all off my goddam aching back!

EMILY: It's not that simple, Sam. . . .

ALFRED: I believe the legendary character is Simple *Simon*, Emily.

SAM: You always got time ta make light of things, don't-cha? Ya always got time for makin' laughin' matters . . . makin' jokes outa serious things . . .

EMILY: Like lovemaking.

SAM: Huh?

ALFRED: I think that'll be just about enough, please. . . .

EMILY: Making a joke out of making love. . . . [*Pauses; to* SAM] Alfred . . . When I first met him, he was a laugh a minute. . . .

ALFRED: I said that'll be enough!

EMILY: Things have slowed down some. [*Pauses.*] Alfred hasn't given me so much as a chuckle in years. . . . [*Pauses.*] Hardly a smile. [*Pauses.*] I think he's lost his sense of humor altogether.

ALFRED: [*Fiercely*] Shut it, Emily!

EMILY: You're going to say it now . . . loud and clear. [*To* SAM] You're going to get your reason now: why Alfred's

here . . . why he came back to Wakefield . . . what he
wants. What he *really* wants, beyond the money, Sam.
Way beyond! [*To* ALFRED; *yells.*] *Now!* Finish *some*thing,
Alfred! You're going to have to finish *some*thing! We
have made an agreement, remember: a contract!

ALFRED: I wish you wouldn't . . .

EMILY: There is a great deal you would like to remember
. . . a great deal that you have forgotten that you would like
to remember. You would like. Sam's got some things that
he would like, too. Sam would like to know what exactly
it is you want, Alfred. . . . [*To* ALFRED] Let's give Sam
something he needs, Alfred: The real reason—why you
came back here—what you want. What you would like.

ALFRED: Please, Emily.

EMILY: I would like, Alfred. [*Screams.*] Begin your sentence with "I would like." [*Screams.*] *Alfred!!!*

ALFRED: I would like . . .

EMILY: Go on . . . *Finish!!!*

ALFRED: I would like . . .

EMILY: My father . . .

ALFRED: My father . . .

EMILY: *All of it!*

ALFRED: I would like . . . my father . . . to die. [*Bows
head.*]

SAM: [*After a pause*] That's it? That's why he came back?

EMILY: Perfect.

SAM: You ungrateful little twat . . . [*Pauses.*] You Pillsbury-
pancakey little tit . . . [*Pauses.*] You only get one father,
pansy. Just one: him.

EMILY: Now, Sam. I have your sacred word. [*Pauses.*] Go
bring it in here, Sam.

SAM: I hate doin' this. I really do. I've done some wicked
things in my day, but I really hate this one.

EMILY: Bring it in here, Sam. Now!

ALFRED: It's here? [*Pauses.*] Sam? Money? For Emily?

SAM: Huh?

ALFRED: Where?

SAM: In the kitchen. All the time.

ALFRED: The money?

SAM: No. [*Pauses.*] Your father. [*After a pause*] He's been
in the kitchen the whole time. Heard every word.
[*Pauses.*] I never liked you, Alfred.

[ALFRED *walks to kitchen door.*
He opens door, looks inside kitchen. EMILY *laughs.*
ALFRED *returns to* EMILY, *faces her.*]

ALFRED: Whose idea was this? Whose splendid idea was this?

[*He moves to chair; sits.*
EMILY *moves behind chair; strokes* ALFRED's *hair.*
She walks to side of chair; stares at ALFRED, *who is staring straight out front.*]

EMILY: This is the first time, in all the years I've known you . . . you've actually looked . . . your age.

[SAM *has been standing, watching them.*
ALFRED *in chair.*
EMILY *behind chair, touching* ALFRED's *hair.*
SAM *at sofa, standing.*
Tableau.]

SAM: [*Moves to kitchen door. He knocks on door—a signal: three knocks.*] Saddest thing I ever seen.

[SAM *opens door.* PA *standing there.* PA *enters room. Wears greatcoat. Holds arms inside.*
Tableau.
SAM *leads* PA *to sofa.*]

SAM: He heard every word.

[SAM *pauses. Stations* PA *at corner of sofa.*]

SAM: You better hurry, Alfred. Ain't got much time left. [*Pauses.*] You can't look at me accusingly. The whole thing's your fault. [*Pauses.*] He's failing. Hmmm. That's right.

EMILY: [*Pauses.*] This is the worst I've ever done to you, isn't it?

ALFRED: No. [*Pauses; looks at her.*] Not the worst. [*Head down now*] No.

PA: Look at me, Alfred. Pick up your head and look at me.

SAM: Look at your father, sonny.

[SAM *pauses. No response.*
ALFRED *continues to look at his shoes.*]

SAM: You hear me, sonnyboy? I told you ta look at your father!

PA: You're going to have to face it, son. [*No response*] I'm sorry, Alfred, but I'm going to have to make you remember exactly what it was you did. [*Pauses.*] I'm sorry. I really am.

SAM: I can vouch for that, Alfred. There isn't a sorrier son
of a bitch in th' whole Commonwealth of Massachusetts.
[SAM *pauses; no response from* ALFRED.]

SAM: You gotta pick up your head and look at your father,
Alfred. You're gonna haveta face both him and the facts.
Ain't much of a list ta choose from, but there it is. . . .
[*Pauses.*] Alfred?

PA: Alfred?

EMILY: Alfred?

SAM: Alfred?

PA: [*Angrily*] Alfred!
[ALFRED, *in chair, head down, slowly lifts his face and
looks into* PA's *eyes.*
SAM *watches and then bows head.*
EMILY *watches and then bows head.*
Tableau.
The lights fade to black.]

END OF SCENE 1

Scene 2

Living room.

Later, just before dawn.

Three sharp knocks are heard.

Stage remains in darkness.

*First words of scene—*PA's*—are heard.*

PA: My days of protecting you are comin' to a close.
[*Lights to full, suddenly.* ALFRED *in chair, head bowed.*
PA *sits on end of sofa, back against arm, nearly reclining.*
Faces ALFRED. *He holds one arm with his other arm,
both inside ill-fitting greatcoat.*]

ALFRED: [*Slowly looking up. Their eyes meet.*] I want you
to know why. I didn't mean it.

PA: Mean what?

ALFRED: What I said. What you heard. I was tricked into it. I was tricked.

PA: Makes no difference.

ALFRED: It does to *me*. It really does. I want you to understand.

PA: But it makes no difference to me, Alfred. And what makes no difference to me . . . well . . . makes no difference. [*Pauses.*] I want *you* to understand.

ALFRED: Oh, I do. I really do.

PA: Oh, you *don't*. You really *don't*. [*Pauses.*] There's no *time* left for what makes a difference to *you*. I'm through taking the blame. I'm through lying.

ALFRED: She was my mother.

PA: She was what?

ALFRED: My mother.

PA: *SHE WAS MY WIFE!*

[ALFRED *turns his back to* PA, *who is outraged by the move. Yells suddenly.*]

PA: *Do you goddammit! understand me???*

ALFRED: Yes, sir. I'm . . . sorry.

[ALFRED *and* PA *look at each other.*]

PA: I never ever heard you say things like "Yes, sir," or "I'm sorry" . . . not when you had some *position*.

ALFRED: No, sir . . . I mean . . . I'm sorry, sir. . . .

PA: When I was your age, I could . . . [*Pauses.*] When I was forty, I was . . . [*Pauses.*] Hope you've learned something, Alfred. When I choose to go . . . when I die . . . and you get your power back . . . *real* power, I mean . . . hide it. [*Pauses.*] Never let it be counted. [*Pauses.*] Never let them know the limits. [*Pauses.*] I never did. [*Pauses.*] That was my secret. [*Pauses.*] You know how old I really am? [*No response*] Take a guess.

[PA *laughs softly. After a moment's silence,* ALFRED *speaks.*]

ALFRED: When you were sixty-three, I was just getting myself born. You'd been away four months already. [*Pauses.*] Can you imagine? [*Pauses.*] By the time my ship, as they say, sailed into port, you were four months gone. [*Pauses.*] My mother said you'd run away . . . run away from home. [*Pauses.*] A man your age. [*Pauses.*] You missed my most important birthday, Pa. I've often

wondered exactly what it was I'd done that offended you
. . . that drove you away. . . .

PA: I can explain that. . . .

ALFRED: [*Explosively*] Don't you *goddammit!* interrupt me!
I loathe being interrupted by you! [*Pauses.*] Apologize!

PA: [*Quietly*] I'm sorry.

ALFRED: I said *apologize!*

PA: I'm . . . I'm sorry.

ALFRED: You never let me finish.

PA: I'm sorry. I'm sorry I took the blame for you, son. I'm
sorry I lied. I was wrong. Dead wrong.

ALFRED: I don't understand.

PA: Open your eyes, Alfred.

ALFRED: What the hell are you talking about?

PA: My wife . . . your mother.

ALFRED: Oh, really? You think about her much? You miss
her? Do you see her in your dreams?

PA: Wouldn't be much point in it, Alfred. She's dead.

ALFRED: What goes through your mind when you *do* think
about her?

PA: But I *don't*. I said I don't.

ALFRED: But when you *do* . . .

PA: But I *don't!*

ALFRED: [*Screams.*] *I want an answer!* [*No response*] Okay,
Pa. Stay crazy. [*Pauses.*] I think about the box we put
her in and whether or not it was really airtight, like they
promised us . . . like it said in the brochure. [*Pauses.*]
I kept the brochure for years. . . . [*Pauses.*] How much
flesh is left now? That's quite another question high on
the list of things I think about. [*Pauses.*] What color is
it? Are the maggots still nibbling away and, if so, what
specific kind of maggot is attracted to my ma: grub or
larva; blue-bottle maggot or cheese-fly maggot? [*Pauses.*]
I've done quite an exhaustive study. I've become quite
an expert in the long overlooked field of body rot.
[*Pauses.*] No one really knows how the maggot gets in:
how it penetrates the sealed box. Nobody knows where
the maggot comes from, period. Nobody even knows
where the *word* "maggot" comes from. Etymologically
speaking, the maggot is a mystery. [*Pauses.*] So's my
mother, thanks to you. [*Pauses.*] It's as though I never

had one . . . as though she never, well, existed. [*Pauses.*] I'm bringing her back. Sorry.

PA: Sorry? Why?

ALFRED: Everything born dies. Once you've seen the thing itself, you can't pretend. Can you? [*Yells.*] *Can you?*

PA: No, you can't pretend.

ALFRED: Let me get to my essential question, please. Cremation or burled walnut, Pa? Which do you prefer?

PA: Is that a question that needs to be answered?

ALFRED: Cremation certainly has its good points. It's maggot-proof and quite tidy. We should be realistic in these matters. . . . [*Pauses.*] And I could scatter your ashes, if you'd like. I'd do that for you. [*Pauses.*] I could maybe hurl them into the wind and scatter them over Quannapowitt. Or Good Harbor Beach down in Gloucester. . . . Maybe even Gloucester harbor during the Greasy Pole Contest. Or maybe Magnolia? Or Wingaersheek Beach? Or Crane's, down in Ipswich? [*Pauses.*] Course, I'd be running the risk that the wind would turn against me . . . that your ashes might blow back into my face . . . into my eyes . . . cause me to blink and maybe miss something that was really *considerable*. [*Suddenly*] I could promise you *any*thing, couldn't I? Just the way you promised *her*? [*Softly*] I just don't understand how you can feel nothing.

PA: You don't believe it, do you, son? You really can't open your eyes to it, can you?

ALFRED: I was there, Pa. I have eyes. I have a memory.

PA: Look at the cap, Alfred. Try it on. It was yours, Alfred, remember?

[ALFRED *holds cap—does not place it on his head.*]

PA: No? You will. Sooner or later you will. You'll have to.

[SAM *and* EMILY *enter, together.* ALFRED *looks at* EMILY, *angrily.*]

ALFRED: You!

EMILY: [*To* ALFRED] Is it over?

ALFRED: I feel cold.

EMILY: Pa?

SAM: He looks pretty bad. . . . Nearly finished. [*Pauses.*] Crow's *already* dead. Just saw him layin', feet curled under, West Ward path. All buggy already, too. [*Pauses.*]

Old people layin' down sick, all over town. Looks as if everybody's gettin' set for the big change. [*Pauses.*] Guess we'll all go now. [*Pauses.*] Course, when *I* go, I do have a plan. Wanna hear it?

PA: No.

SAM: No?

PA: No.

SAM: It's wrong. It ain't fair. It's wicked. It angers me somethin' awful. I know the man's a liar, a cheater, and a fornicator, but this is too much . . . *too much!* [*Pauses.*] What did he ever do, really, ta deserve this kinda pain and punishment? A ton of horrible lies does *not*, in *my* book, add up ta this horrible ending. Not for such a man. [*Pauses.*] Your father was a good man, Alfred. He lived a good, clean-and-moral, hard-working life. Lies, cheating, and fornication to the wind . . . [*Pauses.*] It simply ain't fair.

PA: What ain't fair, Sam?

SAM: The life.

PA: The life?

SAM: The life.

PA: Shut up, Sam.

SAM: About what happened . . . I couldn't stop it. . . .

PA: I saw that okay. But why'd you have to start it?

SAM: Been with this man nearly all my life. I know he's a liar, but all the same . . . [*Pauses.*] I've never known a man with his qualities. [*Pauses.*] I'd be . . . nothing . . . without him. [*Pauses.*] Everything I got, I owe to him. Even though he's a liar. . . . [*Pauses.*] He . . . well . . . taught me everything I know. [*Pauses.*] Liar or not, this man's a saint. [*Pauses.*] He's the one I'd burn for. [*Pauses.*] I never married because of him. . . . [*Pauses.*] He . . . satisfied . . . me.

[SAM'*s hand is on* PA'*s cheek, his thumb near* PA'*s mouth.* PA *bites* SAM'*s thumb.*

SAM *squeals and yips.*]

SAM: The filthy bitch just bit me!

PA: And I'll do it again.

SAM: [*Mortified; outraged*] That bite might have just cost you the best friend a man ever had.

PA: Who? You? Man's best friend?

SAM: I hated that crack. [*Pauses.*] That crack did it.

[*Pauses.*] I'm gettin' outa here. I've had enough. [*Pauses.*]
Sixty-one years. Sixty-one miserable years.

[SAM *moves to* PA; *points his finger at* PA.]

SAM: You lied to me, Tommy. You goddam lied.

[PA *bites* SAM's *finger.* SAM *squeals and yips.*]

SAM: *Doggone! This bullshit artist drew blood!* [*Pauses.*]
Doggone. [*Pauses.*] This is curtains, partner. [*Pauses;
looks at his finger.*] Doggone.

PA: [*Laughing*] Get outa here, Sam. [*Pauses; smiles.*] I've
had enough.

SAM: Sure. [*Pauses; to* PA] I'll go. [*Pauses.*] I'm on my
way. [*No response*] I'm blowin' this town. [*Takes five
steps in silence.*] Doesn't bother me a bit. [*Five more
steps. At door now*] I ain't usually a quitter, but sixty
years is where I draw the line. [*Pauses.*] Tom?

PA: Yuh, Sam?

SAM: God bless. [*Pauses.*] Tommy?

PA: Yuh, Sam?

SAM: It kinda annoys me that you're . . . well . . . but,
long as you are, well . . .

PA: What, Sam?

SAM: You gonna let me?

PA: Let you what?

SAM: Finish?

PA: Can you?

SAM: It came to me just after noon. After all these years
of work I have it. I swear to God: the greatest story
ever told!

PA: Go on, Sam . . .

SAM: Oh, God . . . [*Pauses; grinning now.*] When you take
an idea like this, as I have, and work on it and work on
it and work on it, as I have, it just gets better and better.
[*Pauses.*] A small perfection is what's comin'. . . .

PA: Go on, Sam . . .

SAM: Okay, okay. [*Pauses. Poses.*] I've always felt that the
best way out of this wicked awful mess called the life
was out route one-twenty-eight, Lynnfield way and right
up the Newburyport Turnpike . . . that's route one . . .
straight up into New Hampshire. . . . [*Pauses.*] You
wanna know where ta go from there?

PA: Where, Sam?

SAM: [*To* ALFRED] *You* wanna know?

ALFRED: Where, Sam?

SAM: [*To* EMILY] *You* wanna know?

EMILY: Where, Sam?

SAM: [*Taking stage fully now*] Here it comes . . . "The
Way Outa Wakefield!" . . . the greatest story is finally
gettin' told. The ending . . . the punch . . . the capper
. . . the over-the-top . . . the *risus puris!* [*To* PA] Ask me
again, Tom.

PA: Where, Sam? Did you forget the ending, Sam? The
punch? The capper? The *risus puris?* He forgot!
[*There is a long, painful pause, in which it becomes quite
obvious that* SAM *has forgotten the ending to his joke.*]

PA: He forgot.

SAM: [*Shocked and dejected*] Oh, my dear God. Oh, my
dear sweet God. . . . [*Pauses; moves to side of stage in
false exit. He stops. He returns again to the center of the
stage.*] If I ever *EVER!* try that one again, I'm gonna
take a little more time settin' it up! [*Pauses; moves to
side of stage. Stops. He turns to* PA.] You'll see.
[SAM *exits the play.*]

PA: [*After a pause*] Used to keep disbelieving that Sam's
really crazy. . . . [*Pauses.*] Lately, it's been harder than
ever to disbelieve. . . . [*Pauses.*] Alfred?

ALFRED: Right here.

PA: Sam left, huh?

ALFRED: Sam left.

PA: He's gone, huh?

ALFRED: He's gone.

PA: He lied, ya know. He's really a hundred. I'm a hundred
and three.

EMILY: Sam's gone.

PA: Man's been tryin' ta kill me for years now. Sixty, maybe
sixty-one. . . . [*Pauses.*] Accomplished th' opposite. Kept
me alive. Kept me alive and then some. [*Pauses.*] Every
day, day after day, he put six drops of poison . . . strychnine . . . in my mornin' glass of Wakefield water. [*Pauses.*]
Caused me some pain at first, but with some interestin'
side effects. Strychnine was the ticket. Doctors were
amazed. [*Pauses.*] Made me potent. Able and anxious ta
please . . . every woman in town. Stoneham and Reading,
as well. [*Pauses.*] Made a real lover of me. [*Pauses.*] To
make a lover of a man who's so full of hate is quite a

thing. [*Pauses.*] Sam did that for me. [*Pauses.*] Sixty-one years, six drops a day, never missed a mornin'. . . . [*Pauses.*] That's friendship. [*Pauses.*] Gone now, I guess. [*Pauses.*] Is he outa sight?

EMILY: Sam's gone.

ALFRED: He's gone, Pa.

PA: Emily?

EMILY: Open your eyes, Pa. . . .

PA: Can't . . . Don't want to . . . Not now. . . .

EMILY: You've got to . . . tell me. Now. Did Alfred kill his mother?

ALFRED: Stop it . . .

EMILY: You promised me . . . to tell me . . . out loud . . . NOW!

ALFRED: [*Softly; intensely*] Back off from him . . .

EMILY: Nobody knows but you. . . . Alfred can't remember. Will you for *Christ's* sake open your eyes!

ALFRED: You stay away from him! [*Moves to her.*] Do you hear me?

[*She turns.*]

ALFRED: Step back.

EMILY: Please, Pa, answer me.

ALFRED: Hey!

EMILY: Answer me!

ALFRED: Hey!

PA: Okay, what's your question?

EMILY: Did Alfred kill his mother?

ALFRED: Hey!

PA: [*To* ALFRED] Stop making noises! . . . [*Pauses.*] Yes. [*Pauses.*] Yes, he did.

ALFRED: [*Quietly.*] That's not true. [*Bows his head.*]

PA: He thought he was doin' me a favor, I guess. [*Pauses.*] He was just a kid.

ALFRED: That's not true.

PA: He killed 'em both. Stabbed them with his Scout knife while they were in bed together. [*Pauses.*] My bed. He musta thought I wanted that: Wanted them punished. [*Pauses.*] He was protecting me from knowing.

ALFRED: That's . . . not . . . true.

PA: Sam and me, we took the blame for it. I told Sam I'd done it. Sam never knew the real truth. I spared him from that. [*Pauses.*] If Sam'd known, he never woulda

stayed with me. I had to hide it from him. [*Pauses.*]
Sam trusted me. He always did. Gone now. . . . [*Pauses.*]
Alfred was only ten then, that's all. No point in making
a boy ten suffer. I wanted to protect him: the boy:
Alfred. [*Pauses; screams.*] *I made a mistake!!!* [*Pauses;
quietly again.*] Alfred did the murders. I took the blame,
but he's got the guilt. And that's the truth. [*To* ALFRED]
There it is, Alfred. In the open now. The cap probably
still fits. Try it. [*To* EMILY] His cap. He wrapped his
Scout knife and best baseball cards in it. Put it all in a
cigar box. . . .

EMILY: Dutch Masters.

PA: Yuh. Dutch Masters. How'd you find it?

EMILY: I was persistent, Pa. That's my nature.

ALFRED: [*To* EMILY; *deliberately*] I want you . . . out of
my life. [*Pauses.*] Goodbye, Emily.

EMILY: Alfred, I . . .

ALFRED: [*Cutting her off*] I said *goodbye.*

PA: You'd better go. . . . If you want to punish Alfred for
what I told you, that's *your* business. My business is
ending now. I want to be with Alfred for a bit. [*Pauses.*]
I'm sorry to have to give you such . . . bad news. . . .
[*Pauses.*] A father should die with his son nearby. You're
not my son. Alfred's my son. You'd better go. I'm gettin'
close now. . . .

ALFRED: I . . . want . . . you . . . out . . . of . . . here.
. . . [*Pauses; turns to* PA.] Okay, Pa? Did you hear me?
[*To* EMILY *again*] I want you out of my life. [*Yells.*] *Do
you hear me?*

EMILY: [*After a long pause*] Fine, Alfred, fine. [*Smiles.*]
Perfect. [*Pauses.*] I know it all, Alfred. All the pieces
have finally fit together. I know all about the Widow
O'Brien Scandal, Alfred. I know it's true. *Did you hear
me, Alfred?* I said that I know. I do. . . . I know why
you had to marry me, why you forced me, why you
held me down. I even know why my babies died. I know
it all.

ALFRED: [*A circus barker's voice*] Goodbye, Emily!

PA: Emily?

EMILY: What?

PA: What is it you want, Emily? What is it you *really*
want?

EMILY: Pa . . . [*Moves to side of stage.*] I never thought you'd ask. [*Turns to* ALFRED.] I shall destroy you, Alfred. I swear it. It's going to take time and money, but I've got both . . . lots . . . I'm going to destroy you, Alfred. I really shall. [*Pauses.*] No one will be able to stop me, Alfred. Not you. Not me. No one. [*Pauses.*] I swear it. [*To* PA] Pa? You asked and now you know: Alfred dies. I swear it.

[EMILY *goes to* PA. *She kisses him.* EMILY *goes to* ALFRED. *She kisses him.* EMILY *exits the play.*]

ALFRED: [*After a long pause*] She's gone, Pa. Emily's gone. [*Pauses.*] It's just us now. Just family.

PA: Tell me what to do, Alfred. It's just us now. Family: father and son. No one's tricking you now. It's just us. Tell me straight. I want to leave it to you.

ALFRED: I don't understand. Leave *what* to me?

PA: The decision. Live or die. Which?

ALFRED: *What the hell are you talking about?*

PA: Me. . . .

ALFRED: What?

PA: No one here now . . . just you and me. . . . Tell me!

ALFRED: Pa, please don't . . . Just be quiet now. . . . Shhhh.

PA: Quick, Alfred! Live or die! [*Gasps for breath.*] Put it simply. . . . Tell me simply. I want to hear it from your lips . . . your mouth . . . your mind. . . .

ALFRED: *I don't know!*

PA: Think!

ALFRED: I don't know!

PA: Hurry!

ALFRED: Don't, Pa!

PA: I have to!

ALFRED: You don't . . . !

PA: I *want* to!

ALFRED: We never talked!

PA: Don't be stupid! [*Pauses.*] *Do you hear me???*

[*There is a long pause;* ALFRED *places cap on head.*]

ALFRED: Yes. [*Pauses; realizes.*] They were all together: buried. In a Dutch Masters cigar box. Sealed. Wood. I remember now, the cap, the knife, my best baseball cards. I must have figured they'd punish me—catch me —The cards were there, Pa—I'd forgotten—All signed and wrapped in alphabetical order. I was neat—ordered.

Joe Cronin, Dom DiMaggio, Bobby Doerr, Bob Ferris, Mickey Harris, Higgins, Wally Moses, Johnny Peskey, Wagner, Ted Williams, Rudy York. [*Pauses.*] It's true, Pa, isn't it? *I* was the one who did it. I did. [*Pauses.*] I'd forgotten. I killed your wife . . . my mother. . . . You've been protecting me, haven't you? [*Pauses.*] Pa? It still fits, Pa. [*Pauses; waits.*] Pa? Look, Pa. [*Softly*] Pa? Get up. Don't die. [*Suddenly angry*] You've got no right to do this! *What I did I did for you!* I thought you were . . . a great man. [*Changed tone*] Get up, Pa. I don't want to stay alone with this. Pa? [*Pauses.*] Pa? I don't. I really don't. [*Pauses; smiles.*] I'm very successful, Pa . . . I've been very lucky. I am quite a successful young . . . man. [*Pauses; softly.*] Pa? I've gotta be punished, Pa. . . . [*Pauses.*] Pa? I've gotta . . . [*Softly*] Pa, it's me: Alfred.
[*Silence.*

PA, *on sofa, absolutely still.* ALFRED, *on sofa, unmovingly. A moment passes.*

ALFRED *stands, moves to chair, sits, removes cap.*
He moves his face toward the auditorium, stops, stares straight out front.
He bows his head.
Tableau.
The lights fade to black.]

THE PLAY IS OVER.

Paris, Chicago, New York City, Gloucester— 1971–1978.

The Wakefield Plays, Part V

ALFRED DIES
A Play in Three Acts

For Martin Esslin.

The People of the Play

ALFRED: Forties, thin, once elegant.
LYNCH: Forties, thick, tough.
ROXY: Ancient.
EMILY: Forties, thin, once elegant.

The Place of the Play

A makeshift prison room; set in the storage room under the lanternlike cupola bandstand, the Common, Wakefield, Massachusetts.

The Time of the Play

End of June, start of July.

An aged man is but a paltry thing,
A tattered coat upon a stick, unless
Soul clap its hands and sing, and louder sing
For every tatter in its mortal dress,
Nor is there singing school but studying
Monuments of its own magnificence:
And therefore I have sailed the seas and come
To the holy city of Byzantium.

—Yeats

ACT I
Scene 1

Prison room. Dawn. Stage in darkness.

Three sharp knocks are heard. Same sound will precede each scene of play.

Church bells in distance, four chimes.

*First words of play—*ALFRED'S*—are heard in darkness.*

ALFRED: [*Yells.*] Anybody out there? [*Pauses.*] Hello!
  [*Lights to full, suddenly.*
  Storage room for park benches, under the bandstand, under the Common, Wakefield, Massachusetts.
  The room is circular, stone-walled.
  A makeshift prison has been constructed in the room of equidistant metal bars. The floor space of the prison cell occupies one half of the entire floor space of the room.
  There are two doors in the room, no windows. One door is upstage right, connecting the room to a staircase leading to the outside. The second door is on the upstage left, in the cell, leading to an unlit back room.
  There is a door to the cell, downstage center, constructed of equidistant bars, held closed with lock and key, plus a padlocked heavy chain.
  Park benches are stacked along the walls outside the cell. Three benches are lined one in front of the other, downstage left, for use by those outside the cell.
  There is no furniture in the cell.

197

A small table is set, downstage left, upon which a telephone sits.

Opposite, a small court stenography machine is set on
a proper table, with a stenographer's chair set under.
Both table and chairs are castered.

Crates are stacked along the wall between the door to
the room and the stenography table. One of the crates
is a portable refrigerator for food storage.

A long pole, padded at one end, leans against the stage-
right wall.

There are three overhead light sources visible: one lamp,
exceedingly bright, hangs center of cell; a second, downstage right, over benches (it is not on at start of play):
and a third light hangs over stenography table. Cell light
and stenography table light are lit.

A ventilation duct is seen overhead, near where pole is
leaned. Possible to open duct for fresh air by poking
same with pole. Also possible to poke caged person in
cell with pole.

Weather in room cool and damp: unusual in contrast to
July's heat in world above ground.

Sense of absolute silence wanted, when no one creates
sound in room. No sounds from outside world above
evident during play until its conclusion.]

ALFRED: [Calling from offstage, behind door] Anybody out
there?

[Three sharp knocks again. Source revealed now as
ALFRED knocking on back of door, which suddenly flies
open.

ALFRED hurtles out onstage, self-propelled, stopping at
downstage bars of cell.

The lights hurt his eyes. He shields them, not blinking.

He is shocked and amazed to discover that he has been
caged.

He moves about the inside circumference of the cell,
feeling the bars as he goes.

His eyes adjust to the new lighting. He studies the room
outside of the cell. He calls again.]

ALFRED: Hello?

[There is no reply.

Pause.

He moves to the open door on upstage wall of cell.

He peeks outside, calling, with head offstage, poked into darkened room above cell.]

ALFRED: *Anybody out here either?*

[*There is no reply.*

ALFRED *exits into upstage darkened room. For a moment, there is no one onstage.*

ALFRED'S *voice, heard calling in darkened room:*]

ALFRED: *Anybody hear me?*

[*No reply. Silence.*

The downstage left door opens quietly. LYNCH *enters.*]

LYNCH: Hello?

ALFRED: [*His voice from back room. He thinks he has been answered.*] Hello!

[LYNCH *looks around room and into cage.*

ALFRED *runs onto stage.*]

LYNCH: Alfred!

ALFRED: [*Delighted to see another person in room*] Hello!

LYNCH: Hey, Alfred. It's me! [*Moves to bars of cell.*] Don't you recognize me?

ALFRED: [*Confused*] I beg your pardon. . . .

LYNCH: It's me: Lynchie. . . .

ALFRED: Lynchie?

LYNCH: Lynchie. Lynchie. From West Ward School. . . .

ALFRED: I didn't go to West Ward School. I went to Warren School. . . .

LYNCH: [*Takes bulb from paper bag, exchanges same in downstage-left light. He stands on chair.*] Lynch, for Christ's sakes! From church league basketball . . . Saint Joe's!

ALFRED: I certainly didn't play for Saint Joe's!

LYNCH: Lynch, Alfred, Lynch! From B.C.!

ALFRED: B.C.? [*Pauses.*] I never went to B.C. [*Pauses.*] I've parked at B.C. . . . nights . . . on dates. . . . But that was a long time ago. [*Pauses; smiles.*] I think there's been a tremendous mistake here.

LYNCH: I know you know me. Look at me. Look at me. [*He stands in front of cell now, smiling.*]

ALFRED: Well, there is a look of the familiar about you.

LYNCH: I'm Margaret's brother.

ALFRED: Excuse me, but did you say you were Margaret's brother?

LYNCH: [*Laughing now*] You remember, now, huh?

Lynchie. We use'ta have terrific fistfights, you and me, right? . . . I use'ta win.

ALFRED: Your sister? . . . Your sister was Margaret? Lynchie? *That* Lynchie? You're Margaret's brother? The brother that's my age . . . roughly?

LYNCH: [*Deadly serious now*] Yuh, Your age, roughly. I'm six weeks older than you. Six.

ALFRED: My God . . . I just . . . Well, look at you!

LYNCH: [*After a long pause; with tremendous hostility*] How's your pecker?

ALFRED: Excuse me?

LYNCH: [*Smiles.*] We'll talk about Margaret in due course, huh? [*Attitude changes drastically; he laughs.*] You're lookin' great, Alfred . . . just great!

ALFRED: [*Half laughs.*] You don't look so bad, yourself, Lynchie. Good ta see ya. . . . [*Smiles; looks around.*] What is this place, anyway? Some kind of . . . prison?

LYNCH: Yuh, 'tis.

ALFRED: Where are we, anyway? Are we in Wakefield?

LYNCH: What kind of dumb question's that s'posed ta be?

ALFRED: What kind of dumb question? I don't actually *know* what kind. Are we, Lynchie? Are we in Wakefield?

LYNCH: Yuh. We are. We're in Wakefield. In the storage room for park benches, under the bandstand, center of the Common, right overlookin' Lake Quannapowitt. I built this on commission. . . .

ALFRED: *What?*

LYNCH: The pen. Your cage. I built it on commission. Specially built prison, just for the occasion. No expense spared. Pretty good, huh?

ALFRED: [*Looking at his cage; feeling bars to it*] You did this, huh? You seem to know your way around a tool. [*Smiles at* LYNCH.] You in construction?

LYNCH: In what?

ALFRED: Your line of work: construction?

LYNCH: Opposite.

[ALFRED *looks at* LYNCH *blankly.*]

LYNCH: *Destruction.* [*Smiles.*] I take things down.

ALFRED: But in the case of this . . . prison . . . you put things up?

LYNCH: Well, yuh. I mean, you can't learn one thing without learning the other . . . the opposite. Right?

ALFRED: Yes. I definitely agree. I wish I knew to what, exactly, but let's just move along. . . . [*He pauses.*] We're in Wakefield, Massachusetts, under the bandstand, in the Common, underground? That's where we are?

LYNCH: Who told you that?

ALFRED: You told me that.

LYNCH: I've never been able to control my mouth. Yuh. It's true. Mother Earth is just above us.

ALFRED: Lynchie . . . uh? . . . Could I possibly risk another dumb one? Another dumb question? There's one burning inside me right now.

LYNCH: Shoot! It's a free country. Never let it be said I don't still have my sense of humor, huh? Remember?

ALFRED: [*Smiles.*] I sure do.

LYNCH: I remember takin' apart your 'thirty-seven Chevy Coupe . . . a two-seater, right? . . . and puttin' it back together again up on Buzzy Whatsis's barn roof. . . . [*He laughs.*] That was hilarious!

ALFRED: [*Stares at* LYNCH *awhile before speaking.*] Uh, Lynchie?

LYNCH: Yuh?

ALFRED: Am . . . uh . . . Am *I* inside the cell or are *you* inside the cell? [*Silence.*] It's a little difficult to tell from here. [LYNCH *stares at* ALFRED.] I knew you were going to think it was kinda a dumb question. . . .

LYNCH: [*Astonished*] Am *I* or *you*? . . . [*Laughs.*] That's really rich! [*Roars.*] You are one hilarious son of a bitch! No *wonder* Alfred L. Webber got rich and B. J. Lynch got nothin'!

[*After laughter subsides,* ALFRED *and* LYNCH *stare at each other.*]

ALFRED: My guess is me.

LYNCH: Right.

ALFRED: Could I ask you for how long?

LYNCH: How long you've *been?* Or how long you're *gonna be?*

ALFRED: Either, Lynchie. I'll take either.

LYNCH: You've *been* maybe three days now. Mostly sleeping. [*Pauses; scratches head.*] How long you're *gonna be* . . . depends.

ALFRED: On what?

LYNCH: Don't be a joker, Alfred. Not all the time. Air's

getting foul. . . . [*Pokes ventilator duct open.*] Some
things are not laughing matters, huh?

ALFRED: Would you believe me if I told you I don't know
a single bit of what's going on? This is a *total* blank to
me. . . .

LYNCH: That should be your case, then.

ALFRED: Case? I'm arrested? For what? Could I ask you
for what?

[LYNCH *tries phone.*
As the men talk, ALFRED, *at first discreetly and then
openly, tests the strength of the bars that define his cell.
Neither will comment on this action.*]

LYNCH: Insanity.

ALFRED: What?

LYNCH: Insanity. [*Tries phone again.*]

ALFRED: I've been arrested for insanity?

LYNCH: That should be your case.

ALFRED: *No*body gets arrested for insanity! [*Pauses.*] Most
people are *rewarded* for insanity. Given better jobs:
positions of leadership and control. [*Pauses.*] Political
power. [*Pauses.*] Professions such as law and medicine:
crawling with the demented and the insane. [*Pauses.*]
It's a fact. [*Pauses.*] What case?

[*The phone is dead.* LYNCH *turns to* ALFRED.]

LYNCH: Here's what, if I was you . . .

ALFRED: Were.

LYNCH: Huh?

ALFRED: [*Steps back three steps and then runs his body
into the upstage-left bars. They do not budge under the
force of his weight.*] If I *were* you . . . [*Smiles.*] Subjunc-
tive. [*Pauses.*] Sorry. It's the one case I tend to believe
in. . . . [*Smiles, embarrassed by his own digression.*]
In which I tend to believe. Am I in danger?

LYNCH: Twenty years ago, you were as normal as any of
us. That's what the city does ta you, Alf. . . .

ALFRED: [*Sits on floor; pauses.*] Uh . . . Lynchie?

LYNCH: Yuh?

ALFRED: Could you try never to call me that?

LYNCH: Huh?

ALFRED: What you just called me.

LYNCH: Alf? [*Pauses.*] Everybody calls you Alf.

ALFRED: I don't think so.

LYNCH: Are you kidding me?

ALFRED: No, I really don't like that so much: being called that.

LYNCH: Alf? You don't like "Alf"?

ALFRED: It really annoys me. . . .

LYNCH: Alf? "Alf" annoys you?

ALFRED: . . . Runny.

LYNCH: Wha's'at?

ALFRED: Runny. Unless my memory fails me . . . Runny.

LYNCH: I wouldn't, Alf. . . .

ALFRED: "Runny Lynch. . . . The nose that flows like the Mystic River." Wasn't that the way you were known in some circles?

LYNCH: Okay, Alfred. Okay.

ALFRED: [*Smiling*] Okay, Lynch. [*Suddenly*] What the hell did I do? Who brought me here? When? I feel like I've been drugged! Or hit over the head? Did somebody hit me over the head? Huh? Huh? [*Leans in.*] Someone will be held responsible here. . . . I warn you.

LYNCH: *You* warn *me*?

ALFRED: "Imbroglio" is the word that springs to mind.

LYNCH: What's that supposed to mean? Like a barbecue? You hungry?

ALFRED: Hungry? I am. Yes.

LYNCH: Well, I suppose I could go into town and try to scrounge something up . . . maybe at Hazelwood. Sun's up. They're open. What kind of food you like?

ALFRED: Could you just give me a hint?

LYNCH: You mean like pancakes?

ALFRED: What on earth are you talking about?

LYNCH: What on earth are *you* talking about?

ALFRED: I asked you first.

LYNCH: I'm talking about breakfast.

ALFRED: I'm talking about why I'm here. Just a hint, Lynchie?

LYNCH: What was the word that sprung to your mind?

ALFRED: I'll tell *you*, if you tell *me*.

LYNCH: C'mon, Alf . . . I'm not s'pose'ta be talking to you at all. . . .

ALFRED: Runn*yyyy* . . .

LYNCH: C'mon, Alfred. I can't. I could get into real trouble.

ALFRED: For an old pal? What am I here for? How come I'm in jail?

LYNCH: I can't. I really can't.

ALFRED: I'm going to find out anyway, right? For an old pal, Lynchie. Come on. . . . I'll count to three and you say your word and I'll say my word. Come on, Lynchie. . . .

LYNCH: I dunno. . . .

ALFRED: Lynchie. Lynchie - Lynchie. Lynchie - Lynchie - Lynchie . . .

LYNCH: At three. Okay. Count.

ALFRED: One . . . two . . . *three! Imbroglio!*

LYNCH: Didn't know you could count that high. [*Laughs.*]

ALFRED: You cheated me, Lynch. You goddam cheated me. [LYNCH *laughs.*]

ALFRED: I gave you my word, Lynch. A deal's a deal. . . . [LYNCH *laughs again.*]

ALFRED: You're welchin' out! [*Pauses.*] You're pullin' a Guinea-give. . . . [*Pauses.*] You're Scotchin' me. . . . [*Pauses.*] You're Jewin' me. . . . You're Jappin' me. . . . [*Pauses.*] I'm gettin' a Sheenie-screwin'. . . . Baptist bee-bop. . . . [*Pauses.*] This is Polack pudding. . . . [*Pauses.*] You're a nigger in a woodpile, Lynch. . . . [*With sudden anger*] Now you open your goddam dumb mouth and you speak words, dolt!

LYNCH: [*After a pause*] I don't like your attitude. I would try a little more respect, if I was—*were*—you. [*Smiles.*] You ain't exactly able to call your position *prime*, ya know.

ALFRED: Have I been charged?

LYNCH: For what? For *this?* [*Pauses.*] This is being paid for. . . . [*Laughs.*]

ALFRED: Have I been charged *with something* is what I meant. Not *for something.* [*Pauses.*] The state's paying for this, right? There'll be a judge, right? [*Pauses.*] Lynchie, for the love of God, *I really don't know!*

LYNCH: I'm not supposed to be talking to you, Alfred. . . . I'm even a little sorry I mentioned the bandstand to ya. . . . Maybe that was a mistake, ya know?

ALFRED: But I'm in trouble. . . .

LYNCH: That's an understatement, if I ever heard one. . . .

ALFRED: Then the state *is* paying for this, right?

LYNCH: I can't talk.

ALFRED: I mean, that's just *assumed*, right?

LYNCH: Sorry, *Alf.* [*He crosses to desk and telephone; sits.*]

ALFRED: You mean that somebody else is? . . . Somebody else is footing the bill for this . . . ? [*Pauses.*] A private person . . . party? [*No response.*] It is, isn't it? What's in the back room behind me? I can't see anything in there. Where does it lead to?

LYNCH: You're gonna haveta figure things out for yourself.

ALFRED: Sure. [*Pauses.*] Okay. [*Pauses.*] I don't mind at all. . . .

[ALFRED *moves upstage and exits into the darkened room.* LYNCH *watches a moment and then goes to telephone. He dials a number on the telephone, waits a moment, listens.*]

LYNCH: What's'a matter here? [*Jiggles the receiver on and off the cradle, breaking the connection; he listens for a dial tone. There is none.*] What's'a matter here?

ALFRED: [*Calling from darkened room, upstage*] Hello? Anybody here?

LYNCH: [*Looks up to cell. Moves from telephone to bars and tries to look into darkened room. Calls into room.*] Alfred!

ALFRED: [*Calling from room, offstage*] Hello?

[*There is a silence.* ALFRED *reenters cell, onstage. He shields his eyes from the bright onstage light.*]

ALFRED: Where's the door? I've just felt my way around in there. No door. . . . [*Moves around cell, feeling bars.*] No breaks in bars. . . . [*Stops; looks at door.*] Just one door between room and cage. . . . [*Looks at* LYNCH; *smiles.*] You must have rebuilt this whole room for me, huh? All this welding . . . all those bricks laid in there. . . . [*Motions to back room.*] Highly skilled work . . . backbreaking, too, I should think. . . .

LYNCH: Not too bad. . . .

ALFRED: Somebody must be very anxious to . . . well . . . hold me down.

LYNCH: You hungry?

ALFRED: I believe we've been through all that. . . .

LYNCH: You didn't give me your order. . . .

ALFRED: Do I have choices?

LYNCH: How do you feel about meat?

ALFRED: Meat? [*Pauses.*] Neutral. [*Pauses.*] I am quite neutral on the subject of meat. [*Pauses.*] It's Emily, isn't it?

[LYNCH *turns to* ALFRED *and smiles.* LYNCH *walks to telephone and tries to dial a number.*]

LYNCH: What the hell's the matter here? [*Slams receiver down on its cradle.*] Phone's outa whack! Three days now. The whole goddam week before the goddam Fourth of July is a waste, far's I'm concerned. . . . They oughtta just skip from June thirtieth ta July eighth . . . and that'd be *it!* . . . How da they expect me ta operate without a phone?

ALFRED: Two Whiting's milk cartons and string? Semaphore flags? Finger-taps in Morse Code. [*After a stare from* LYNCH] Where is she, Lynch? I'd sure hate to celebrate Independence Day without my Emily close by. . . .

LYNCH: [*Moves again to the telephone, made nervous by the mention of the name* EMILY. *He picks up the phone, but it is dead.*] Crappola! [LYNCH *violently rips the phone from the wall and throws it onto the floor.*] Conditions are wicked awful nowadays!

[ALFRED *stares incredulously at* LYNCH, *who kicks the fallen telephone, crosses to the crates, stage left; sits.* ALFRED *stares after him awhile.*]

ALFRED: [*Smiling.*] You've grown into quite an ignoramus. [LYNCH *turns to him; stares.*]

ALFRED: You were kinda a dumb but likable kid. [*Pauses.*] I remember. [*Pauses.*] It's amazing how the worst multiplies. Whatever was likable was probably beaten down and out. . . . Was that it? Beaten? [*Pauses.*] What's left is really horrifying, Lynch. [*Pauses.*] You've become a veritable mutant. You've become to man what margarine has become to butter. . . . [*Pauses.*] It is incredibly difficult to believe that we're even close to the same age, Lynch. Incredibly difficult to believe. . . . You look just awful, Lynch. Awful. What did they *do* to you . . . to make you look so awful?

[LYNCH *bows his head.*]

ALFRED: Where is she, Lynch? Where's Emily? I want to know where Emily is, Lynch. I want to see Emily.

LYNCH: [*After a pause, looks up.*] I don't know what you're talking about, Alfred. [*Pauses; smiles.*] You're not making any sense. . . . [*Pauses. Stands.*] I don't know any Emily. [*Smiles again.*] She someone local or is she a visitor? [*Moves to door.*] I don't know what you're talking about, Alfred. . . . [*Hand on doorknob*] You're not making any sense.

[*There is a silence in which* ALFRED *and* LYNCH *look at one another.*]

LYNCH: [*Moves to cage. Uses confidential tone.*] Alfred?

ALFRED: [*Moves to him, thinking he will get information.*] What do you want?

[LYNCH *spits at* ALFRED, *wetting* ALFRED's *face. There is a pause.* ALFRED *smiles, stares at* LYNCH.]

ALFRED: Nice. Really nice.

[*The two men stare at each other.*
Tableau.
Blackout.]

END OF SCENE 1

Scene 2

Later.

Stage in darkness.

Three sharp knocks are heard.

*First words of scene—*ALFRED's*—are heard in darkness.*

ALFRED: It's very comforting for me to know that you're out there. . . .
[*Lights to full, suddenly.*
ALFRED, *in cell, standing, leaning against bars of stage-right wall.*
He stares at EMILY, *who sits in middle bench, outside of cell.*

Her legs are up on bench in front of her.
There is a brown-paper bundle of food in cell, stage left.
ALFRED's *beard has begun to fill in.*]

ALFRED: I feel quite comfortable, really, knowing you're
out *there* and I'm in *here*. [*Pauses.*] I'd always wondered
why there were people who insisted on being jailed, time
and time again. [*Pauses.*] Now I know. [*Pauses.*] It's the
comfort of the situation. [*Moves to food bundle.*] Food?
[*Lifts it as best he can.*] Yes, it certainly is. You're too
kind to me, Emily. Far too kind. [*Sniffs bag. Opens bag:
a cheeseburger.*] Something Oriental? I think it is! Quite
a change of pace from what I've been eating. . . . [*Looks
at* EMILY.] You do know what I've been eating, don't
you? [*Smiles.*] Nothing.

[EMILY *sits, watching, silently.*

ALFRED *eats voraciously; ravenously. When he is again
aware of* EMILY's *presence, he is embarrassed.*]

ALFRED: Look at *me*: eating like a bird: a raven . . . a
vulture . . . a condor. . . . [*Pauses; smiles. He stands; faces*
EMILY.] Look at *me* . . . awful. Needing a shave, as I
do. Very sloppy. . . . [*Bows head.*]

EMILY's *feet down now; replaced by her hands, as she
leans in against bench in front of her.*]

ALFRED: Been quite a while, hasn't it, Emily? [*Pauses.*]
I hope you take this remark in the right spirit. . . .
[*Pauses.*] You look . . . older. [*Without warning*] Is this
your idea of a *joke*? Is this your idea of something *funny*?
[*Angrily*] This is hardly a joke, Emily! This is hardly
funny! [*Pauses.*] What is it about you that moves me to
such . . . anger? To such heights of rage and revulsion?
[*Pauses.*] Maybe it's the funny little way you wear your
hair. Or the way you have me hit over the head and
tortured. The way you build jails and have me locked
up like some sort of criminal. Maybe that's it. Or maybe
it's just your face, which I suddenly discover I can't . . .
stomach.

[EMILY *stands; walks to door, exits.*
There is a long pause.]

ALFRED: [*Calls after her.*] Em-i-leee!
[*Lights quickly fade to black.*]

END OF SCENE 2

Scene 3

Later.

Stage in darkness.

Three sharp knocks sound as soon as lights have gone to black at end of preceding scene.

*First words of scene—*LYNCH's—*are heard in darkness.*

LYNCH: You're gonna haveta pay some attention!
  [*Lights to full, suddenly.*
  ALFRED, *on floor, dozing in cell.*
  LYNCH, *standing at bars to cell, poking inside at* ALFRED
  with ten-foot pole. ALFRED, *struck by the pole, stirs.*
  LYNCH *pokes him violently.*
  ALFRED *raises his head, suddenly. His beard is filling in
  now, considerably.*]
LYNCH: Shake a leg!
ALFRED: Huh?
LYNCH: Wiggle it! [*Pokes him.*] Move your ass! [*Pokes him
  again.*] Get a move on!
ALFRED: What do you want?
LYNCH: Let's have a little hustle.
ALFRED: What for?
LYNCH: It's morning. . . . [*Pauses.*] Rise and shine. . . .
ALFRED: Stuff it closed, will ya, Lynch? . . .
LYNCH: [*Poking at* ALFRED *with the pole*] Up and Adam
  and Eve!
ALFRED: *Lynch, God damn it! Knock it off!*
  [LYNCH *pokes* ALFRED *again.*]
ALFRED: C'mon!
  [LYNCH *pokes him again.*]
ALFRED: Knock it off!
  [LYNCH *pokes him again.* ALFRED *leaps to his feet.*]
ALFRED: Okay, *okay,* I'm up!
LYNCH: [*Removes pole from cell and leans it against wall,
  next to his desk.*] I got some duties for you. [*Pauses.*]
  Boss's orders. . . . [*Produces leather travel kit with shav-
  ing cream, towel, razor. No mirror.*] You gotta shave.

ALFRED: Shave? [*Pauses.*] Why? [*Pauses.*] For whom? For you?

LYNCH: I only deliver the messages, Alfred. [*Pauses.*] C'mon, you gotta. . . . [*Hands razor, shaving cream, etc. through bars.*]

ALFRED: [*Taking supplies*] Maybe if you didn't start off with "You gotta" . . . [*Pauses.*] I don't "gotta" . . . [*Pauses.*] Nobody's "gotta" . . .

LYNCH: Now that's where you're wrong, Alfred. . . . [*Moves to other side of room.*] Everybody's gotta. . . . [*Finds broom against wall.*] That's the truth. . . . [*Begins sweeping room.*] You think I wanna do this? [*Pauses.*] I gotta. [*Pauses.*] You think I wanna spend my time poking you with a pole?

ALFRED: Call me crazy for saying this, Lynchie, but I do. I really do. I really think you enjoy spending your time poking me with what appears to be the legendary ten-foot pole. I think it pleases the living piss right outa you.

LYNCH: Yuh . . . [*Smiles.*] That's true, too. [*Laughs.*] I gotta admit, you got me there, Alfred. [*Laughs.*] You've got a hell of a way with words, too. . . . *Ten-foot pole!* [Laughs.] I'm enjoyin' this all right. [*Pauses.*] But I don't enjoy working for a woman. I've got to tell you that. I don't enjoy working for a woman at all.

ALFRED: Especially *that* woman.

LYNCH: Yuh. True, again. You've got a knack for hitting the nail right on the head.

ALFRED: And you've got a knack for hitting *me* right on the head.

LYNCH: Hey, listen. . . . It's my job, you know?

ALFRED: Hey, listen. . . . I can remember when you did it without pay.

LYNCH: Times change.

ALFRED: "Times change"? You've got quite a way with the word yourself, Lynchie. Quite a way.

LYNCH: How'd you ever get stuck with her, Alf?

ALFRED: Me? [*Smiles.*] Stuck with Emily? [*Pauses.*] I forget. We've been stuck together for so long, I actually can't remember the first sticking. . . .

LYNCH: I gotta.

ALFRED: Huh?

LYNCH: Work for her.

ALFRED: Oh. [*Shaving now*] Could I ask you something, Lynch?

LYNCH: [*Sweeping*] Sure.

ALFRED: Isn't there something better I could do with my shit? [*Pauses.*] Maybe if you put a light in there . . . so I could at least *see* where it was going . . . [*Pauses.*] *Could* we get a light back there? It would be a hell of a lot better if I could . . . you know. . . . Could you ask Emily for a light?

LYNCH: I'm not even supposed to be talking to you, ya know, let alone askin' favors. . . .

ALFRED: Oh, you're supposed to be talking to me, all right. . . . [*Pauses.*] Emily's too smart to trap me in a place with somebody like you and have you not talking. . . . [*Pauses.*] I should not worry, if I were you, Lynch: you're doing good work.

LYNCH: Thank you.

ALFRED: Don't mention it.

LYNCH: God knows I try.

ALFRED: I said "Don't mention it."

LYNCH: Huh?

ALFRED: By my calculations, today is Thursday, right?

LYNCH: I can't tell you.

ALFRED: Am I at least warm? July Fourth will be Friday this year, right?

LYNCH: Can't say.

ALFRED: Cold then? July Fourth isn't Friday? It's Monday? Thursday? [*Pauses.*] Today is Monday, isn't it? Those are my two guesses: Thursday and Monday. [*Pauses.*] C'mon, Lynch. . . . Give me a break, huh?

LYNCH: Sorry, Alfred . . . I ain't fallin' for it. [*Pauses; smiles.*] You must figure me for a dope . . . a real dumbell.

ALFRED: You have uncanny perceptiveness. . . . [*Wipes remainder of lather from his face with towel.*] No mirror, huh? [*Smiles.*] Just as well [*To* LYNCH] Any nicks?

LYNCH: [*Studies* ALFRED's *face.*] Couple of suds still. . . . [*Points.*] There.

[ALFRED *wipes his face.*]

LYNCH: You got 'em.

ALFRED: Thanks.

LYNCH: Pleasure.

ALFRED: I'll just bet.

LYNCH: You'll have to give me back the razor now. . . .

ALFRED: That's ridiculous. . . .

LYNCH: Sorry. . . .

ALFRED: My beard's just going to appear again tomorrow.
. . . [*Pauses; smiles.*] That's the way a beard works,
Lynch. . . .

LYNCH: You bet. [*Pauses.*] Gimme the razor. [*Pauses.*]
Give it over, Alfred!

ALFRED: The actual mechanism of a man's beard is quite
fascinating. . . . [*Smiles.*] Don't you think?

LYNCH: Razor.

ALFRED: How the good Lord can be so divinely and supremely clever, God only knows! To have the skill and
cunning to insert exactly the right length of hair for sixty,
seventy, eighty, a hundred years of life. . . .

LYNCH: Huh?

ALFRED: All coiled in the jawbone . . .

LYNCH: What the hell are you talking about?

ALFRED: . . . serpentine . . . [*Pauses.*] Didn't you know?
A-head is full of curled hair.

LYNCH: You're cracked . . . you're mental. . . .

ALFRED: Where'd ya think your beard was comin' from,
Lynch? Your underarms and your crotch as well?
[*Pauses.*] Thin air? Magic? Religious fervor? Patriotic
passion? A vehement belief in order, such as in the old
Quaker quantum: the tidier the house, the longer the
beard; the sloppier the house, the more pubic the
beard. . . . [*Smiles.*]

LYNCH: Gimme the goddam razor, Alfred!

ALFRED: [*Suddenly*] *Why'd she want me clean today,
Lynch???*

LYNCH: Just gimme!

ALFRED: *Plans today? Big boggling plans today???* [*Leans
in.*] *What are they, Lynchie? What? What? What?*

LYNCH: *Gimme the goddam razor!!!*

ALFRED: Frightened of an untimely end, are you? Frightened of suicide? Wouldn't you just be in the shit for that,
huh?

LYNCH: Just gimme the goddam razor, Alfred!

ALFRED: No! [*He smiles; walks to back wall holding razor.*] No.

LYNCH: [*Tries a new tone; a new tactic to get razor from* ALFRED.] This doesn't give me any pleasure, you know?

ALFRED: I should think not.

LYNCH: I mean you . . . you were kinda my . . . well . . . you were kinda my *ideal* . . . when we were younger, I mean. When you were getting your picture in the papers . . . when you were always bein' mentioned on the television . . . practically every night . . . back then. [*Pauses.*] I used to be able to say to people: "Alfred and I played together as kids." [*Laughs.*] "I used ta beat him up!" [*Pauses.*] I used ta get a kick outa feelin' close to you and all. . . . My whole family did. Most of Wakefield did. . . . You were a famous guy: eighteen years old and already a millionaire. Hey, didn't this town hate your guts when you sold the swamp by the lake, huh? Eighteen years old and already made a cool million. . . . [*Whistles appreciatively.*] "Boy Wonder" is what they used to call you in these parts. "Boy Wonder . . ." [*Pauses.*] Look at you now.

ALFRED: Lynchie . . . There's something I really need to know for old time's sake, huh? Why does Emily want me shaved today? Why does she want me all cleaned up? You can tell me, sport, huh? Is there an event coming? A special day? Is there a dignitary visiting? A Saltonstall? A Lodge? A Lowell? A Kennedy? A Cushing? A Bishop? A Pope? A Dryden? A Swift?

LYNCH: You know I'd tell you if I could, Alf. . . . [*Pauses.*] There's no dignitary comin' here. . . . [*Pauses.*] Your days of gettin' dignitaries to visit are all over, Alf. [*Quietly.*] The razor. [*No reply*] You know something, Alf? Once I was getting fired . . . I was workin' at Crystal Cement as a loader. It was Christmastime and I was gettin' fired. [*Pauses.*] Sons a' bitches! [*Looks up at* ALFRED; *smiles.*] I'm sittin' 'cross the desk from old Kiley. . . . He was running the crew assignments then. He's tellin' me how bad times are. I'm gettin' two and a half bucks an hour and not even half a weeks work and *he's* tellin' *me* how bad things are. . . . [*Pauses.*] I'm lookin' at my shoes, 'cause I know what's comin'. The radio's on in the background. Kiley cryin' the blues . . . and the next thing I know, old Alfred—you—on Kiley's radio. You were being interviewed. [*Smiles.*] Kiley asks if you're the same Alfred who was my sister Margaret's sweetheart and I say "yes" and one thing leads to another and I get to keep my rotten job. [*Pauses.*] You saved my ass, Alfred. [*Quietly*] The razor.

ALFRED: Why am I being cleaned and shaved today, Lynchie? What's going to happen? *Please!*

LYNCH: You're being charged today. Your trial begins. Now, gimme . . .

ALFRED: Oh. I see. My trial. I'm being charged.

LYNCH: I shouldn't be telling you. You gotta pretend you don't know. I could get into awful trouble. . . .

ALFRED: Don't you worry, Lynch. You don't have a worry in the world. [*Smiles.*] I swear to God. [*Pauses.*] Lynch? [LYNCH *looks up.*]

ALFRED: Charged with what? I'd really like to know. What crime, Lynch? Just give me the word.

LYNCH: I can't.

ALFRED: The word, please, Lynchie. . . .

LYNCH: I can't. Really.

ALFRED: [*Screams, suddenly.*] I'll call Kiley! I will! You'll never work again in the cement business, Lynch! You'll be ruined in this town, Lynch. I gave you *my* word and you cheated me. You lied! Now, you . . . goddammit! . . . give me the word.

LYNCH: Razor, Alfred.

[LYNCH *reaches through the bars.* ALFRED *extends the razor and they both hold the handle of same, as two young boys might hold a baseball bat in the air, waiting for the other to let loose.*]

ALFRED: The word, Lynch.

LYNCH: Murder.

[ALFRED *lets loose his grip on the razor.* LYNCH *takes it from him at once.*

ALFRED *repeats the following lines, moving his head from side to side, as though a machine.*]

ALFRED: This is *déjà vu.* . . . [*Repeats exactly the same*

tone.] This is *déjà vu.* . . . [*Again*] This is *déjà-vu.* . . .
[*Again*] This is *déjà-vu.* . . . [*Smiles.*] That's French. . . .
[*Pauses.*] *C'est déjà vu, mon cher* Lynch. . . . [*Repeats.*]
C'est déjà vu, mon cher Lynch. . . . [*Smiles.*] Of whom?

LYNCH: Of *whom?* As if you didn't know . . . [*Smiles.*]
. . . of *whom.* . . .

[LYNCH *moves to position in front of* ALFRED; *stops. He smiles.*]

LYNCH: Ten years, I worked on the cement trucks: you
know that? I wasted ten years. [*Pauses.*] Your fault,
Alfred. Your fault. [*Pauses.*] You wrecked my life. You
ruined me. I was almost outa there too. . . . [*Pauses;
smiles.*] That's a fact.

ALFRED: I want a lawyer. I know my rights. I want a
lawyer. . . .

LYNCH: What rights? Rights here? [*Laughs.*]

ALFRED: So. This is really happening, is it?

LYNCH: I know I shouldn't have talked, Alfred. I shouldn't
have told you. [*Pauses.*] I shouldn't have spilled any
beans. . . . [*Pauses.*] But it was really worth it . . .
[*Pauses.*] . . . to see your face. . . . [*Pauses.*] I wish you
could see your face. . . .

ALFRED: I'm sure it's amusing. . . .

LYNCH: Amusing? [*Smiles.*] Amusing? [*Smiles.*] Oh, it's
much more than that, Alf. [*Pauses.*] It's the best thing
I ever did. [*Pauses.*] In my whole life, this is the best!
[*Pauses.*] By the time we're through with you, Alfred,
you are gonna wish you never set foot back here in
Wakefield, Massachusetts, again. . . . [*Pauses.*] Really.
[*Smiles.*] I give you my word.

[LYNCH *stands downstage left, near table, looking up at*
ALFRED, *who is in downstage-left-most position in cell.*
ALFRED *looks away and down.*
ALFRED's *head bows.*
LYNCH *watches a moment, then he too looks away and
his head bows as well.*
Tableau.
Lights fade to black.]

END OF SCENE 3

Scene 4

Later.

Stage in darkness. Three sharp knocks are heard.

*First words of scene—*EMILY's*—are heard in darkness.*

EMILY: I think you'd better start taking this seriously.
  [*Pauses.*] It's not going away.
  [*Lights to full, suddenly.* EMILY *stands at table, down-stage left.*
  Beside her sits ROXY, *an old woman, who records all dialogue on a courtroom stenography machine.*
  ROXY *is given to clearing her throat and her chest of bronchial mucus and phlegm.*
  SHE *is corpulent: obese.*
  LYNCH *reclines on middle bench, with his feet dangling over bench in front of him. He appears to be sleeping.*
  ALFRED *stands facing bars, upstage of* EMILY *and* ROXY, *same side, looking away from them intentionally.*]

EMILY: [*To* ROXY] Did you get that?

ROXY: [*After a great deal of coughing and clearing of her throat and chest, looks at long tape that has been folding into stenography machine's tray. She tries to read same but cannot.*] I can't see without my glasses.

EMILY: [*After a long pause in which she and* ROXY *stare silently at each other*] Do you have them?

ROXY: [*Pauses.*] My glasses?

EMILY: Yes, of course, your glasses. . . .

ROXY: They're in my bag. [*Displaying oversized satchel-pocketbook*] Here.

EMILY: Put them on, please. . . .

ROXY: Certainly. [*She does.*]

EMILY: Now have a look and read back what you've got. . . .

ROXY: The whole thing?

EMILY: Just the last part, please. . . .

ROXY: [*Reading*] "I think you'd better start taking this seriously. . . . It's not going away."

EMILY: Could you read before that, please. . . .

[ALFRED *on his hands, feet against wall.*]

ROXY: How afar before that?

EMILY: Use your own discretion. . . .

ROXY: [*Rummaging through tape now, reading to herself. She coughs a great deal and then reads aloud.*] "Alfred? Are you paying attention to me?" . . .

ALFRED: [*Rights himself onto his feet.*] Huh?

ROXY: [*Still reading*] "This is Roxy. Roxy, this is Alfred. Alfred, this is Roxy. . . ."

ALFRED: Oh. You're reading. . . . [*To* LYNCH] She's reading. . . .

ROXY: [*Continuing*] "How-dee-do," *I* said and "It's a pleasure, dear lady," *he* said. I then said, "I've heard a lot aboutcha," and he then said, "This is attractive, Emily . . ."

ALFRED: [*Interrupting*] Wrong!

[ROXY *and* EMILY *turn to* ALFRED.]

ALFRED: "This is *atrocious*, Emily." . . . That's what I said. . . .

EMILY: That's what he said.

ROXY: That's *not* what you said!

LYNCH: [*Calling across room*] That's what he said!

ROXY: [*Calling to* LYNCH] You just keep your trap shut, okay?

LYNCH: Okay by me. . . .

ROXY: *Do it, then!!!*

LYNCH: Okay . . .

ROXY: Don't answer me back!

[LYNCH *waves his hand at her in sign of disgust. Slouches back into chair.*]

ROXY: That's better. [*To* EMILY] Where were we? [*Coughs a lot, clearing throat and chest of phlegm.*] Then Emily butted in here and says, "You remember Lynch, don't you, Alfred? His grandfather was the hangman who hanged his own son . . . for whom the very act of lynching was named."

LYNCH: [*Jumps up.*] Come on, God damn it!

ROXY: Then Lynch jumps up and yells, "Come on, God damn it!" Then Emily continues here with "Lynch will be chief guard, custodian-at-large, trochee judge, and executioner." . . . [*Pauses.*] Emily butts in again here with "Not a *trochee* judge, but a . . ." [*Looks at* EMILY.] Still can't read the word.

EMILY: *Troika* judge. . . . [*Smiles; to* ALFRED] Three judges, one judgment. [*Pauses; to* ROXY] *Troika.* . . .

ROXY: That's what *I* said!

EMILY: You said *trochee.* . . .

ALFRED: [*Standing; watching*] Too poetic . . . [*Smiles.*] *Trochee.* [*Pauses.*] A trochee is a foot of two syllables. . . .

ROXY: What's he saying?

ALFRED: Metrical measure. The word "trochee" is from the Greek. You've heard of the Greeks, Roxy. They're the folks who put white cheese next to black olives and call it salad.

[ROXY *laughs.*]

ALFRED: A trochee, Rox, is a foot of two syllables. A long followed by a short in quantitative meter . . . such as "Sooooooo-eeee-soooooooo-eeee." [*Makes the sound of a hog caller.*]

[LYNCH *laughs.*]

ALFRED: Or a stressed followed by an unstressed in accentual meter, like Emily and me; the unstressed following the stressed . . . Are you paying attention, Roxy?

EMILY: Just write the word "Babble" into the record.

ROXY: Thank God.

ALFRED: "Thank *God*" is unnecessarily reverential, Roxy, but I'm sure Emily accepts your gratitude.

EMILY: I call your attention, Roxy . . . and Mr. Lynch . . . to Alfred's inability to stop his incessant—continual and repeated—babble. [*Pauses.*] It gets a bit tiring, Alfred, after fifteen or twenty years. [*Pauses; smiles.*] I hope you understand. [*Pauses; to* ROXY. *Her attitude changes.*] Skip ahead, now, Roxy. Skip ahead and read, please. . . .

ROXY: From where.

EMILY: From the charges against Alfred. I read them into the record yesterday morning.

ROXY: The what?

EMILY: The charges.

ALFRED: For what? [*Pauses; smiles.*] The amusement? . . . I'm being charged for the amusement? . . . How much you chargin' for this animal act, Emmy? . . . A buck an hour?

EMILY: Mr. Lynch!

ALFRED: Emily, come on, now . . . Emily?

EMILY: Mr. Lynch! I would like Alfred touched . . . deeply.

LYNCH: [*Stands.*] Okay.

> LYNCH *moves to wall behind bench, from which he removes the long pole.*
>
> *He inserts the pole into the cell and chases* ALFRED *down, tripping him and then finally punching him to floor with end of pole.*
>
> *When he has finished beating* ALFRED, *he returns to bench, where, after setting pole back into its position against wall,* LYNCH *rests again on bench in recline.*
>
> ALFRED *lies in pain, on floor of cell.*]

EMILY: Roxy?

ROXY: [*Continues to read.*] ". . . because he has murdered . . ." [*Looks up.*] Anywhere here?

EMILY: Alfred, are you paying close attention?

ALFRED: [*Looking up from floor*] Rapt.

EMILY: What was that?

ALFRED: Rapt attention.

EMILY: [*To* ROXY] His mother . . . [*Nods.*]

ROXY: [*Repeating* EMILY'*s words*] . . . his mother . . .

EMILY: . . . his father . . .

ROXY: . . . his father . . .

EMILY: . . . his friends . . .

ROXY: . . . his friends . . .

EMILY: . . . his children . . .

ROXY: . . . his children . . .

EMILY: Are you reading?

ROXY: Reading . . . [ROXY *has been staring at* ALFRED *and repeating* EMILY'*s words, not reading.*]

EMILY: I asked you to read, please. . . .

ROXY: Huh? Oh. I was just watching him . . . I'll read. [LYNCH *stands at attention.*]

ROXY: [*Reads.*] "Because he has murdered his mother, causing the curse that fell upon the people of his town . . . because he has murdered his father, and his close friends . . . [*Pauses.*] Because he is responsible for the deaths of those who have died . . . [*Pauses.*] He then too must . . . die."

ALFRED: Emily, could I have a moment with you?

EMILY: What?

ALFRED: Could I possibly have a moment with you?

EMILY: But you've already had *years* with me. . . .

ALFRED: Alone?

EMILY: That too. [*Pauses.*] I don't think so, Alfred. [*Smiles.*] A person's got to know when to draw the line. . . . [*Pauses.*] I've drawn mine.

ALFRED: [*To* EMILY] How far are you planning to take this, Emily?

EMILY: How far? [*Pauses.*] All the way.

ALFRED: Don't you find all this a trifle . . . suburban? [EMILY *sits with her back to* ALFRED.]

ALFRED: Excuse me. Emily? [*Still no reply; louder*] Excuse me . . . Emily? Lynch, poke Emily.

LYNCH: [*Starts for pole; realizes. Calls across to* EMILY, *who is lost in a memory.*] Emily! Alfred's calling you!

EMILY: [*To* ALFRED] What?

ALFRED: I'm going to have to leave you all for a while. . . .

EMILY: You're what?

ALFRED: Going to have to say "Excuse me," *Je m'excuse,* but I'm . . . well . . . going off for a while. [*Smiles.*] Into the other room.

EMILY: To do what?

LYNCH: To do what?

ROXY: To do what?

ALFRED: Rest.

EMILY: Rest?

LYNCH: Rest?

ROXY: Rest?

EMILY: In there?

LYNCH: In there?

ROXY: In there?

ALFRED: You three should really work on that routine. . . . [*Pauses.*] Rehearse it. [*Pauses.*] Perfect it. [*Pauses.*] It's quite amusing. Nearly funny. [*Pauses.*] Makes me . . . happy. . . . [*Pauses.*] It really does: I'm happy. . . . [*Pauses; smiles.*] Especially now that you've added the hog to your animal act. [*To* EMILY] The gorilla made me smile, but not laugh. . . . [*To* LYNCH] No offense. [*To* EMILY] The addition of the hog was a sensational touch. . . . A masterstroke. . . . [*Moves back three steps.*] Look at you three: the perfect blend of python, gorilla, and hog. . . . [*Backs up a few more steps; smiles and points finger in schoolteacherish manner.*] Practice: that's the

ticket. . . . [*Smiles.*] You kids have got it! . . . The goods!
The stuff! The talent! That magic *quelque chose!*
[ALFRED *exits into the back room, closing door tightly
shut behind him.*
There is a ten count of silence.
EMILY *nods to* LYNCH.]
EMILY: Mr. Lynch?
LYNCH: Huh?
EMILY: Secure the lock.
LYNCH: Hmm?
EMILY: Alfred's door. Lock it.
[LYNCH *stands, takes pole, reaches into cage, pokes door
latch closed.*
He returns to his seat; sits.
There is another ten count of silence.
ALFRED'S *coughing and retching is heard from back room.*
The sound grows more sonorous.
ALFRED *is now pounding on the inside of the back door,
trying to open same.*
LYNCH *looks at* EMILY; *smiles.*
ROXY *looks at* EMILY; *smiles.*
Tableau.
EMILY *bows her head.*
The lights fade out.]

END OF ACT I

ACT II
Scene 1

Later. Stage in darkness.

Three sharp knocks are heard.

*The first words of this act—*ALFRED'S—*are heard in darkness.*

ALFRED: [*Screams; off*] If I have to break it down, *I God damned will!* [*Louder*] Do . . . you . . . hear . . . me???
[*Lights to full, suddenly.*
At same moment, door bursts open and ALFRED *bursts with it, onto stage, into visible portion of cell.*
EMILY *sits in cell with her back against upstage-right section of the wall that is now covered by door* [*door opens in against wall*].
ALFRED *will not see* EMILY *until she slams door closed and noise of door slamming will startle him.*
LYNCH *reclines in center bench.* ROXY *is at her machine. Both are dozing.*]

ALFRED: [*Adjusting eyes to light; to* ROXY] Where is she? Where is she? [*Pauses; screams.*] Where . . . the hell . . . is she???

LYNCH: She's right in front of you, Alfred.

ROXY: Here I am, Alfred.

LYNCH: You're all hot and bothered, Alfred. . . .

ROXY: You oughtta calm down. . . . [*Pauses.*] You could have yaself a stroke. . . .

ALFRED: [*Screams.*] Where is she??? Answer me!!! [*Leans*

222

in toward ROXY *and* LYNCH.] *God damn you!!! Where
. . . is . . . she???*

LYNCH: You better learn ta calm down, Alfred. Bad for the ticker.

ROXY: [*Giggles.*] What a temper!

[EMILY *slams door closed, revealing to* ALFRED *that she is where she is.*

There is a long pause.

ALFRED *turns, slowly, and stares at her.*

EMILY *smiles.*]

EMILY: Here I am, Alfred.

LYNCH: There she is, Alfred.

ROXY: There she is, Alfred.

ALFRED: What the hell *is* this? You, too? Did they lock *you* up, too?

EMILY: Oh, nooo. I'm just visiting. Today is visitors' day.

ALFRED: I could kill you now, if I wanted to . . .

EMILY: Well, there it is: the first thought-out sentence you've spoken. The first premeditated thought expressed. [*Smiles.*] The killer returns to the sense of the crime. [*Pauses.*] Irrefutable witnesses, this time, Alfred. [*To* ROXY *and* LYNCH] Repeat Alfred's threat, please.

ROXY: He said he could kill you now.

LYNCH: [*Correcting* ROXY] No. He said he could kill her now . . . if he wanted to.

ROXY: That's exactly what *I* just said!

EMILY: Type it into the records, please. I want all threats of physical harm in the record. . . . I must insist.

ROXY: [*Stands; shuffles to her stenography machine and types statement.*] Okay. Done.

LYNCH: Did you get the "if I wanted to" part?

ROXY: I really think we could keep things straighter if you'd just let me use a tape recorder. . . .

EMILY: No. I want all the twistings and turnings of a human touch. Those are the rules, Roxy.

ALFRED: Emily, I am so completely traumatized, I think what I think is that I've stopped thinking. . . . [*Pauses.*] I've stopped all thought. [*Pauses.*] I . . . [*Stops; looks at* ROXY.] You needn't copy down any of this. . . . [*To* EMILY] I'm a little self-conscious about things being written down. . . . [*Pauses.*] I guess that's your idea. . . . [*Pauses.*] It's working. . . . [*Bows head.*]

EMILY: Rap the gavel, Roxy.

[ROXY *crosses to table, picks up a wooden gavel; raps three times.* ALFRED *looks up.*]

EMILY: Better. Wonderful gavel. Burled walnut. [*To* ALFRED] You're going to face it *all*, Alfred. All the twistings and turnings, all the amazing details, all the surprises, all of your absolutely incredible lies. . . . They're all coming back.

[ALFRED *looks up at her.*]

EMILY: Roxy, Lynch and I all have . . . complaints. [*Pauses.*] Mr. Lynch?

[LYNCH *looks up.*]

EMILY: Your complaints now. Briefly, please.

LYNCH: Briefly? Sure. [*Officious tone; clearly*] Sister, father, family name . . . Alfred killed them all. [*He glares at* ALFRED.]

ALFRED: Lynch . . . You can't be serious.

EMILY: I'd suggest that you just listen, Alfred. Roxy?

ROXY: How much of it?

EMILY: The barest bones for now, please. . . .

ROXY: Let's see . . . barest bones? Okay. All of my husbands, several of my children, and, of course, me. Alfred killed us all.

ALFRED: Emily, it is somewhat anxiety-producing to realize that the entire world's gone berserk. . . . I really don't know what anyone here is saying. None of you . . .

EMILY: Alfred, I suggest you listen carefully to my complaints.

ROXY: Ready. [*She sits at stenography machine.*]

EMILY: Four stillbirths, Alfred. Your fault. [*Pauses.*] If four stillbirths sound like a lot, you ought to try *feeling* them. They *feel* like a *hell* of a lot. [*Pauses.*] Four. Each one dead in the seventh month. Twenty-eight months of feeling your children inside of me . . . kicking . . . punching . . . sucking away . . . until they stopped. . . . And stop they did, didn't they? Had to. Every last one of them. [*Suddenly; her tone changes.*] I know the truth, Alfred. I know exactly why . . . why they died.

ALFRED: [*Quietly*] Emily, I . . .

EMILY: Did you say "Emily, I . . ."? [*Smiles.*] How like you. Generous to the last. [*Pauses; attitude changes again.*] I was always shamed. You did that, Alfred. You

shamed me. [*Pauses.*] I remember, 'round about our
fourth or fifth child I had a real catastrophe . . . both a
miscarriage *and* a stillbirth: a double treat. I remember
. . . how it was to watch you be not able to face it . . .
to join me. [*Quietly*] I took a taxi, alone, to the hospital.
I didn't have any money with me for the fare. I just
didn't *have* any. I had probably a hundred different
credit cards, but not a dime in hard cold cash. The driver
was furious. Thanks to my prior annual visits, the old
doorman knew me . . . remembered me. He coughed up
the money. . . . Quite a lot, I recall. Ten or twelve
dollars. . . . [*Pauses; smiles.*] The back seat of the cab
was ruined, Alfred. Drenched with blood. You should
have seen the driver's face, when I lifted myself from
his seat. "You wrecked my goddam seat, lady! What the
hell's the matter with you?" [*Pauses.*] I asked the doorman for enough money to replace the seat. The driver
yelled at me: "That'll be a hundred bucks, you know
that?" [*Smiles.*] I didn't know that. The doorman told me
he only earned a hundred a week. Can you imagine that?
A hundred for one whole week of opening doors for
women like me: bleeders, sufferers, complainers. I'd
spent more than a hundred on my pocketbook . . . almost
that for my credit-card case. [*Pauses. She is smiling.*]
I was ashamed I'd bled on his seat . . . ashamed I asked
the doorman for the fare . . . ashamed to have had the
doorman have to tell me his salary . . . ashamed to own
my pocketbook . . . my wallet . . . my shoes . . . my dead
baby in my broken stretched-out bleeding body. I was
ashamed! I was ashamed! *I . . . was . . . ashamed!*
[*Pauses; attitude changes.*] Looking at you now. Alfred
. . . knowing what I know about us . . . what you've done
. . . *what you've done!* . . . [*Screams.*] *I . . . am not . . .
ashamed!!!* [*After a long pause, she smiles.*] Mr. Lynch,
I'd like to leave the cage now.

LYNCH: Right.

[LYNCH *stands; gets long pole.*

ALFRED *backs up; frightened.*]

ALFRED: Don't, Lynch! Emily, tell him "Don't!"

[LYNCH *moves to edge of cell with pole.*]

EMILY: Stand with your face against the wall, Alfred. [*Motions to back wall.*]

ALFRED: [*Looks first to wall and then to* EMILY.] I . . .
[*Stops his voice.*] Okay.
[*He walks to back wall, faces same.* LYNCH *places end of
pole just behind* ALFRED's *head.*]

LYNCH: Any kind of funny business, I push. If I push, your
face ain't gonna look like much in the paper tomorrow
. . . if ya know what I mean.

ALFRED: This is the most extraordinarily infantile and
sick . . .

EMILY: You may be wondering why, out of all the possible
Wakefieldians I could have employed, I've employed
Roxy and Lynch. Roxy, Lynch, and I have made an
amazing pact. Remember the word "pact," Alfred. . . .
You'll be hearing it again. [*Moves to cell door, unlocks
it. Moves to* ROXY, *inspects tape.*] This tape will be history, Alfred. Every word Roxy writes here will get out
of this room . . . will be read and reread . . . will be
discussed and chewed over and digested. It's a fact.
You're a famous fellow. People will be interested in
what's gone on here . . . now . . . and *before* now. What
you've done. [*Pauses; with hostility*] Mr. Lynch, see to
it that he doesn't sleep. I want him standing, face to
the wall. . . . No rest. [*To* ROXY] Take a break, Roxy.
Work begins at nine. Did you get that?

ROXY: First you said for Lynch to smash his face into the
wall and get some sleep . . . and then you said . . . let's
see . . . [*Reads.*] You said, "Work, Roxy. We'll take a
break at nine." Then you asked, "Did you get that?"
[*Looks up at* EMILY.] And I answered, "Yup."

[LYNCH *is disgusted.*

ALFRED *turns helplessly; his eyes meet* EMILY's. ALFRED
bows his head.

The lights fade out.]

END OF SCENE 1

Scene 2

Later. Stage in darkness.

Three sharp knocks are heard.

*The first words of the scene—*EMILY's*—are heard in darkness.*

EMILY: Mr. Lynch, I blame you for this!
  [*Lights to full, suddenly.*
  ROXY *sits center stage, at stenotype machine, staring into cell.*
  LYNCH *is sitting in bench across from* ROXY, *asleep.*
  EMILY *is standing at table, gavel in hand, staring angrily at* LYNCH.
  ALFRED *is sitting asleep on floor of cell, his back against the back wall. His clothing is somewhat scruffier; his beard fuller.*
  EMILY *calls* LYNCH's *name again and raps gavel on table.*]
EMILY: *Mr. Lynch, dammit!*
LYNCH: [*At once alert*] What? What is it?
ROXY: [*Typing and talking at same time*] You're being blamed.
LYNCH: For what? [*To* EMILY] For what? [*Sees* ALFRED *asleep on cell floor.*] Again? [*To* EMILY] Sorry. I'll fix it.
  . . . [*Lifts pole, walks to cell, pokes* ALFRED *forcefully, waking him.*] Get up, you.
ALFRED: What? . . . Ughhh . . . *Hey!* . . . Emily . . . *heyyy!*
  [*Rises to his knees.*] *Heyyy!*
LYNCH: *Up!*
ALFRED: *Heyyy, c'mon* . . .
LYNCH: I don't wanna hurt you, Alfred!
ALFRED: But you are! You really are!
LYNCH: Then stand up!
ALFRED: [*Rising*] Okay!
LYNCH: [*Screams.*] Do it!
ALFRED: [*Stands and screams.*] *Okay!*
  [LYNCH *stops;* ALFRED *faces him.*]

ALFRED: Okay. [*To* EMILY] Okay?

EMILY: Good afternoon, Alfred.

ALFRED: Afternoon?

EMILY: Put your pole back now, Mr. Lynch. And thank you. . . .

LYNCH: Sorry I dozed. I got dozy.

ROXY: The nose that flows dozed.

LYNCH: What's that s'pose'ta be, blimp? A name-joke? [*To* ALFRED] You remember her name when she was substitute-teachin'? They called her Graf Zeppelin: the blimp that burned. [*Laughs.*] Graf Zeppelin . . . quite a catastrophe.

EMILY: [*To* ALFRED] We're ready to continue our interview, Alfred. . . .

ALFRED: Is it really afternoon, Emily? I really don't know. I can't tell . . . I'd like to know.

EMILY: [*To* ROXY] Did you get that?

ROXY: [*Reads.*] "Is it really afternoon, Emily? I really don't know."

ALFRED: [*Interrupts* ROXY's *reading.*] It makes me terribly nervous to have her writing all of this down. . . .

EMILY: If interviews made you nervous, you certainly opened yourself up for a lot of anxiety over the years! [*To* LYNCH] He was interviewed every five minutes. He set them up himself.

LYNCH: I don't blame you, Alfred. If you don't push yourself, who's gonna, right? I don't blame you. . . .

ALFRED: Why is it that all the uninterviewed are always telling all the interviewed "I don't blame you"? [*Pauses.*] Who do you blame, Lynch?

LYNCH: For what?

ALFRED: For your being nobody. . . . [*Pauses.*] A man of your years, too . . . being nobody. [*Pauses.*] Who's ever heard of you, Lynch? [*Pauses.*] Hardly a soul. [*Pauses.*] You almost never happened, Lynch. [*Pauses.*] Must be awful, huh?

LYNCH: It is. [*Sadly*] It's awful.

EMILY: Who do you blame? Roxy, write Lynch's answer, please.

LYNCH: Myself. [*Pauses.*] I do. I blame myself. [*Pauses.*] I shoulda listened. . . .

EMILY: To whom?

LYNCH: Everybody. . . . My teachers . . . my father . . .

ALFRED: Who was he, Lynch? Your father: who was he?

LYNCH: Are you kiddin' me?

ALFRED: I mean *really* . . . who was your father, *really?*

LYNCH: *He was somebody!*

ALFRED: You don't say?

LYNCH: Write this down! Greasy-pole champion, two times. [*To* ROXY] Write this . . .

[*All are staring at* LYNCH; *he continues, nervously.*]

LYNCH: Gloucester. Every June. They run a greasy-pole contest. The St. Peter's Club . . . mostly Italians. . . . They nail a telephone pole down to a floating wharf out in the harbor . . . and grease it. [*Pauses.*] Any man who can make it out to the end of the greasy pole and grab the red flag—they have a red flag at the end—wins.

ALFRED: Wins what?

LYNCH: Wins. [*Pauses.*] Wins. [*Pauses.*] My father won once and then he actually won again, five years later. [*Pauses.*] I was five the first time; ten, the second. [*To* ROXY] Don't smirk! It ain't that easy, ya know. Damn near impossible.

ALFRED: You ever try it yourself, Lynchie? . . . [*Pauses.*] You know: after he . . . your father . . . died?

LYNCH: I . . . well . . . yuh, I did.

ALFRED: Tried for his record?

LYNCH: It woulda made him proud, yuh.

ALFRED: After he was dead?

LYNCH: What are you sayin'?

ALFRED: Do you think it would have made him proud after he was dead? [*Pauses.*] Was that an important . . . consideration?

LYNCH: What?

ALFRED: Paternal pride after death!

LYNCH: I don't have to take this kind of guff from anybody, bub. Especially *you!* [*To* EMILY] My father was *somebody* and that's the truth!

EMILY: [*After a long pause*] I don't think you'll have to transcribe any of that.

LYNCH: [*To* ROXY] Write it.

EMILY: Mr. Lynch, really . . .

LYNCH: I want my father's story written here: Willie-Boy Lynch: a champion.

EMILY: All right. Write out your statement in longhand and I'll see to it that Roxy types it into the record later. I think that's fair, Lynch.

ROXY: Fair's fair, Lynch.

LYNCH: Don't "fair's fair" me, blimp, or you'll have a fat lip to worry about!

ALFRED: I believe that Emily requires that all threats of physical harm go into the record as well. . . . Fair's fair, Emily. You had her type mine. . . .

ROXY: That's right! I'm putting that right in, Lynch! [*Types.*] "Fat lip ta worry about." It's all in there now to hang you.

LYNCH: It's all in there to *what* me, bitch?

ALFRED: Whoops! I think you said the magic word, Rox!

ROXY: What magic word? [*Realizes.*] I get it!

LYNCH: You get what? Bad breath in the morning? A cruller with your coffee? No kicks from champagne? What? What do you get?

ROXY: [*Smiling into* LYNCH's *remarks, and then*] "Hang" is the magic word. Isn't it?

LYNCH: I'm gonna rip her tits off!

ALFRED: [*Nodding up and down*] Another threat, Em!

LYNCH: I'm gonna unscrew her head and flush it down the hopper!

ALFRED: A *definite* threat there, Em. . . .

LYNCH: I'm gonna take a greasy pole and shove it right up.

EMILY: [*Interrupting*] That will be *quite* enough, Mr. Lynch!

[LYNCH *makes a slow deliberate move toward* ROXY.]

EMILY: I want some order here. . . . Sit down, Mr. Lynch!

ALFRED: Emily has an order, Lynch!

LYNCH: What's that? [*He stops, in front of* ROXY.]

ALFRED: She orders you to sit down, Mr. Lynch.

LYNCH: [*Amazed. To* EMILY] You *what* me?

ALFRED: Emily wants you to take her order. She used to be an absolute fiend for a Brigham's sundae. . . . Chocolate mint chip, wasn't it, Em?

EMILY: You seem to be losing some of your reticence.

ALFRED: You seem to be losing some of your control. Just helpin' out. . . . [*Nods toward* ROXY *and* LYNCH.]

LYNCH: [*Stands in front of* ROXY *now.*] Say you're sorry!

ROXY: When I grow a head under my arm is when I'll say I'm sorry!

LYNCH: You've already got a head growin' under your arm! You want another head there? Like Siamese twins?

EMILY: Mr. Lynch!

LYNCH: What?

EMILY: You can be easily replaced.

LYNCH: What's that s'pose'ta mean?

EMILY: Guess. [*Smiles.*] In or out?

LYNCH: Of what?

EMILY: This . . . bit of history. . . . [*Pauses.*] Our . . . trial. . . . The trial of Alfred L. Webber, boy wonder. [*Pauses.*] In or out?

LYNCH: In.

EMILY: Sit.

[*He sits.*]

EMILY: Stand.

[*He stands.*]

EMILY: Sit.

[*He sits.*]

EMILY: Stand.

LYNCH: Come on, lady . . .

EMILY: Mr. Lynch . . . ? Alfred doubts my control here. *Stand!*

LYNCH: [*Stands.*] You got yourself quite a little wife here, Alfred. . . . My heart goes out ta ya. . . .

ALFRED: Emily? She's all right. . . .

LYNCH: You got the prize here! I gotta admit it: you get the goddam prize. . . .

EMILY: [*To* LYNCH] Sit.

[*He sits.*]

EMILY: Not there. [*Points to step near door.*] There.

LYNCH: [*Moves to step; sits.*] No wonder you got rich. Bein' married to her, you probably never came home. Probably worked 'round the clock, twenty-four hours a day at four bucks an hour, that's nearly a hundred every day . . . seven hundred a week . . . [*Pauses.*] No wonder. [*Pauses.*] I guess what they say is true: It's the woman behind the man. . . .

ALFRED: [*To* LYNCH] Stand!

[LYNCH *stands.*]

EMILY: Sit!

LYNCH: C'mon, *goddammit!*

EMILY: *Sit!*

LYNCH: [*Sits.*] As far as I'm concerned, you two should split the trophy right down the middle. . . . The Most-Likely-Ta-Drive-Everybody-Nuts Award. . . . The gold cup for Alfred and the brass balls for you, lady!

EMILY: Mr. Lynch?

LYNCH: [*Stands.*] Okay?

EMILY: Why are you standing?

LYNCH: You just told me to. . . .

EMILY: I most certainly did not. . . .

[LYNCH *sits.*]

EMILY: Now then, Alfred. Roxy's testimony is first. The subject is Alfred's mother.

ALFRED: I beg your pardon?

ROXY: It's not just his mother. It's his mother, her murder by him . . . and the curse it put over this town. Also, the other people he slaughtered along the way. . . . [*Smiles.*] I'm ready.

EMILY: Tell us what you saw. . . . No interruptions, please, Alfred.

ROXY: I was hemming one of her just-below-the-knee skirts . . . a very bold plaid, if I recall. . . . [*Smiles.*] I had one of those chalk markers with a squeegee on a stand. . . . Alfred's mother—Sophie—stood on a little platform and I knelt down below with my chalk marker.

[ROXY *has been staring at* ALFRED, *absentmindedly. Smiles to* EMILY.]

ROXY: I haven't really seen his face close-up like this . . . not for a long time. . . . He looks older. [*Clears her throat.*] There was a clickety-clickety at the window. Him.

EMILY: Him? Alfred?

ROXY: Oh, no: him . . . Willie-Boy Lynch. *His* father. [*Nods to* LYNCH.] My boyfriend. . . .

LYNCH: I don't like this. . . .

ROXY: Breaks my heart to type it in the record, but it's true. My boyfriend was having a love affair with Alfred's mother. . . .

ALFRED: [*Quietly*] Emily, I hope you don't take this as misbehavior on my part, but I am incredibly angered to have you drag my mother's memory through this little mudwrestle of yours!

LYNCH: And my father's memory, too! I don't like the mud thrown there either, ya know! I've heard some wicked crap in my life, but nothin' never . . . *ever* . . . like the dung she's dumping now!

EMILY: Mr. Lynch, either you shut that halitositic mouth of yours once and for all, or you leave! Now which will it be: shut or leave?

LYNCH: [*After a pause, he goes to door, stands a moment.*] Shut.

[*He settles back; disgusted, beaten.*

ALFRED *smiles.*]

EMILY: As for you, Alfred, the more humiliated Mr. Lynch becomes, the more enraged he becomes. The more enraged he becomes, the more likely he is to hurt you.

LYNCH: I wouldn't mind.

ALFRED: I understand.

EMILY: Please, go on, Roxy. You won't be interrupted again.

ROXY: They went off upstairs together. I followed. I know I shouldn't have. I should have just let them go. But I was young and hurt. . . . We were in love, me and Willie-Boy Lynch. [*Suddenly; to* EMILY] I was young once, too, ya know. You're not the only one ever had looks and youth. I had 'em. . . . [*Quietly*] He was handsome. [*To* LYNCH] Not like his children. The tree don't necessarily fall anywhere near the apples, ya know. . . . [*To* EMILY] I was a simple dressmaker and Willie-Boy was a simple bread-truck driver . . . and *by God!* we had something good. . . . [*Pauses.*] I followed. Alfred was in the hallway, hiding. I saw him. He had his Boy Scout knife open. Ten years old, and ready to kill. And kill he did. Killed 'em both. . . . [*Pauses.*] The rest is history.

LYNCH: [*Has had his back turned to* ROXY; *suddenly turns toward her, enraged.*] The rest is horseshit! [*To* EMILY] She's lyin' about my father. I want this record straight, you get me? My father, Willie-Boy Lynch, never *ever* went near this fat bitch . . . not unless he had her price in his hand. Quarter, fifty cents . . . [*To* ROXY] Now I want this goddam record straight and I want it straight *now! YOU TYPE THIS!!!* "I have never in my miserable

life heard such horseshit!" [*To* EMILY] She was a hooker,
down in Reading, near the head of the lake. Once they
threw her outa Nazareth, she hooked full-time. [*To*
ALFRED] Alfred killed my father and his own mother . . .
that's true . . . and it was in *his own* house: that's true
too. But as far as my father goin' near this fat old bitch
. . . old Graf Zeppelin Roxy . . . well, that's just a crock
of you-know-what . . . unless he had the quarter in his
hand and was in the you-know-what house, down in
Reading. [*To* EMILY] Cheap! That was Roxy's main
quality: cheap. Simple dressmaker? *Horseshit!* You think
somebody named Roxy's gonna turn out ta be a simple
dressmaker? *Horse*shit! That's a definite hooker name.
A prostie. A lovelady. [*To* ROXY] A *hooore* . . .

[ROXY *stands up and faces* LYNCH, *who faces her. A moment of silence.*

LYNCH *smiles.*]

LYNCH: If you raise so much as a pinky to me, you're
gonna be a flabby pancake.

[ROXY *stops.*]

LYNCH: Think about it.

[ROXY *returns to table. She sits.*

LYNCH *turns to* ALFRED.]

LYNCH: If I remember correctly, it was a certain Tommy
Webber who was truly nuts over *this* one, right? [*To*
ROXY] *RIGHT???*

ROXY: I did have an uncontrollable romantic streak. I still
do.

ALFRED: [*Shaken*] Did . . . uh . . . ? Roxy, did Lynch say
you got thrown out of Nazareth?

LYNCH: Yuh. That's what I said, Alfred.

EMILY: I've done my homework, Alfred. Nazareth Academy is Wakefield's Catholic girls' school, remember?
Nuns with sticks and other famous catechetical methods.
Teachers and pupils together, so to speak, sailing one
holy ship of clitoridean panic. Girls in little blue uni-
forms, Alfred? How can you have forgotten?

ROXY: He didn't forget. . . .

LYNCH: He didn't forget.

ROXY: He didn't forget.

LYNCH: He didn't forget.

ALFRED: Roxy, I . . . If you're *that* Roxy, you must be nearly a hundred . . .

ROXY: Thanks to you.

ALFRED: It's hard to believe I could have forgotten you . . . your face . . .

LYNCH: Stops your clock, doesn't it? It's true! That fornicating bitch was supposed ta be substitute-teaching my sister Margaret. My Margaret was a Nazarite, studyin' to become a nun. 'Stead of teachin' her the Catechism, she taught her the oldest profession of them all: hookin' . . . hookin'! [*Enraged*] WRITE THIS IN!!! . . . WRITE THIS IN!!! Between them . . . your Alfred and your Roxy, they took my Margaret . . . a seventeen-year-old virgin so pure you could show her to God himself . . . and they ruined her! RUINED HER! They made a fornicating bitch of a whore of her! [*To* ROXY] YOU WRITE IT! YOU WRITE EVERY WORD!!!

ROXY: [*Frightened* LYNCH *will hit her; she transcribes, looking to* EMILY *for help.*] Okay, Lynch. Okay . . .

LYNCH: Better.

EMILY: I'm glad you're starting to remember, Alfred. How much of this sounds familiar?

[*No reply.* ALFRED *stares at* EMILY.]

EMILY: Okay then. How much of this sounds fami"l"*ial?*

ALFRED: Why is it that at the center of even total lunacy, there's always a scrap, a shard, a remnant, a vestige of something that was . . . well . . . true? [*Pauses.*] Most of what Roxy said was absolute first-level crap . . . demented. . . . But some of it was true. [*Pauses.*] My mother certainly did have a friend and it certainly was Lynch's pop: Willie-Boy. And Roxy did make my mother's skirts. . . . And I *was* just ten when it all . . . happened. . . . [ALFRED *pauses; bows his head. There is a short silence in which* EMILY, ROXY, *and* LYNCH *all stare at* ALFRED. ALFRED *faces them again.*]

ALFRED: Most of what Lynch said was crap, too. But, some of it was true. My father, Tommy Webber, did have a fling with Roxy. And Lynch's sister Margaret and I did have a high school indiscretion. She did have to leave Nazareth before graduation. It was taken care—aborted —up in New Hampshire. Route one-twenty-eight, Lynn-

field way, then straight up the Newburyport Turnpike . . .

EMILY: Alfred, I think your mind is slipping.

ALFRED: You *think* my mind is slipping? You *think* my
mind is slipping??? Climb into my mind awhile if you
want to know what slippage *is*! My mind is the quint-
essence of slip!

[ALFRED *reaches to grab* EMILY *through the bars.*
LYNCH *moves for the pole.*]

ALFRED: No, Lynch! Don't poke me! Tell him not to poke
me, Emily! I'm sorry, sorry. I apologize. I know you're
angry. I'd forgotten that you were so deeply involved
with your sister. I'm sorry. [*To* EMILY] Lynchie and
Margaret were close. I forgot. I'm sorry.

LYNCH: You ain't payin' off the kind of debt you owe to
me with no "I'm sorry" pally-pal. Believe you me . . .

ALFRED: I'd forgotten. Willie-Boy's family . . . Lynch . . .
Margaret . . . all of them . . . intertwined. It slipped my
mind. They lived in the Italian section of town: Guinea
Gulch the kids called it. We all passed the Lynch house
on the bus every day . . . on the bus to Woodville school.
The kids all held their noses and made farting sounds.
. . . Kids are wonderful. . . . They called the Lynch house
"The Town Dump"! Margaret, God bless her, they called
her "The Town Pump." Willie-Boy Lynch was the town's
leading lunatic. That's why it was so upsetting to me
when my mother found him to be so . . . well . . .
attractive. So did Roxy . . . I forgot. . . . [*Pauses.*] Roxy
and Willie-Boy had a child together. . . .

ROXY: Two. We had two. I told you we were in love. . . .

ALFRED: My mind. I forgot it all. All intertwined. . . . The
word was that Margaret and her husband had blood
between them: incest. All through their family. Before
she married her husband . . . so the word went . . .
Margaret and her brother, Lynchie, were . . . well . . .
doin' it.

LYNCH: This is stoppin' and it's stoppin' right now! [*Moves
to cell, unlocks door.*]

EMILY: What are you doing, Mr. Lynch?

LYNCH: There's no way I'm lettin' history get written the
way it's gettin' written here. [*Enters cell.*] I'm s'pose'ta

be settin' the history books straight on Lynches and lynchin', right?

[*He moves to* ALFRED, *who backs to wall.*]

LYNCH: *You know what? You know what?* I think the record's lookin' *worse* . . . every minute . . . not better . . . *WORSE!* [*To* ALFRED] No more talk, Alfred. No more waitin'!

ALFRED: Emily?

EMILY: Mr. Lynch, you're highly overwrought. I must *demand* you back off. . . . *Get out of there, Lynch!*

[LYNCH *removes his belt and moves to* ALFRED.]

EMILY: God damn it, you agreed! If you wanted to just kill him, you should have done that weeks ago! We have a pact here!

LYNCH: [*Ties belt around* ALFRED'S *neck.*] Shove your pact.

EMILY: You're a greedy son of a bitch!

[ALFRED *stumbles out of cell, belt around his neck, end dangling.* ALFRED *runs to door.* LYNCH *follows.* ALFRED *pulls at the door. It is padlocked closed.*]

LYNCH: It's locked, Alfred. Locked it myself. [*Laughs; turns to* EMILY.] This isn't for me: this is for my father . . . Willie-Boy Lynch: a champion . . . and for my sister, Margaret . . . a saint . . . a virgin and a saint and a Nazarite, too. . . . And for Lynch, itself—the sacred family name. . . . *ARE YOU WRITING THIS IN???* [ROXY *does.*

ALFRED *crawls to position behind cell door. He pulls himself to his feet; smiles at* LYNCH.]

LYNCH: What the hell are *you* doing?

ALFRED: Stay back, Lynch! [*Hops behind open cell door, thinking he has moved into cell itself.*] I'm just going back inside. . . .

LYNCH: [*Confused*] What the hell do you think *you're* doing?

ALFRED: [*His back is against front of cell. He has pulled the cell door against his belly and peers through the bars of cell door at* LYNCH. ALFRED *seems relieved.*] Better inside. It's better. More relaxed. Safer. . . . [ALFRED *exhales, relieved. He smiles.*]

LYNCH: This is the fuckin' one-time-only *limit!* [*Moves to* ALFRED; *faces him through bars of door*] Look at me,

Alfred; Lynchie. We were kids together, Alfred . . .
Bottom of West Ward School hill. . . . I know every
detail, Alfred, don't I? [*Screams.*] LOOK . . . AT . . .
ME!! LOOK! LOOK! LOOK!

[LYNCH *bangs on the bars as he screams.* LYNCH *slams
cell door closed.*

ALFRED *stands facing* LYNCH *now, his back against bars,
front of cell.*

LYNCH *tightens loop of belt around* ALFRED's *neck.*]

LYNCH: *C'MON! C'MON! C'MON! C'MONNNNNNN!*

[EMILY *arrives at desk, opens drawer, removes gun.*]

ROXY: Jesus, it's *the* gun . . . *the* gun.

EMILY: Yes. It is. Thirty-two-caliber. Not a lot, but enough.
. . . [*Calls across.*] Mr. Lynch?

[LYNCH *laughs. He pulls* ALFRED *between* EMILY *and
himself, so that if* EMILY *shoots gun, she must first hit*
ALFRED. LYNCH *holds belt tightly, choking* ALFRED.]

LYNCH: You want to shoot me, Emily? Great! Terrific! Do
it! Only thing is, you're gonna have to send the bullet
through Alfred to get to me. Okay? Come on. Do it!
Save me some trouble!

EMILY: You bricked up the door. How do you plan on
leaving here?

LYNCH: Any man who knows how ta brick a door, knows
how ta *un*brick a door. Can't learn one without learnin'
t'other. The opposite.

EMILY: We have a pact, Mr. Lynch: a firm and solid
pact. . . .

LYNCH: [*To* ALFRED] She's got us down here on a suicide
pact. Can ya believe it? A suicide pact. She thinks I'm
s'posed ta die in here with you. . . . *I'm* goin' out: I've
got a great hiding place . . . my house. Nobody's gonna
find me there 'cause nobody even knows I exist. That's
what forty years in Wakefield did for B.J. Lynch: He's
safe in his own house. . . . [*To* ALFRED] I'm going to
kill you now, Alfred. [*Begins to choke him. To* EMILY]
If you had the guts to shoot me, Emily, you would've
done it as soon as you picked up the gun. . . .

[*There is a pause.* EMILY *is unable to kill* LYNCH.]

EMILY: Why . . . can't I . . . pull the trigger?

ALFRED: Emily, please. . . .

EMILY: I can't, Alfred. . . .

[ROXY *moves to* EMILY: *takes* EMILY's *hand with gun in it in her own hand.*

LYNCH *begins choking* ALFRED.

GUNSHOT. Both ALFRED *and* LYNCH *fall, at once.*

LYNCH *is dead.* EMILY *steps back, three steps.* ROXY *stands alone, holding pistol in hand.*

ALFRED *is unable at first to open his eyes. He lies next to the dead* LYNCH, *eyes clenched closed.*]

ALFRED: Emily? Are you hurt? Emily? [*He opens his eyes.*] Lynch . . . all bloody . . . he's dead, Emily. . . . Emily?

ROXY: Silly to worry, right? Silly to think of a woman of my age getting punished for anything, right?

ALFRED: I . . . I don't know why you did what you did, Roxy . . . but . . . thank you.

EMILY: I . . . I . . . thank you. . . .

ROXY: After all, a mother has certain obligations, right? A mother has an obligation to protect her daughter. No matter what. . . .

[*She looks at* ALFRED, *then to* EMILY. *She touches* EMILY's *arm.*]

ROXY: No matter what.

[EMILY *and* ALFRED *look at* ROXY; *then at each other. All bow heads. Tableau. The lights fade to black.*]

END OF ACT II

ACT III

Later. Stage in darkness.

Three sharp knocks are heard.

*First words of this act—*ROXY's—*are heard in darkness.*

ROXY: I blame you, Alfred.
  [*Lights to full, suddenly. Cell door is open.* ROXY *in chair pulled in front of cell. Her stenotype machine is in front of her, as she gives testimony and records her words, simultaneously.*
  EMILY *sits on desk, watching.*
  LYNCH's *body is gone from room.*
  ALFRED *in cell. His clothing is scruffy. His beard quite full again. He is groggy.*
  ROXY *turns to* EMILY.]
ROXY: He's not listening to me.
EMILY: [*Raps with the wooden gavel on the desktop: three sharp raps.*] Alfred! Look at my mother, Alfred!
  [ALFRED *looks up, meekly.*]
ROXY: It's true. [*Pauses.*] It is true, too.
EMILY: [*To* ALFRED] Look at her. [*Pauses.*] She's telling the truth. [*Pauses.*] Look at her!
ROXY: It's *you* who's responsible for our troubles here . . . and that's the truth of it. [*To* EMILY] It's him. [*Pauses; to* ALFRED *again*] Old folks livin' way beyond their prime . . . way beyond their wildest dreams! *You* did that! [*Pauses.*] Look at me: nearly a hundred and sunk since

240

the age of fourteen. Is that a life? Is that a pleasure? Is that any goddam reward for my suffering? [*Pauses.*] I blame *you*, Alfred. [*Pauses.*] No one else.

ALFRED: [*Lies down on floor.*] . . . so tired, Emily . . . want to rest . . . want to sleep . . . please . . . no more of this . . . so tired . . . no more . . . let me rest . . .
[EMILY *stands, takes long pole.*
ALFRED *looks at her. He recoils.*]

ALFRED: No! Don't! [*Looks up at her again.*]

EMILY: Stand up, Alfred. You're on the ground.
[*He does.*]

EMILY: Better.

ALFRED: Emily, I can't be responsible for what I did when I was ten. Ten, Emily. Ten. Surely, you can see. I forgot. I'd forgotten. I'd blocked it out . . . pushed it under. . . .

EMILY: You are responsible. . . .

ALFRED: I . . . yes. I am. [*Pauses.*] I thought it would please him . . . my father . . . to punish her . . . my mother. I did it for him. . . . [*Looks at* EMILY.] I did do that . . . my mother . . . killed her . . . I did do that . . . but the rest, Emily, the rest . . . didn't . . . didn't . . . don't know why I'm being punished . . . not for the rest. . . .

EMILY: Your father.

ALFRED: My father? No. You mean my mother. . . .

EMILY: Father.

ROXY: Who killed him, Alfred?

ALFRED: Who killed my father? Is that what you're asking me?

ROXY: That's it.

ALFRED: Emily . . . Over and over . . . I can't take it. . . .

EMILY: Each crime must be counted . . . over and over again. [*Pauses.*] Your father. Who killed him? Who put him in a home and let him rot for thirty years?

ALFRED: I . . . [*Pauses.*] For the love of God! [*Pauses.*] I . . . I feel responsible.

EMILY: [*To* ROXY] Did you get that? In the record?

ROXY: [*Stops typing; reads.*] "I . . . for the love of God . . . I did it . . . I killed my father."

ALFRED: I feel responsible! I did not say I killed him. I said I feel responsible.

ROXY: [*Pointing gun at him. To* ALFRED] What's the difference? [*To* EMILY] What's the difference? [*To* ALFRED] I don't see any difference.

[ALFRED *bows his head.*]

ROXY: Do you? [*To* EMILY] Do *you?*

EMILY: There seems to be an entire family to account for, Alfred. . . .

ALFRED: For which to account.

EMILY: [*Pauses.*] Everyone who died, Alfred. What of them?

ALFRED: [*Angrily*] Yes. Me. My fault. I . . . All of them. Me . . . [*Pauses.*] My fault.

EMILY: I'd like now to point to the family tree, Alfred. I know it well. I've studied it. Become an expert. I've actually climbed it and a hard climb it was, too. Once I started climbing the tree, Alfred, I . . . well . . . you know me . . . sooner or later I had to find the absolute top. . . .

ALFRED: Yes, I do know, Emily. When she said it . . . Roxy . . . your mother . . . it all fit. [*Pauses.*] Roxy, your mother: Willie-Boy, your father. . . . [*Pauses.*] It all fit together. [*Pauses.*] My fault. I killed your father, didn't I? I did that.

ROXY: What?

ALFRED: My fault.

[ROXY *laughs;* ALFRED *looks up at her.*]

EMILY: Sorry, Alfred. You can't close your eyes to it anymore. . . . [*Pauses.*] Wrong father.

ROXY: Wrong father.

EMILY: Tommy. Tommy. My father . . . our father. Pa. Tommy Webber. We share the same Pa. Remember?

ALFRED: [*After a pause. He is shocked; shaken.*] Emily, I . . . I didn't know. Emily, I . . . [*He looks away.*]

ROXY: He's known that all along, Emily. No way he could have forgotten: not known.

ALFRED: I . . . didn't . . . know.

EMILY: One child after the other. [*Pauses.*] I always wondered why. [*Pauses.*] One child after the other. [*Pauses.*] So close to being born. But never quite. [*Pauses.*] Always spared the shame. [*Pauses.*] I always wondered why. Didn't you?

ALFRED: Yes.

ROXY: Nobody could ever keep the family ties straight. . . .
[*Laughs.*] The ties that bind, they say. Well, that's true
enough, isn't it? [*Pauses.*] We could never keep them
straight . . . unknotted. [*Pauses.*] We used to pretend
it didn't matter. But we were all old enough to know
better . . . to know it did matter . . . but we closed our
eyes to it . . . pretended. [*Pauses.*] We couldn't stop it
anyway. Nothing we could do. Not after *you* started it,
Alfred. Not after you killed your mother. It seemed to
me, at the time, like the end of something. . . . [*Pauses.*]
I was wrong. It wasn't. [*Pauses.*] Opposite. [*Pauses.*] It
was the start of something. A curse! [*Pauses.*] Thirty
years, no births, no deaths. . . . We grew older. That's
for sure. But no one . . . got out. Only those without
our blood. That's what you started. [*Pauses.*] Awful thing
to watch. [*Pauses.*] Awful thing to watch. [*Pauses.*] Awful
thing to watch. [*Pauses.*] I never could keep it straight
. . . who was family . . . who was even mine. . . . [*Pauses.*]
Seein' Emily again . . . here . . . now . . . suffering, as
she is . . . seeing my face on hers . . . that face . . .
that face . . . [*Pauses.*] I know it well. [*Pauses.*] I love
her, Alfred. I love my daughter. . . . [*Pauses.*] I love you,
Emily. . . . [*Pauses.*] Oh, God! Oh, God! Oh, God,
forgive us. . . . [*Bows her head; weeps. Looks at* ALFRED.]
Lynch's grandfather tried to stop it . . . the incest. . . . His
children, all mutant. Awful thing to watch. [*Pauses.*]
Hanged one of his own sons. . . . He got caught doin'
it. . . . [*Pauses.*] There was no way of stoppin' the
incest. . . . So it seemed. [*Pauses.*] I knew what we were.
My own father told me. He gave me over to the Car-
melites, down in Ipswich, but I talked. They gave me
over to the Sisters of Charity and I tried to stick it out
. . . to never *ever* have babies. [*Pauses.*] But I couldn't
resist the pull. [*Pauses.*] I wanted to. I couldn't. I couldn't
resist the pull. [*Pauses.*] Baby after baby, they just kept
comin'. [*Pauses.*] I gave them away . . . each of them . . .
I couldn't *look* at them. I'm in the Guinness Book of
World Records. Oldest Living Mother. Fifty-seven when
I had Emily. [*Pauses.*] You're the first I've had to look
at in all these years now, Emily. . . . Having to sit
across from you, Alfred, lookin' exaxtly as your Pa . . .
and Lynch, Jesus-God forgive him, lookin' exactly like

his Pa . . . and Emily, all the look of me, when I was
. . . well . . . *then. Such a thing!* [*Pauses.*] I never thought
it could grow worse, Alfred, but you saw to it it did.
[*Pauses.*] The day you killed your mother, we were
cursed. I swear we were. Thirty years . . . no births, no
deaths, unless by murder. [*Pauses.*] *It's you I blame!*

ALFRED: I can't be blamed.

EMILY: Not true.

ALFRED: I didn't know.

EMILY: Not true.

ALFRED: I was led to it. . . . Out of my control. . . .

EMILY: Not true. . . .

ALFRED: Emily, please. . . .

EMILY: You chose me. You tracked me down. You forced
me. You stopped me. You forced me. You forced me.
You forced me.

ROXY: You must be blamed, Alfred.

EMILY: You knew *before* you ever married me, Alfred.
You wanted us to be married in spite of what you knew.
. . . [*Pauses; then pleading*] For God's sakes, Alfred . . .
don't close your eyes to it. Not now! Give . . . me . . .
*some*thing!

ALFRED: [*After a pause*] I did. I knew. I'd blocked it out
. . . forgotten. [*Pauses.*] I lied. [*Pauses.*] You'd just returned from the hospital . . . another stillbirth . . .
another one lost. . . . We were sitting in a restaurant . . .
only us . . . staring . . . lost in a memory. . . . [*Pauses;
quietly*] I thought I was looking into a mirror but my
hair seemed too long . . . extraordinarily so . . . hanging
over my eyes. . . . [*Pauses.*] I moved it up, across my
forehead wedging it behind my ear. . . . [*Pauses.*] My
reflection didn't move, Emily. . . . It was you . . . me
. . . *us.* . . . [*Pauses.*] Same face . . . same eyes . . .
same lips . . . all the same. I remembered. I knew.
[*Pauses.*] I'd grown up with a photograph of you . . .
large . . . tinted with pastels . . . hanging in the hall
outside my room. [*Pauses.*] It was the kind of hall that
was taken for granted. Pictures and photographs on the
walls . . . never really looked at . . . taken for granted
. . . forgotten. [*Pauses.*] Your hair was brown . . . your
loose blouse white. [*Pauses.*] You were looking at a bird:

a robin. [*Pauses.*] I knew you were my father's child. . . .
The photograph was his. My mother forgot to take it
down. . . . She'd told me that you were his . . . and that
your mother had . . . given you away . . . to a home
. . . in Boston. [*Pauses.*] I was so frightened that my
mother would give me away, too. . . . [*Pauses; smiles
bravely.*] She didn't. [*Pauses.*] When I was ten, I murdered my mother. Found her in bed with Willie-Boy
Lynch: a champion. I killed them both with my Boy
Scout knife. I thought it would please my father. I
thought she'd betrayed him and had to be punished.
[*Pauses.*] My father took the blame . . . told the police
he did it. He was too old for jail . . . too crazy. He went
to the asylum on the hill. . . . Rotted there . . . thirty
years, before he died. He took the blame . . . held it
for thirty years. He protected *me* from it . . . protected
me from the blame. He felt responsible. Almost every
memory I had before the day I killed my mother . . .
well . . . disappeared. The day itself was a complete
blank. [*Pauses.*] Emily, you were the most exciting crea-
ture I'd ever laid eyes upon. [*Pauses.*] It *had* to be that
way. Our whole family punished for what I did. [*Pauses.*]
It had to be that way. [*Pauses.*] When I did finally remember, that was the start of it. From the moment of
remembering, things . . . well . . . changed between
us. I found you revolting. I began to remember . . . all
of it. [*Pauses.*] I'd forgotten my father was alive. . . .
Forgotten I'd killed my mother . . . all of it. The first
fact that came back to me was you: that we were brother
and sister, husband and wife. [*Pauses.*] I feel responsible.
I *am* responsible. I shouldn't have lied. I should have
told you. Who did?

EMILY: Pa. Our father. Pa.

ALFRED: [*After a long pause*] God . . . [*Pauses.*] Let . . .
me . . . be . . . dead. Let me die!

EMILY: He will, Alfred. He'll let you die. There are just
a few interesting steps to go: to take. . . . I have it all
planned . . . beautifully planned. [*Smiles.*] It's rare, in
this life, that it becomes really and truly possible to
blame *any*one for *any*thing. . . . In the matter of twenty
years of my life, Alfred, I blame you. I hold you re-

sponsible . . . *accountable*. [*To* ROXY.] It's your time,
Mother. . . .

[ROXY *stands, moves to* EMILY. *They embrace. They kiss.*]

ROXY: If I had to live my life over, Emily, I would try
hard to make it different. . . . [*Pauses; moves to cell.*]
If I had to live my life over . . . I would.

[*She faces* ALFRED, *stares a moment, kisses him. She
moves into back room, behind the cell.*

ALFRED *waits a moment and then turns, facing* EMILY.]

ALFRED: Where's she going? There's a door? All the time,
there was a door?

[*He moves into back room. There is a pause.* ALFRED's
voice heard offstage.]

ALFRED: [*Off*] Roxy? I can't see anything! Roxy? . . .

[*The sound of a gunshot.*
Silence.

EMILY, *alone on stage, staring at door to back room.*

ALFRED *staggers out of door into cell.*]

ALFRED: Emily! Your mother . . .

[*He stops at bars to cell; stares at* EMILY. *There is a
moment between them.*]

EMILY: I know. We have a pact: Lynch, my mother,
and I.

ALFRED: She had this with her . . . this gun. . . . I didn't
. . . [*Frightened that* EMILY *will think he killed* ROXY,
ALFRED *tosses gun onto floor near* EMILY's *feet.*] Emily,
I . . .

EMILY: [*Pauses.*] It has to stop, Alfred . . . this path for
me. . . . It has to stop. . . . I've had all I can bear. . . .
[*She moves to cell.*] The lock.

ALFRED: [*Clicks the lock closed.*] Done.

EMILY: There's one more, Alfred. One to go.

ALFRED: One more what, Emily?

EMILY: Murder. [*Pauses.*] The supreme kill . . . the over-
the-top kill. . . . [*To* ALFRED] the *risus puris*. . . .
[*Pauses.*] Alfred?

ALFRED: [*Accepting his fate; quietly*] Yes.

EMILY: Me. [*Moves to stage-right door.*] There is something special about this door. . . . [*Smiles.*] Something
you should know. . . . [*Opens the stage-right door. It
opens onstage, hinged on the upstage edge of door. It*

*is now revealed that opening that was doorway has been
cemented, space is filled in. Cement blocks and stucco
form a solid impenetrable wall.]* Like it? I do. Expensive
but well worth the price. . . .

ALFRED: I . . .

*[He moves slowly to stage-left lower wall of cell, grip-
ping bars for support as he goes. He stops: stares at
plugged doorway.*

EMILY *leaves door opened, against stage-left wall.]*

EMILY: *[Moves to table: picks up gavel again, raps three
knocks on tabletop.]* Like it? Guaranteed impenetra-
bility. I asked for granite . . . *[Pauses.]* From Rockport
. . . *[Pauses.]* Had to settle for cement . . . from Wakefield . . . native. . . . *[Pauses.]* The price of granite has,
as they say, mushroomed. *[Smiles.]* Mr. Lynch did this.
He bricked the door. Good worker, Mr. Lynch. Pity.
He died.

*[EMILY raps the gavel against the tabletop sharply; three
knocks.*

ALFRED *blinks three times, clenching his eyes closed, and
then open.]*

EMILY: Stop blinking. . . .

[ALFRED's eyes open and close, rapidly.]

EMILY: Stop blinking!

[ALFRED clenches his eyes closed.]

EMILY: You've closed your eyes. . . . Fine . . . just fine.
[Pauses; coughs.] The air is awful already. Awful.

*[ALFRED moves from side to side of his cell, feeling his
way along the front edge, eyes clenched closed.*

*When he has completed traveling the full surface and
has returned to his starting position, center of cell's
downstage wall, he stops, gripping the bars above and
outside his shoulders.*

He opens his eyes.

He looks at EMILY a moment in silence.

Speaks again, rapidly now.]

ALFRED: I tried to tell you before this . . . I did: I really
did. You wouldn't listen. Wouldn't hear it. *[Pauses.]* I
never thought it was natural: pairs. You and me, you
and anybody, me and anybody. In alone, out alone.

EMILY: Alfred. I am . . . somebody.

ALFRED: [*After a long pause*] Never, not in my entire life,
   did I ever have to *say* I was somebody. [*Pauses.*] I just
   . . . was. [*Pauses.*] Sorry, Emily. . . .

EMILY: Alfred, *I am somebody.*

ALFRED: How can we get out of here? [*Pauses.*] How can
   we get out of here? [*Pauses.*] How can we get out of
   here?

EMILY: [*Slowly*] How can you be so . . . hopeful?

ALFRED: I have no intention of ending it here, Emily. Not
   in Wakefield, not in this room, not in front of you. . . .
   [*He circles the cell, furious, finally comes to rest. Pauses.*]
   How?

EMILY: Neither of us can or will leave this room. [*Pauses.*]
   Not you nor I. Neither. [*Pauses.*] It's possible, of course,
   in a few months' time, someone might blast a way in
   . . . just to have a peek . . . and pull us out. Maybe in
   November, to put the park benches away for winter.
   [*She begins packing tapes into box.*] For the moment,
   polymer . . . a sealed tomb: the perfect compound . . .
   us and our history: Roxy's report. It'll be quite a find:
   big news. [*Pauses.*] An average man of average weight
   and height could stay alive, say, one month. [*Pauses.*]
   You are, of course, not average. [*Pauses.*] You are, at
   this particular juncture in your life, less than average.
   [*Pauses.*] Three weeks I'd say. Three weeks. Your body
   can devour itself, in place of food, for three weeks. [*She
   stacks bottles near cell.*] Without water, less. That's why
   you'll notice that there is an adequate supply of water
   set in these bottles. [*There are now eight bottles of
   water, set against the upstage wall of the cell.*] If you
   have the . . . you know . . . desire to hurry . . . [*Smiles.*]
   If you . . . well . . . [*Pauses.*] . . . find the courage . . .
   just . . . [*Pauses; smiles.*] . . . don't drink the water.
   [*Pauses.*] I have no doubt as to the outcome. . . . [*Pauses.*]
   You'll sip away. . . . [*Pauses.*] You'll remain . . . hopeful . . . until the last. . . . [*Pauses.*] One day . . . in the
   next twenty or twenty-one . . . you'll understand. . . .
   It will all become comprehensible . . . [*Smiles.*] Coherent.
   [*The sound of explosions from above: dull thuds, as
   though bombs were exploding somewhere a great distance away.*]

EMILY: The fireworks have started, Alfred. [*Looks up to ceiling; smiles.*] It's the night of the Fourth. Today is Independence Day. . . . Parade floats . . . majorettes twirling their aluminum sticks . . . senators, marching. . . . All above us. Everyone . . . smiling. . . . [*Pauses.*] I don't have what it takes to kill you . . . not directly, not face-to-face. I knew that when I stood facing Lynch. I wanted him dead. I couldn't. [*Pauses.*] It seems that I'm just not . . . allowed. [*Pauses.*] I've figured this way instead: *my* death will kill you, too. [*Pauses.*] It *will*, you know.

ALFRED: Emily . . . Forgive me . . . I shouldn't have lied . . . forgotten . . .

EMILY: I forgive you, Alfred. I do. [*Pauses.*] Forgiveness is all I have for which to be proud . . . of me. Forgiveness is my last and final right on this habitable earth. . . . I know you'd love to go on and on . . . to live. I know you'll hope for it . . . struggle . . . fight it out until the end. . . . [*Pauses.*] But you can't go on, Alfred. You have to die. Both of us. It has to end with us. [*Pauses.*] Really, Alfred. Trust me. Somebody has to stop it, here and now. There's always a possibility that one child might make it all the way . . . be born . . . start it again. I can't take the chance. I have to be certain. You're going to be so much happier . . . I promise you. [*Walks to desk and takes revolver from desk drawer.*] Look at me, Alfred. . . .

ALFRED: Emily, for the love of God . . . [*Panic now*] Emily! [EMILY *places the revolver against her breast. She turns from desk and moves directly to* ALFRED, *smiling. She stops at bars in front of him.*]

EMILY: Sorry it's a gun. [*Pauses.*] Sorry it couldn't be something more . . . you know . . . imaginative . . . [*Pauses.*] . . . something less . . . modern. [*Pauses.*] These are inferior times. . . . [*Pauses.*] I have to be . . . certain. [*Pauses.*] Alfred?

ALFRED: [*Stares at* EMILY.] Don't, Emily . . . please don't . . .

EMILY: [*Slowly; clearly*] Emily . . . dies.
[*She fires the revolver into her breast: one sharp report;* EMILY's *body jerks backward against desk and she*

*slumps into chair. Drops gun. Clutches chest. She is
dead.*

ALFRED *stares at* EMILY'*s body.*]

ALFRED: I wish you hadn't done that, Emily. I do wish
that.

[*He walks to back wall, presses face against same, clenching eyes closed.*

He suddenly turns, blinks eyes open, as if EMILY *might
be gone.*]

ALFRED: Still there.

[*He inhales and exhales through his nostrils.*

*He walks to water bottles, lined in a row at edge of cell.
He nonchalantly opens one, drinks from it, relids bottle,
replaces same in row, but at other end: closer to* EMILY.
He bends, reaches across, touches EMILY'*s hair.*]

ALFRED: This is attractive, Emily. Wrong! This is *atrocious,*
Emily. That's what I said. That's *not* what you said!
That's what I said! [*Pauses.*] Losing my grip.

[*He takes gun from beneath* EMILY *and stands.* ALFRED
places barrel of gun in his mouth.

*He holds his breath, weeps. He cannot pull the trigger.
He places the gun's barrel against the palm of his hand,
walks to back wall, stoops, pulls trigger twice: two
reports.*

*He turns, faces front, blood dripping from his wounded
hand.*

He looks at EMILY, *smiles.*]

ALFRED: Better. *Kneels on floor, next to her, carefully.*]
I would like this in the record, please: I feel somewhat
better. I have taken positive steps to ensure the loss of
my grip. . . . [*Looks at* EMILY. *Pauses; stands, looks at
hand dripping blood.*] What have you done, Alfred?
[*Smiles.*] Five, the first time. Didn't know why. [*Pauses.*]
Knife on table, eyebrow-high. Watched it, tiptoe. Sounds
all empty. Colors mute. Smells to rancid. Tiny chest
thumping. [*Pauses.*] Knife in hand, curled in fingers.
Sounds, colors, smells, all gone. [*Pauses.*] Point pricked,
no pain. Full thrust, no blood. Eyes clenched, no scream.
Me, alive, always spared. [*Pauses.*] I could have stayed
away, you know. I could have kept my eyes clenched
closed. . . . I needn't have ever looked at it again. [*Pauses.*]
I wanted to come back here . . . to Wakefield . . . and

see them and tell them . . . everybody . . . that it was all right. That's what I wanted to do. [*Pauses.*] It wasn't all right. I didn't tell them so. [*Pauses.*] Look at us. [*Pauses.*] You are Emily and I am Alfred. [*Pauses.*] We were cursed, Emily. Your mother was right. We were cursed. [*Pauses.*] By whom?

[*He is weak now. He looks at his hand dripping blood.*]

ALFRED: My hand. [*Pauses.*] What have you done, Alfred? [*Tries to stand; cannot.*] Too weak.

[*The sound of Fourth of July celebration—faintly, dully —overhead.*

The dull thuds of the final fireworks display, overhead.]

ALFRED: Finished.

[ALFRED, *sitting on floor next to* EMILY. *The bars of the cage separate them. He now hears the music. He looks up, suddenly. He is hopeful.*

Tableau.

The lights fade to black.]

THE PLAY IS OVER.

Paris, New York, San Francisco, Milford, Gloucester—1971–1978

The Wakefield Plays, Part VI

STAGE DIRECTIONS
A Play in One Act

For Edith Fournier.

The People of the Play

RICHARD: A thin, hawklike man, forties.
RUTH: A thin, hawklike woman, thirties.
RUBY: A small, wrenlike woman, twenties.

The Place of the Play

Living room, New England home, overlooking Lake Quannapowitt, Wakefield, Massachusetts.

The Time of the Play

Late afternoon, fall.

Note to Director

The people of the play will speak only words that describe their activities and, on occasion, emotions. No other words or sounds are permitted. By definition, then, all activity and conveyed emotion must be born of spoken stage directions.

Lights fade up.

Sofa, slightly right of room's center.

Bar wagon and liquor, upstage right.

Overstuffed chairs, right and left of sofa, slightly downstage.

Large framed mirror, 24" x 36", draped in black fabric, upstage-left wall.

Equal-sized framed photograph, draped in black fabric as well, opposite wall, upstage of center of sofa.

China cabinet filled with bric-a-brac, wall beside upstage chair (optional).

Single door to room, upstage-right wall.

Copious bookshelves and books, wherever space permits.

General feeling wanted that room belongs to bookish person.

Small desk downstage right. Writing stand, memo pad, stationery, on same. Wastebasket at upstage-front foot.

Oriental carpet, subdued tones, under all of above.

RICHARD: [*Enters.*] Richard enters, quietly. Looks about room to see if he is alone. Certain he is, closes door. Pauses, inhales, turns and leans his back against door, exhales, sobs once. He wipes his eyes on his cuff, notices black armband, which he removes and into which he blows his nose. He then stuffs armband into pocket of his overcoat which he then removes and folds somewhat fastidiously over back of sofa. He pauses, looking about room, taking a private moment: possibly adjusting his underwear and then discovering and dealing with a day-old insect bite in the pit behind his knee. A fly buzzes past his nose, breaking into his thoughts. He swats at fly carelessly, but somehow manages to capture same in hand, which he brings down and then up close to his eye. He opens hand ever so slightly, watching fly awhile. Although it appears certain that he will open hand allowing fly her freedom, he suddenly smashes hands together, finishing fly and causing clap to sound in room. He walks to desk and using slip of memo paper from pad, he scrapes fly from palm and into wastebasket at foot of desk. He inspects stain on palm, lowers hand to side, pauses, returns to chair, sobs once, sits, bows head, notices shoe, removes same, places single shoe in his lap, sobs again, searches for and finds lightly plaided handkerchief into which he blows nose enthusiastically, unclogging same and producing substantial honking sound in room. He settles back in chair, stares vacantly up at ceiling.

RUTH: [*Enters.*] Ruth enters, quietly, closing door with her heel. She looks cautiously about room to see if she is alone, sees Richard sitting in chair.

RICHARD: Richard quickly bows his head and assumes somewhat grave look on his face, rather a studied vacant stare at his black-stockinged foot.

RUTH: Ruth smiles, as though she has been acknowledged.

RICHARD: Richard flashes a quick look at Ruth, to be certain it is she who has entered.

RUTH: Ruth catches Richard's glance and smiles again.

RICHARD: Richard is forced to return her smile and does. He then returns to former position in chair, head-bowed, eyes vacant, staring down toward black-stockinged foot.

RUTH: Ruth leans her back against door, exhales.

RICHARD: Richard adjusts his underwear, discreetly.

RUTH: Ruth sighs.

RICHARD: Richard wipes the palm of his hand behind the knee of his trouser leg, accomplishing both a wipe and a rub of the day-old insect bite.

RUTH: Ruth touches her black armband to be certain it has not been lost, sighs again.

RICHARD: Richard glances at his hand to be certain now that fly stain has been completely removed. Satisfied, nonetheless, he wipes his hand on his trouser leg again.

RUTH: Ruth pretends to be removing her overcoat while never removing her stare from the back of Richard's head. She slips her hand inside her coat and discreetly adjusts her brassière . . .

RICHARD: . . . just as Richard turns to her. . . .

RUTH: She recoils quickly, pulling her hand from her coat.

RICHARD: Seeing that he has startled her, he turns away, reviving his former position, head bowed, vacantly staring at his black-stockinged foot.

RUTH: Ruth pauses a moment and then moves directly to bar and surveys liquor supply atop same.

RICHARD: Richard senses her presence at the bar and turns to look disapprovingly at her.

RUTH: Ruth, sensing his disapproval, quickly pours an inch of bourbon, which she downs in a gulp.

RICHARD: He continues his disapproving stare, while unconsciously touching his nose.

RUTH: She raises her glass toward him, nods: blatantly hostile. She smiles, unconsciously touching her nose as well.

RICHARD: She is smiling, deliberately handling her nose. . . .

RUTH: He turns away, pompously. . . . She clears her throat, attempting to regain his attention, but he remains unmoved, disapproving. . . . She pulls open her coat and adjusts her brassière. . . .

RICHARD: Raising his hip and thigh, slightly and quickly, he adjusts his briefs, scratches his day-old insect bite, and then spits directly on to his palm and fly stain, wipes his hand on his trouser knee, smiles. . . . He turns now and faces her directly, but she is pretending not to notice, not to be paying attention to him. She searches for and finds a rather gaudy orange nylon handkerchief, into which she indelicately honks her hooked nose. . . .

RUTH: He removes his sock and pulls at toes, playing with same. . . .

RICHARD: She flings her coat sloppily over back of sofa. . . . His other shoe off now and . . .

RUTH: [Note: Words and actions overlap competitively.] Ruth removes her gloves . . . and hat . . .

RICHARD: [Overlapping] . . . placing it precisely beside his first shoe . . .

RUTH: [Overlapping] . . . tossing them in a heap on the sofa . . .

RICHARD: [Overlapping] . . . He then peels off his other sock . . .

RUTH: [Overlapping] . . . She then hoists her skirt and unhitches her stocking top from the front and back garters on her garter-belt . . .

RICHARD: [Overlapping] Richard averts his eyes!

RUTH: Ruth stares at the back of Richard's head, directly. The affect should be one of deep hostility. She is, however, surprised to notice that she is weeping.

RICHARD: . . . as is Richard.

RUTH: There is a moment of absolute silence. [Five count]

RICHARD: Sock clenched in fist, Richard will pound the arm of his chair, three times. He stares straight ahead, eyes unblinking. Three . . . dull . . . thuds. . . . And then silence. [*Five count*]

RUTH: Ruth approaches Ruby's chair, stands behind it a moment, pauses.

RICHARD: Richard turns to her and their eyes quietly meet.

RUTH: Ruth is the first to turn away.

RICHARD: Richard bows his head.

RUTH: Ruth walks quickly to the bar wagon and liquor supply, pours two inches of bourbon this time, tosses bottle cap onto floor, and then returns to Ruby's chair.

RICHARD: Richard does not look up. He picks at a loose thread on his trouser knee.

RUTH: Ruth sits, crosses legs, removes shoes, floors them.

RICHARD: Richard turns his body away from her, staring off vacantly.

RUTH: Ruth notices now she wears one stocking pulled taut, the other dangling loose by her knee. She removes first stocking and allows it to stay on floor near her foot. She reaches under her skirt and unhitches other stocking from her garter belt.

RICHARD: Richard glances at her, discreetly touching his nose.

RUTH: She senses his glance, but neither looks up nor acknowledges same. She instead removes stocking which she crunches and holds in same hand with glass of bourbon.

RICHARD: Richard suddenly stands, floors shoes, crosses room to bar.

RUTH: Ruth watches him, unconsciously touching her nose.

RICHARD: Richard searches for and finds small clear bottle of club soda, which he neatly uncaps, pouring liquid into small clear glass. He recaps bottle, replacing same precisely where it was found. Taking glass in hand, returns to chair, sits, sips.

RUTH: Ruth sips her bourbon and notices stocking crunched in hand. She reaches down and finds other stocking, joining both in loose knot, which she flings on to sofa seat.

RICHARD: Richard stares at her disapprovingly.

RUTH: Ruth remembers armband on coat. She stands, goes to it.

RICHARD: Richard stares after her.

RUTH: Ruth begins to remove armband, but thinks better of it, returns to chair, begins to sit, thinks better of it, drains glass of its bourbon, returns to bar, pours three inches of fresh bourbon into same glass.

RICHARD: Richard turns away from her.

RUTH: Ruth glances at back of Richard's head.

RICHARD: Richard rubs his knee.

RUTH: Ruth tosses bottle, now empty, into wastebasket.

RICHARD: The sound startles Richard, who turns suddenly . . .

RUTH: . . . startling Ruth, who recoils, spilling her drink . . . on the rug.

RICHARD: Richard stares at stain [*Yells; amazed.*] . . . *on the rug!*

RUTH: Ruth rubs stain with her toe.

RICHARD: Richard turns away.

RUTH: Ruth turns, cupping her forehead in the palm of her right hand. She then moves her hand down over her nose and mouth and sobs.

RICHARD: There is a moment of silence, which Richard breaks first by dropping his glass onto floor.

RUTH: Ruth looks quickly in direction of sound.

RICHARD: Richard is amazed. He grabs his nose.

RUTH: Ruth smiles.

RICHARD: Richard leans forward and picks up glass.

RUTH: Ruth drains her glass of its remaining bourbon, one gulp.

RICHARD: Richard wipes his stain on rug with his socks, never leaving his chair, but instead leaning forward to his stain.

RUTH: Ruth, for the first time, notices his body, now stretched forward. Her smile is gone.

RICHARD: Richard seems perplexed. He pulls at his earlobe.

RUTH: Ruth places glass atop bar. She searches for and finds dish towel, which she aims and pitches onto floor near Richard's stain.

RICHARD: Richard looks first at dish towel, then at Ruth, disapprovingly. He then picks up dish towel and covers his stain with same.

RUTH: Ruth crosses to Ruby's chair, sits. She is weeping.

RICHARD: Richard, too, is weeping.

RUBY: [*Enters.*] Ruby enters, somewhat noisily, clumsily.

RUTH: Ruth turns to her from chair, smiles.

RUBY: Ruby returns the smile.

RUTH: Ruth looks away.

RUBY: Ruby looks about the room until her eyes meet Richard's.

RICHARD: His expresson is cold, the muscles of his face taut, his mouth thin-lipped, angry.

RUBY: Ruby nods to Richard.

RICHARD: Richard turns away, fists clenched on knees.

RUBY: Ruby closes door, bracing back against same.

RUTH: She has Richard's enormous Tel Avivian nose . . .

RICHARD: . . . Ruth's hawklike eyes, her hopelessly flat chest . . .

RUTH: . . . Richard's studied pomposity: his gravity . . .

RICHARD: . . . Ruth's unfathomable lack of courage . . .

RUTH: Richard's incomprehensible lack of feeling . . .

RICHARD: . . . Ruth's self-consciously-correct posture . . .

RUBY: Rich girl's shoulders.

RICHARD: Richard loathes Ruby.

RUTH: As does Ruth.

RICHARD: Evident now in his stern glance.

RUTH: As in Ruth's sudden snap from warmth to disapproval: from passion to ice.

RUBY: Ruby moves four steps to center of room and then stops, suddenly, somewhat squashed by their staring. [*Note: The following speeches are to be spoken as though interruptions, often overlapping, as often blending. No considerable movement wanted during this section.*]

RICHARD: N.B. Richard was first to hear news of father's death . . .

RUTH: N.B. Ruth heard news of plane crash and mother's death from Richard . . .

RUBY: N.B. Ruby was last to hear news of plane crash and mother's death . . .

RICHARD: . . . Mother's call put through by Betsy—the secretary—Mrs. Betsy Day, the secretary—Conference room, cigar smoke thick, business trouble, no time, distractions impossible . . .

RUTH: . . . Richard's phone call, Asian Studies Office, University of Vermont, town of Manchester, employed as nobody, researching nothing, touching no one . . .

RUBY: . . . Read news in Chicago *Sun-Times*. Heard same on FM station, midst of news, interrupting Bach's *Concerto in D Minor for Three Harpsicords and Orchestra, Alla Siciliana,* my name, them famous, now dead, now famous death . . .

RICHARD: . . . Father's body must be gotten. Died in Hot Springs, Arkansas, getting cured . . .

RUTH: . . . Ruth had not known her father had died . . .

RUBY: . . . Flew from O'Hare International to Logan International, United Air Lines, 707, morning flight, a clot of double-knit-polyester-leisure-suited businessmen, whispering loudly. Her second flight only, entire lifetime . . .

RICHARD: . . . Arranged for mother to fly to Hot Springs, Arkansas, to collect father's body, fly it home . . .

RUTH: . . . Ruth had not even known her father had been ill . . .

RUBY: . . . Her first flight was three years prior, visited father, first news of illness . . .

RICHARD: . . . Had reserved and paid for American Airlines First Class ticket. Had ticket hand-delivered to mother, two days prior . . .

RUTH: . . . Had years ago conquered fear of air travel. Had flown to and from all continents of the earth . . .

RUBY: . . . Met with doctors, disease incurable, all hope lost . . .

RICHARD: . . . Had summoned surviving siblings to family home, New England September, all chill . . .

RUTH: . . . Had preferred Asia to all others. Had preferred living in countries possessing languages she could neither read nor speak . . .

RUBY: Brother Robert, gone as well, same disease, spared no pain, three years prior, family . . . curse . . .

RICHARD: . . . Had not spoken even one word to Ruth in four years' time, since her third divorce . . .

RUTH: . . . Had preferred most of all living within Cantonese dialect, Northern China, most difficult, words impossible to separate, blend together, word as din . . .

RUBY: . . . Missed brother Robert's funeral, fear of airplanes, trains too slow, Jewish custom, grave by sundown, arrived during night . . .

RICHARD: . . . Had not spoken even one word to Ruby in four years' time, since her first divorce . . .

RUTH: . . . Had stayed in room once, one full month, three years prior, Northern China, never straying, never speaking, not one word, not aloud, voice postponed . . .

RUBY: . . . Jewish Law, beat the sundown. Only mirrors, covered, missed her absence . . . All else saw . . .

RICHARD: . . . Had not spoken even one word to father in five years' time, since news of father's irreversible disease . . .

RUTH: . . . Ruth had loved her brother, Robert, deeply . . .

RUBY: . . . Family shocked by Ruby's absence, never forgiven, never heard . . .

RICHARD: . . . Richard was first to hear news of plane crash, second half of ticket, both together, Ozark Mountains, hillbillies found them, picked their clothing clean of money, pried their teeth clean of gold . . .

RUTH: . . . Mourned brother Robert's death, deeply, endlessly, silently . . .

RUBY: . . . Ruby, youngest, most degrees, Ph.D., Modern British, Joyce and Woolf her favored pair . . . cheerleader, once, Wakefield High School, F, now depressed.

RICHARD: . . . Pried their teeth clean of gold . . .

RUTH: ' . . . Never forgiven parents' not reaching her in time. Never said "Goodbye" to Robert . . .

[Note: Overlapping ends here.]

RUBY: . . . One brief marriage, to a surgeon . . .

RICHARD: . . . Mother's death . . .

RUTH: . . . Never reached her . . .

RUBY: . . . Engendered nothing, born barren, ovaries broken at birth . . .

RICHARD: . . . Richard feels responsible . . .

RUTH: . . . Ruth feels angry . . .

RUBY: . . . Ruby left husband; she, first to door, first to street, first to forget . . .

RICHARD: . . . Richard feels responsible . . .

RUTH: Ruth feels angry . . .

RUBY: . . . Lived with friends, always male . . .

RICHARD: . . . Richard feels responsible . . .

RUTH: . . . Ruth feels angry . . .

RUBY: . . . Loved her brother, Robert, deeply. Mourned his death, not forgotten. Parents and siblings never forgiven, they never forgave . . .

RICHARD: . . . Richard feels responsible for his parents' death . . .

RUTH: . . . Ruth feels anger at her parents' death . . .

RUBY: . . . Jet from Chicago, late as usual, missed their funeral, struck again. Ruby still stunned, unable to weep . . .

RICHARD: . . . Richard feels responsible for the death of his parents . . .

RUTH: . . . Ruth feels anger at the death of her parents . . .

RUBY: . . . Ruby is unable to weep at the death of her parents . . .

RICHARD: N.B. All of above.

RUTH: N.B. All of above.

RUBY: N.B. All of above.

RICHARD: Richard glances at Ruby.

RUTH: Richard smiles, seeing Ruby's pain . . .

RICHARD: As does Ruth.

RUBY: Ruby regains her strength. She moves to the sofa where she flings her black coat, after tossing small Vuitton weekend case to the floor beside sofa.

RICHARD: Richard is contemptuous of her gesture . . .

RUTH: As is Ruth, who is, however, somewhat amused at the same time and is surprised to find herself smiling. She adjusts her skirt.

RUBY: Ruby adjusts her skirt, retucks her blouse into skirt by reaching under skirt, pulls down blouse ends from bottom, straightening blouse perfectly into skirt and, at the same time, pulling blouse tightly over her breasts.

RICHARD: Richard studies her breasts, certain there is no brassière supporting them.

RUTH: Ruth studies her breasts, certain there is no brassière supporting them.

RUBY: Ruby adjusts her brassière.

RUTH: Ruth adjusts her brassière.

RICHARD: Richard scratches his chest and coughs.

RUBY: Ruby moves to bar and pours glass full with ginger ale. She lifts brandy decanter from shelf, holds and studies same, somewhat lovingly.

RICHARD: Richard glances at dish towel . . . on his stain . . . on his rug . . . near his foot.

RUTH: Ruth looks cautiously at her own stain.

RUBY: Ruby drops decanter . . . accidentally. It crashes

down on bar top, causing loud noise to sound sharply in room.

RICHARD: Richard turns quickly to see what Ruby has done.

RUTH: As does Ruth.

RUBY: Ruby is amazed by what she has done. She takes the bar towel and feverishly wipes the spilled liquid.

RICHARD: Richard bows his head. He removes wallet from pocket, studies photograph of daughters and former wife, replaces wallet in pocket.

RUTH: Ruth bows her head. She pauses. She quietly slips from her chair and removes black veil from mirror. She studies her own image.

RUBY: Ruby moves discreetly behind Ruth, so that she is now able to see her own image in mirror as well.

RUTH: Ruth sees Ruby seeing herself and moves away from mirror, turning directly to face Ruby . . .

RUBY: . . . who is unable to meet the stare and turns her face downward, to the floor.

RUTH: Ruth smiles, crosses to sofa; sits.

RICHARD: Richard stands and walks directly to the mirror. He avoids looking at his reflected image, but instead recovers mirror with black fabric veil, moves to Ruby's chair; sits.

RUTH: Ruth crosses to Richard's chair and sits.

RUBY: Ruby clenches eyes closed, three count.

RICHARD: Richard adjusts his underwear.

RUTH: Ruth adjusts her underwear.

RUBY: Ruby crosses to what appears to be second veiled mirror and removes black fabric from it.

RICHARD: Richard averts his eyes from image . . .

RUTH: As does Ruth.

RUBY: Ruby exposes twenty-four-by-thirty-six-inch tinted photograph of their parents, posed, taken on occasion of their fortieth wedding anniversary. Ruby stares at photograph.

RICHARD: Richard is weeping. He silently mouths the word "Mama."

RUTH: As does Ruth.

RUBY: Ruby continues to stare at photograph a moment before taking two odd steps backwards, stiffly. She stops. She silently mouths the word "Papa."

RICHARD and RUTH: [*Silently*] Mama.

RUBY: [*Silently*] Papa.

RUTH: Ruth glances at photograph and then at Ruby. She
faces Richard, three count. She is openly contemptuous
of her sister and brother.

RUBY: Ruby looks first at Richard and then at Ruth. She
replaces veil over photograph. She moves to bar. . . .

RICHARD: Richard follows her with his eyes, openly
staring . . .

RUBY: . . . Ruby leans against bar, somewhat slumped,
anguished . . .

RICHARD: . . . Richard coughs, turns away . . .

RUBY: . . . Ruby covers her eyes with palm of left hand.
Right hand slides discreetly across stomach to waistband
of skirt. She is adjusting and turning same.

RUTH: . . . Ruth remains silent, staring at stain on rug, lost
in a memory . . .

RICHARD: . . . Richard strokes a tear from his cheek.

RUTH: Ruth stands, moves toward Ruby, tentatively: pain-
fully slow, frightened. She plans to embrace her sister,
but will not have the courage to do so.

RUBY: Ruby senses Ruth approaching, turns, faces her,
smiles.

RUTH: Ruth is suddenly stopped.

RUBY: Ruby spies bottle cap on floor, scoops it up, bending
quickly, tosses same easily into wastebasket, leg of desk.
Ruby turns, suddenly facing Richard . . .

RICHARD: . . . who has been discreetly admiring Ruby's
upper thigh, made quite visible during her rapid bend
and scoop . . .

RUBY: . . . Ruby giggles . . .

RICHARD: Richard turns quickly away from her, outraged.

RUBY: Ruby contrives a serious stare in his direction, but
giggles again.

RUTH: Ruth is now holding her hand to her mouth, attempting unsuccessfully to contain a chortle.

RUBY: Ruby chortles openly.

RUTH: Ruth looks across room to Ruby . . .

RUBY: . . . who looks across to Ruth.

RUTH: Ruth takes a step again in Ruby's direction.

RICHARD: Richard produces a wailing sound, suddenly,
burying his face in his lap.

RUTH: Ruth turns to him and watches him awhile. . . .

RICHARD: Richard is sobbing.

RUBY: Ruby walks to the back of Richard's chair, stops, reaches forward, and allows her hand to rest a moment atop Richard's bowed head.

RUTH: Ruth watches, quietly, disapprovingly.

RICHARD: Richard seems unable to move. He neither turns toward Ruby nor away from her: he is instead frozen. His sobbing is now controlled: stopped, quenched.

RUBY: Ruby is embarrassed, sorry she negotiated the touching of Richard's head. She steps back now, three odd steps, stiffly; stops.

RUTH: Ruth stands staring at Ruby.

RUBY: Ruby looks directly at Ruth now. The sisters' eyes meet and hold an absolutely fixed stare.

RUTH: Ruth neither looks away, nor does she smile.

RUBY: Nor Ruby.

RICHARD: Richard stands and moves directly to veiled photograph . . .

RUBY: . . . Ruby does not break her stare at Ruth . . .

RICHARD: . . . He pauses a moment, touching black fabric with the back of his hand . . .

RUTH: . . . Nor does Ruth break her stare at Ruby . . .

RICHARD: . . . Richard carefully, silently, removes black fabric veil from photograph, allowing fabric to fall to floor beside his feet.

RUTH: Ruth is the first to break the stare between the sisters. She turns now to watch Richard.

RUBY: As does Ruby.

RICHARD: Richard stares intently at the photograph, reaching his left hand up and forward, touching the cheek of the man in the photograph. He rubs his finger gently across the face of the man, through the void between the man and the woman, finally allowing his finger to stop directly on the chin on the image of the woman in the photograph.

RUTH: Ruth stands, head bowed, silently mouths the word "Papa."

RUBY: Ruby stands, head bowed, silently mouths the word "Papa."

RICHARD: Richard turns, stares first at Ruth and then at Ruby. He points at the photograph, but then causes his

pointing finger to fold back into his hand, which he
clenches now into a fist, beating same, three times . . .
against . . . his . . . hip. He relaxes. He silently mouths
the word "Mama."

RUBY: Ruby moves to Richard's chair, sits, allowing her
skirt to remain pleated open, high on her leg.

RICHARD: Richard notices her naked thigh.

RUTH: Ruth notices Richard noticing Ruby's naked thigh.

RICHARD: Richard notices that Ruth has noticed him.

RUBY: Ruby tugs her skirt down to her knee. With her left
hand, she wipes a tear from her left cheek.

RICHARD: Richard moves to the bar. He studies the bottle
of scotch whisky awhile before spilling five inches of the
liquid into a fresh glass. He turns and faces Ruth, lifts
his glass to her, then to his lips, drains it of its contents,
drinking same.

RUTH: Ruth stares, silently amazed.

RUBY: Ruby bows her head and sobs.

RICHARD: Richard walks quietly to his shoes and socks and
collects them. He sits on the sofa, center, and redresses
his feet, sitting carelessly atop his sisters' outer garments.

RUTH: Ruth watches, standing straight now.

RUBY: Ruby notices the towel on the floor next to the chair
in which she is sitting, rubs and moves same with her toe.

RICHARD: Richard looks up from tying his shoe to watch
Ruby nudging his stain with her toe. He stares disapprovingly.

RUBY: Ruby senses Richard's disapproval and stops nudging at the stain. She instead leans forward and rubs the
stain with her fingers, returning same to mouth licking
them with her tongue.

RUTH: Ruth gags.

RICHARD: Richard is disgusted, completes tying his shoes
hurriedly. He stands and tosses on his overcoat.

RUTH: Ruth takes three odd steps backwards, stiffly, stops.

RUBY: Ruby turns in her chair and stares openly at Richard.

RICHARD: Richard walks to bar, finds scotch whisky bottle,
which he raises to his lips and drains, unflinchingly.
Richard moves directly to position beneath photograph
and stares at same, lifting bottle to image of mother and
father.

RUBY: Ruby continues her stare at Richard, amazed.

RICHARD: Richard allows bottle to fall to floor near his feet. He touches photograph, precisely as he did before: man first, then woman. He then bows head, sobs.

RUTH: Ruth bows head, weeps, covering her eyes with palm of right hand.

RICHARD: Richard closes his coat fully now, lifting collar to back of his head. He discovers armband in pocket, removes it, clenching same in fist. He stares at Ruth, arm outstretched in her direction, fist pointing accusingly.

RUTH: Ruth glances up and then, suddenly, down, averting eyes from Richard's, but then looking up quickly, she stares directly into Richard's eyes.

RICHARD: He waits a moment, watching to see if she will have the strength to cross the room to him.

RUTH: Ruth moves one step toward Richard, not breaking their joined stare. But then she does. She stops. She lowers her eyes.

RUBY: Ruby stands, looks at Richard, but remains, unmoving, at the foot of her chair.

RICHARD: Richard watches Ruth a moment and then shifts his stare to Ruby.

RUBY: Ruby smiles.

RICHARD: Richard moves to door, opens same, pauses a moment, turns again into room, unclenches fist, allowing armband to drop to rug, pauses a moment, exits [*off*] never closing door.

RUBY: Ruby moves to door and closes same, leaning her back against it. She stares a moment at armband on rug.

RUTH: As does Ruth.

RUBY: Ruby moves to photograph and stares at same.

RUTH: Ruth finds shoes, slips quickly into same, moves to sofa, rapidly collecting her outer clothing.

RUBY: Ruby, suddenly realizing she might be left alone in room, moves quickly away from photograph, sees Ruth; stops, frozen.

RUTH: Ruth races to redress herself in her coat, jamming hat on to head, stockings in coat pocket.

RUBY: Ruby has her outer clothing now in her hands but realizes she is too late.

RUTH: Ruth has moved quickly and successfully, assuming an exit position at the door, coat buttoned closed.

RUBY: Ruby is stunned and allows her outer clothing to drop back down on to the sofa.

RUTH: Ruth smiles, touches doorknob.

RUBY: Ruby leans over sofa, her back to Ruth.

RUTH: Ruth stares at Ruby's youthful body, her thighs, her straight back, her rich girl's shoulders.

RUBY: Ruby lifts her face, but cannot turn to Ruth.

RUTH: Ruth glances at photograph, but cannot sustain look at same. She straightens her back, inhales, quietly opens door, exhales. She glances a final glance at Ruby. Exits.

RUBY: Ruby hears the door . . .

RUTH: [*Off*] Click . . .

RUBY: . . . finally closed. She turns quickly. Certain now that Ruth has exited, Ruby stands frozen, sad-eyed, staring at the still closed door. She moves to bar and finds glass decanter on it, which she holds a moment before suddenly smashing same on bar. After shock of glass breaking, there is silence in the room. Ruby moves again to photograph, carrying jagged neck of glass decanter with her; considers destroying photograph, but instead softly caresses same with palm of right hand, touching first the image of man, then image of woman, and then again image of man. She moves to sofa, still carrying jagged remains of decanter with her. She thinks to sit but does not, instead turns, faces photograph, fully. Leaning forward over sofa, Ruby allows the weight of her body against the final point of the glass, causing the remains of the decanter to enter her body just below the breast. She turns away from photograph, faces front, allows her body to relax onto sofa. Her hand unclenches. The jagged remains of the decanter fall. Blood drops from hand, staining rug. Ruby faces front, pauses a moment. She opens her mouth, screams, but there is no sound.

[*The lights fade to black.*]

THE PLAY IS OVER.

Waltham, Milwaukee, New York—1975–1977.

The Wakefield Plays, Part VII

SPARED
A Play in One Act

For Lenny Baker.

The People of the Play

MAN: Ancient.

The Place of the Play

Outdoors; near Lake Quannapowitt; Wakefield, Massachusetts.

The Time of the Play

The present.

Note to Director

Voices on tape to be prerecorded by the actor, using high-pitched voice. Laughter and scream both sustained, breathy. Words to be recorded once only, spliced together and repeated *without pause*. Frequency as noted in text.

When actor imitates mother's words, scream, and laugh, imitation must reveal taped voice as his.

Four distinct voices must be developed for performance: old man's narrative voice, harsh, deep, cynical; young man's sincere voice; boy's innocent voice; and gangsterish rather comic voice. These voices should work as warring contraries whenever possible, within sections, even within sentences and phrases. Thus, whenever MAN seems to contradict himself, correct himself, contrary voices need be chosen to personalize conflict.

Dependent on size of theater, platform should be built of the maximum possible height to hold actor's face within sightlines, but to create sense of maximum distance from audience floor. Two instruments for lighting: one straight above, straight down; the second slightly above the first, focused on center of actor's face. Thus, channel of light created to allow actor to lean forward to audience during

more intimate moments. Lights must be low-level, soft
glow, no edges, focused evenly so that no lighting changes
occur with actor's forward movement.

Sense of infinite blackness and space, all around.

If house curtain is used, lights to be preset for start of
play, switched off after gunshot, faded in softly after opening monologue, and left on throughout rest of play. House
curtain can close to end play.

Recommend, however, that final cue be slow fadeout of
lights to blackness, as afterimage in dark useful.

Opening moments of play to be musical images, *not*
slowed in tempo for recognition of narrative. Closing moments opposite.

Auditorium dark. Silence.

*Curtain. Lights to soft glow, revealing man suspended in
space considerably higher than audience level of auditorium. He has a pistol pressed to his temple.*

*But for soft glow, there is darkness and infinite space all
around.*

*Man squints into glow, is at first silent, but then awakens
and speaks.*

MAN: [*Points to pistol pressed to temple: speaks clearly.*]
    I have tried to destroy myself more than sixty different
    times. [*Pulls trigger. Click. No gunshot. He shrugs.*] Al-
    ways spared. [*He lowers gun at his side now. Pulls
    trigger. Blam! Gunshot. Man is amazed. Blackout. Audi-
    torium and stage in darkness. Man's voice heard, high-
    pitched, manic. Speaks rapidly, almost unintelligibly at
    first: A tiny child's singsong voice.*] Five, the first time.
    Didn't know why. Children happy. Laughter all around.
    Me outside. [*Pauses.*] Father then moving. Mother all
    ears. Hugs abundant. Talk endless. Food, as talk. Sister,
    wide-eyed, adoring. Didn't know why. [*Pauses.*] Knife
    on table, eyebrow-high. Watched it, tiptoe. Sounds all
    empty. Colors mute. Smells to rancid. Tiny chest thump-

ing. [*Pauses.*] Curled in fingers. Sounds, colors, smells, all gone. [*Pauses.*] Point pricked, no pain. Full thrust, no blood. Eyes clenched, no scream.

VOICE: [*Speaker No. 1*] Poor child.

VOICE: [*Speaker No. 2*] Poor child.

VOICE: [*Speaker No. 3*] Poor child.

VOICE: [*Speaker No. 4*] Poor child.

VOICE: [*Speaker No. 5*] Poor child.

VOICE: [*Speaker No. 6: shrill scream*]

[*Lights restore to soft glow. Man wears white shirt, enormously outsized pinstriped suit, fat necktie. He stiffens, squints. His arms are outstretched, dangling down into darkness. Legs same, feet over edge of playing platform. Sense that chair and man are suspended in space, floating, is wanted. Voice changes in age, dependent on text. Amplification needed. Speakers surround audience, placed in six positions: one in corner of auditorium, one above audience, one in darkness above man's head. Interruptions marked "Voice" are taped by man, but sound womanly, always kindly and sympathetic. When "shrill scream" called for, sound should again be produced by taped voice of man, but for this occasion childlike scream is wanted: shrill, sustained, anguished, breathless only after count of ten. Accent, if distinguishable, Boston. Man's face unflinchingly confident: head rarely bowed. He looks up and realizes audience is watching him. He smiles and speaks.*]

MAN: Fifteen, the second. Thanksgiving Thursday. Aunts scrubbing, cigar smoke uncles. Fat Charlotte, the cousin, all green and sick.

VOICE: [*Speaker No. 1*] Poor child.

MAN: Skeleton turkey, once dead, now eaten. Laughter all around. [*Pauses.*] Three uncles, back from fishing. Cracked the early ice. Three pickerel. [*Voice to harsh*] Easy catch. Frozen solid. In the surface. Eyes open. Still stiff. Mouths open. Still, as well. Caught together. Near the top. Chipped free. Grave to grave. [*Voice to innocent, young again*] Watched them thaw. Early evening. Never thinking. Eye to eye. [*Pauses.*] Turkey carcass, winter treasure. All still. No scream. [*Pauses.*] Apple-bobbing. All cousins. Heads plunged, eyes clenched, mouths plugged, stuffed, reward. Me, outside. Ever-wondering, still, unspeaking. [*Pause.*] Stood in archway, top curved, me tall, head bowed. All eyes on me, pull me in, push me under, no control, all gone. [*Pauses.*] No ice, no flow, easy now, do nothing. Eyes open. Life to play? [*His voice suddenly shifts to experienced voice.*] All lies! Only apples bobbing by! No breath, no sound, no voice, no scream.

[*Note: Man will hear voices that follow now and be frightened by them. He will recognize same as his own.*]

voice: [*Speaker No. 1*] Poor child.

voice: [*Speaker No. 2*] Poor child.

voice: [*Speaker No. 3*] Poor child. [*Sound reverberates.*]

voice: [*Speaker Nos. 4 and 5: sustained shrill scream*]

MAN: Four years slid. Women now. All in that . . . what's the word? Chokes me still. All in . . . [*Chokes three times, L-sound, sudden return to young voice.*] All in love. Silent then. Not a sound. Eyes all voice. Never closed. Not a blink. Ears a team. Never clogged. Girls all blab. Heard them come, watched them go. Countless thrills: Well . . . fifty-nine. Love her even now. What's her name? Not to worry. Love her still. WHAT'S HER NAME?

voices: [*Speakers Nos. 3 and 5*] Poor child.

voices: [*Speakers Nos. 4 and 6*] Poor child.

MAN: Mary! No. Mae it was. May in June. Twelfth. I think. Two o'clock. Veteran's Field. Sun still high. Number sixty. Mae was chilled, all regret. Me still dumb, staring through. Not to worry . . . WHAT'S HER NAME?

voices: [*Speakers Nos. 1, 2, 3, 4*] Poor child. [*Sound reverberates.*]

MAN: Made a pact, Mae and me. Leap together—from the rocks. Climbed them, smiling. July the Fourth. Parade below. Independence. Father's friends as Indians, marching. John Kennedy, too. Senator then. All applause. Us, above it, bound to leap. Children laughing, balloons wound tight. Mother down there. Then still moving. Aunts and uncles, bellies full. [*Pauses.*] From our perch, we watched them watching. Silent now, our hands ungripped. [*Pauses.*] Mae edged closer, never talking. Hair was brown, her loose blouse white. [*Pause.*] Runaway balloon floating up to us, past us, then beyond. I followed with my eye. When I thought of Mae again, I was alone. She was gone. My lover leaped without me. I was spared.

VOICE: [*Speaker No. 3*] Poor child. [*Sound reverberates.*]

MAN: She was broken near a Four-H float. Not a sound. No cry, no scream.

VOICES: [*All speakers: shrill scream*]

MAN: No pact nor promise since. No hope . . .

VOICE: [*Speaker No. 1*] Poor child.

MAN: No plan . . .

VOICE: [*Speaker No. 3*] Poor child.

MAN: No desire . . .

VOICE: [*Speaker No. 5*] Poor child.

MAN: . . . No scream.

VOICE: [*Speaker No. 6: sustained scream*]

MAN: [*Voice again confident, cynical*] When I was twenty-two, I played a game called Houyhnhnm Roulette. [*Pauses.*] All cylinders of the pistol were filled, but for one. [*Pauses.*] Played the game each night for five consecutive nights. [*Pause.*] Finally, my nerves gave out. Had to stop playing. [*Pauses.*] Never been much of a good-loser. [*Pauses.*] Played another game, six months later. [*Pauses.*] A big talent scout passed through town and picked me for his television quiz show, in Boston. Boston's first. [*Pauses.*] Heartbreak. [*Pauses.*] That was the name of the show: Heartbreak. [*Pauses.*] By answering twenty obvious questions in my choice category, Romantic poetry, specifically, Blake, I won more than eighteen thousand dollars. Cash. [*Pauses.*] All of America watched me win. [*Pauses.*] Outside the studio, I was mugged four times. [*Pauses.*] Twice more at the subway. [*Pauses.*] In the parlor car on the Boston and Maine to Wakefield, the rear pockets were ripped from my trousers. [*Pauses.*] Before leaving the train, a series of Budd-liners hooked together, I was mugged and interfered with seventeen different times. [*Pauses.*] The most bizarre attempt was a sad old lady, who filled a Hefty Bag full with water and then threw it at me. While my trousers were drying, she stole them. [*Pauses.*] I was naked upon arrival in Wakefield. [*Pauses.*] The remainder of the year passed without incident. [*Pauses.*] Twenty-three. All repaired. Emily then. Our town. One son. Brown hair and eyes. Nose mine, enormous. [*Pauses.*] No. No son. Never could.

VOICES: [*Speakers Nos. 1 and 3: shrill scream.* MAN *whacks his head against padded chair back in failed attempt at suicide.*]

MAN: She stayed with me nine years. No point going on. My fault. She was . . . normal. [*Pauses.*] She left as she first came, but nine years older. Neither of us had grown taller. Nothing visibly good had sprung from it. I wonder why we tried?

VOICE: [*Speaker No. 3: female laughing*]

MAN: [*Voice normal again*] I grew narrow. [*Pauses.*] My clothes never fit again. Not ever. [*Pauses.*] During the final month of my thirty-second year, I lost more than one hundred pounds of weight. Never tried to. Did the opposite in fact. Ate like a horse. Also *ate* a horse. Cooked, of course. [*Pauses.*] I lost precisely three point three pounds per day for thirty consecutive days. No matter what I ate, I couldn't stop losing weight. [*Pauses.*] Tapeworms. Two of them. [*Pauses.*] Lucky for me they hated each other. [*Pauses.*] On the thirty-first day of the twelfth month of my thirty-second year, I lost one pound by noon and then no more. [*Pauses.*] The problems seemed to, well, *pass.* [*Pauses.*] No one knows to this day why the tapeworms attacked, nibbled at, and destroyed each other instead of me, but they did. I was spared. [*Pauses.*] Jealousy, perhaps. Maybe just hunger. [*Smiles.*] My weight has never changed again, not an ounce, not in any of the years that followed, right up until today . . . and including today. [*Pauses.*] Which is, I suppose, only to say that in all these years, I've lost . . . well . . .

VOICE: [*All speakers: female laughing*]

MAN: . . . nothing! [*Has been somewhat anxious. Changes attitude, sensing that audience has sensed his anxiety. He is now quite cool.*] During my thirty-third year, I quit all major religions. [*He looks up, suddenly frightened. He genuflects, then rocks back and forth a moment, as might an old Jew. He looks out at the audience and is once again suddenly confident. He gestures a shrug with his hand.*] Pppppppttttt! [*Pauses. Young man's voice used here.*] Thirty-four, cleaning dishes for the

Hazelwood Cottage on Main. One-fifty an hour. *Selling out.* [*Pauses.*] My first earned room. Chestnut Street, top floor right. Cold in winter, warm in summer. No pets permitted, not that I would have. [*Pauses.*] All the Hazelwood food a man might dare. A bit soggy, a trifle—well —*touched.* [*Pauses.*] Food and a room. Never happier. [*Pauses.*] Gus, the short-order German, said I had style. Brought a certain *je ne sais quoi* into the old rathole. Easy for Gus, nose dripping in the *soupe du jour.* [*Pauses.*] I said little, of course, always certain to be caught brooding. These lines in the face, even then. All that *practice!* Never saw wisdom in all that gravity— just couldn't control myself—couldn't stop squinting. Reading books again. [*Pauses.*] My room was perfect to me. Amazing sun in the morning. Sunsets through the window by the stove. [*Pauses.*] Why do I remember all the kitchens of my life? [*Pauses.*] Nancy was the first to visit there. Beautiful thing. Nancy. Long, straight hair, dark brown. Wonderful legs: thick and tight with muscles from her walks. [*Pauses, voice changes to old age.*] Wonderful leg, I should say. I never actually saw both of them together. Within one . . . viewing. [*Pauses.*] I never actually saw her walk, either. [*Pauses, voice younger.*] I'm sure she must have. How else could she have gotten into my room? [*Pauses.*] She had one leg or the other bundled in a quilt most of the time. Maybe *all* of the time. Certainly *most* of the time. *All* of the time *I* was nearby, which is, strictly speaking, *most* of the time. [*Pauses.*] There was *some*thing going on under the quilt. [*Pauses.*] I keep my distance. [*Pauses.*] Warmed her belly with pots of Lapsang Souchong tea I'd read in Boswell, bought in Boston. [*Pauses.*] She loved me for every ounce of it. [*Pauses.*] We had a gentle time at first. A lot of reading. Blake: all of *Jerusalem.* Me, in my orange bathrobe, in the easy chair, reclining. [*Pauses.*] I never liked sitting much then. Standing either: I especially avoided standing. The recline suited me best. [*Pauses.*] The less said about Nancy's body, the better. [*Pauses.*] My Hazelwood days were numbered from the moment I reflected upon the stack. I counted: three hundred dishes, two hundred cups, the same in saucers, and, roughly, countless spoons. [*Pauses.*] I couldn't. I didn't. [*Pauses.*] "Gus,"

I said, "I've got the dread disease." "Gott bless you," he belched. [*Pauses.*] I left immediately. He'd never asked me *which* disease. [*Pauses.*] He trusted me, old Gus. God bless him. [*Pauses.*] She stuck it out with me five months, until the money ran out. First hers, then mine. [*Pauses.*] Hers actually ran out just before I'd met her. Which is to say, just before I found her in my room. [*Pauses.*] That's not quite the case, either. [*Pauses.*] I found the room with Nancy in it. It was a furnished place: easy chair, Murphy bed, naturally, table, silverware and dishes, the usual, plus a plump book of verse, quilt, and, of course Nancy, herself. [*Pauses.*] She said she'd worked the year before in the B.P.L. [*Pauses.*] I believed her. [*Pauses.*] A woman wouldn't lie about working in a library. [*Pauses.*] We kept our little idyll, as they say, *up*, until my ignominious parting from Hazelwood and money. [*Pauses.*] Her note said she'd found work in England. [*Pauses.*] I must not have wanted to follow her, because I didn't. [*Pauses.*] I wonder. [*Pauses.*] In all that time together, we never once raised our voices in anger or regret.

VOICES: [*All speakers: female laughing*]

MAN: Actually, we never much raised our voices at all. I don't really remember much talk beyond the reading. *Jerusalem.* [*Pauses.*] I never warmed to the didactical *or* the symbolical. [*Pauses.*] Thirty-six. Changed rooms. Alone again. Took a smaller one, top floor, down on West Water. Cheaper. [*Pauses.*] Not the only reason. [*Pauses.*] Couldn't stop finding *her* in the old room. Bits and scraps: nothing solid. I mean, nothing like the original find of the quilt and, of course, Nancy herself. A bobby-pin once, dozens of emery boards, a plump book of verse. [*Pauses.*] The painful letter was in it. Tucked. [*Pauses.*] "Dear Nancy. I copied your name and address from your notebook cover. I hope you don't find it too forward (sic) of me, but I found you to be so lovely. I have to try. Would you see me? Perhaps a film together?" [*Pauses.*] His address next, then his telephone, then his name: Blake. [*Pauses.*] What was the honorable thing to do? [*Pauses.*] I telephoned the pompous son-of-a-bitch during the middle of each successive night for thirty consecutive nights. Woke him up. Gave him some-

thing to think about. [*Pauses.*] I never spoke, of course.
[*Pauses.*] He sounded lonely, our Mr. Blake. Jim. He
sounded lonely. Always home when I called. Probably
firing off his letters. [*Pauses.*] I wrote to him in March,
asking for a meeting. Signed a woman's name—Aphra
Behn. I thought it might be nice to have a look. Waited
nearly an hour. He didn't show. [*Pauses.*] Burned the
letter, finally. Nothing solid. Nothing to keep, certainly
not to lug around. [*Pauses.*] I moved. Forty. Went with
Evelyn to Utah. Her people were there. Born there and
stayed. Three generations of them. [*Pauses.*] Not Evelyn.
She was spunky. Met her at Hazelwood, where she
dunked and downed her morning cruller, daily. She'd
come East for money. Worked at the copy-center, Lakeside Office Park. [*Pauses.*] Evelyn was quite something.
Straight back. Rich girl's shoulders. Fantastically limber
legs: two of them. [*Pauses.*] She talked me into the trip
westward *à la puriste*. She'd wanted us to walk to Utah,
but once I'd remembered that walking trips were all the
rage among romantic poets, I had to pass. [*Pauses.*] We
settled on a covered wagon and two donkeys: a lament-
able choice in every way imaginable. [*Pauses.*] Less than
one hundred miles from Wakefield, we discovered our
donkeys were sexually opposed, which is to say, a man
and a woman. [*Pauses.*] They were shameless, even as
donkeys go. [*Pauses.*] We stopped for ten minutes out
of every hour, so "Get Off the Rug" and "You Too" could
have their goes. . . . [*Pauses.*] Those were their names:
"Get Off the Rug" and "You Too." Evelyn had quite a
gift for the odd moniker. [*Pauses.*] Had to arrange for
an illegal abortion for "Get Off the Rug" in Kansas.
[*Pauses.*] At the Utah border a band of hostile Mormons
attacked and shot the poor dumb ass herself. Killed her
as well. [*Pauses.*] "You Too" was desolate upon arrival
at the Great Salt Lake. [*Pauses.*] Once there, Evelyn was
somewhat anxious: frightened of how her folks would
take to me. Baptists, they were. I reminded her that I'd
grown up with Baptists on all sides. Wakefield was a
hotbed of Baptist thought. [*Pauses.*] She warned me
about the Grace ritual . . . not to take down any of their
food without thanking God first. [*Pauses.*] I hated her
for telling me that. [*Pauses.*] Her old man gave me a

brandy and water. I blessed it. "Dear Lord, bless this
brandy-and-water and cause it to bring peace into this
strange land." Then I sang "Rock of Ages." A half-hour
later, I prayed over her mother's clam dip and Fritos,
and then an hour later, I blessed the Puss 'n' Boots they
put out for their cats. [*Pauses.*] Dinner went down without
so much as a nod to God. [*Pauses.*] Left Utah, but stayed
West. Forty-three, talking more than ever. Not saying
much, but speaking well. Easterners grow ten times more
learned west of the Mississippi. [*Pauses.*] Found Los Angeles, and a job. Names from my childhood, to my
amazement, here and well known. Mine, as always, an
unheard-of thing, never pronounced as written, always
misspelled, never listened to, thus never remembered.
[*Pauses.*] One face from fifth grade appeared on my
television screen. The nose known as target of frequent
successful pickings, Warren School, thirty-seven years
before, now wrinkled, perplexed. Above serious lips,
speaking of politics and honesty. Concerned words.
[*Looks around.*] No scream? [*Pauses, voice gangsterish.*]
I never wanted a *social* life, exactly, but I had hoped
for a *life*: [*Pauses, voice again normal.*] My job was
counting. I worked for an inventory service, supermar-
kets our specialty, meat and poultry mine. [*Pauses.*] I
met Ethel there, in the counting. She worked spices.
We met in early morning, one Monday, just before absolute totals. [*Pauses.*] She was fifty, old Ethel. Amazing
tits and ass. She'd been married before. Widowed young.
Three sons not yet grown. I had my first with her. Happened so fast, I can't remember deciding to . . . [*Laughs.*]
Must have, though. [*Pauses.*] We named him Alfred,
after Ethel's father, not quite deceased, which is to say,
still alive. [*Pauses.*] He was in Chevrolets, Ethel's father.
Near a major freeway. Can't remember the name of his
place—just the brand. [*Pauses.*] He was extraordinarily
loyal. [*Pauses.*] Owned four Chevrolets: one for the
missus, one for himself, one for Ethel's retarded brother,
Alfred—oh, yes, the brother was Alfred, too. Alfred the
Third, actually. My poor Alfred was at the end of a
long—as they say—line. [*Pauses.*] Ethel got the coupe.
They were not a family of what you might call your
major-league drivers. [*Pauses.*] Ethel's father, Alfred I,

was, well, grateful. Old Alfred the grateful. He never liked me much, but he was full of shhh . . . well . . . gratitude. Ethel wasn't what you'd call much of a bargain, what with her three imbecile children and her awful malady. [*Pauses.*] Hiccups. Ethel had hiccups. Had them nearly thirty years before I met her. [*Pauses.*] It was funny at first. Cute, I suppose. A large woman, wonderful tits and ass, hiccuping through every sentence. [*Pauses.*] I learned to loathe every hic and belch. After five years, I thought of . . . well . . . destroying her. [*Pauses.*] I tried every known method of cure. Jumping out of closets was kid stuff for me and old Ethel. I once drove the coupe straight off Laurel Canyon Road. Mulholland, actually. Through the white fence and straight over the side. [*Pauses.*] I didn't do it on purpose. I was day-dreaming. Thinking of ways to end her hiccing. [*Pauses.*] Ethel figured it was just another ploy to shut her up— so she wasn't scared at all. [*Pauses.*] She didn't even believe my blood on my face. Or, afterward, this scar. [*Pauses.*] I did it. [*Pauses.*] I did. [*Pauses.*] I could not stand the hiccing . . . or worse yet, I could not stand what came between: the endless babble, the endless babble of Ethel's words. [*Pauses.*] I downshifted the coupe into second gear, pulled left into the fence, drove through, and then threw it into neutral. Ethel landed on my shoulders. I carried her on my shoulders, all the way down. Bizarre. It became a sort of St. Christopher act of self-destruction. [*He hiccups. Pauses: voice now as a child's.*] This purple scar on my face. That's all. [*He hiccups again. Attitude changes again.*]

VOICES: [*Speakers Nos. 2 and 4*] Poor child.

VOICES: [*Speakers Nos. 3 and 5*] Poor child.

[MAN *begins to attempt suicide by choking himself and then whacking his head violently against back of his chair and then choking himself again. When he fails again to die, he will simply shrug.*]

MAN: We divorced immediately. I took nothing, she took the rest. [*Pauses.*] Most of all, old Alfred hated me for wrecking his car. [*Pauses.*] At the airport, all alone. No sound . . .

VOICES: [*All speakers*] Poor child . . .

MAN: . . . no voice . . .

VOICES: [*All speakers*] Poor child . . .

MAN: . . . no scream.

VOICES: [*All speakers: sharp shrill scream*]

MAN: [*Voice old again.*] East, again. The Big Apple. Got
a job selling life insurance. Twenty-payment life my
specialty. Made a fortune. Bought a car: a Ford. [*Pauses.*]
Thirty-five thousand miles the first year and never left
New York for one of them. [*Pauses.*] Just as many dollars
as miles that year and no end in sight. [*Pauses.*] Never
happier. [*Pauses.*] Sold an Executive Planner Policy,
Tarrytown, Tuesday, May eighth. Two hundred fifty
thousand, face value. Borrow cash value, increasing term
rider: very neat. [*Pauses, voice younger.*] Can't remember the street. Wooded, dark. [*Pauses.*] When I got back
to my Ford LTD, there was a small Oriental man in the
back seat. Saying nothing. Worse: not speaking. I asked
him to leave. He wouldn't answer. [*Pauses.*] I asked him
his name. He wouldn't answer. [*Pauses, bows, and
smiles.*] Sobbing, I did what a man in my position had
to do: I handed my keys to him and left the car. He
drove away! [*Pauses, bows, smiles inscrutably, as an
Oriental. He pantomimes driving away in car.*] Good car,
the LTD. [*Pauses, voice old again. Very confident.*] Fifty-
six and back in Boston. Marlborough Street, just before
Kenmore. [*Pauses.*] Old ground. [*Pauses.*] Very confident.
[*Pauses.*] Sold the old policy again out of an office in
Chestnut Hill over Stop and Shop. Very seedy, com-
pared to my old Gramercy Park operation. [*Pauses.*]
Millionaires' club in six months and more than forty
thousand for me, after taxes. [*Pauses.*] Never happier.
[*Pauses.*] Couldn't be. [*Pauses.*] It became more than a
job for me, really. Selling the twenty-payment became
. . . well . . . a mission. [*Pauses.*] Most of my clients
actually died. That doesn't *sound* astonishing, but it was.
Of the hundred and twelve Metropolitan men in my
ordinary district, I was the only one who actually had
a client die. [*Pauses.*] My rate was three a week. [*Pauses.*]
No one who knew my reputation would ever buy a
policy from me. [*Pauses.*] I had to watch my step. I
changed my name several times. Most men my age would
be squeamish about changing names—that late in the
game and all. Didn't bother me at all. Still doesn't.

[*Pauses.*] It did present some minor problems now and again. When I delivered the widow's-money, I'd often have to do a bit of research to find out exactly who I was at the time of the sale. [*Pauses.*] It was also difficult when I sold to family. But those who bought died and the problem came to a natural conclusion. [*Pauses.*] I sold to everyone in my family, parents included. [*Pauses.*] Eventually, by the age of sixty-one, I'd come into a great deal of money. Quite an embarrassment for a man of my years. [*Pauses.*] Three and a half million, precisely. [*Pauses.*] No friends. No time. [*Pauses.*] No family, of course. [*Pauses.*] No complaints from me . . . no time. [*Pauses.*] No scream.

voices: [*Speakers Nos. 1 and 2*] Poor child.

voices: [*Speakers Nos. 3 and 4*] Poor child.

voices: [*Speakers Nos. 5 and 6*] Poor child.

voices: [*All speakers: sharp shrill scream.*]

[MAN *grabs necktie as a noose and tries to strangle himself. He fails. He shrugs.*]

MAN: [*Pauses: tone brightens, straightens tie.*] When I first spoke—first learned—I was very close with people. In the beginning. [*Pauses.*] I asked him, my father, why I was born: what purpose he'd had in mind for me. [*Pauses.*] He slapped me. [*Pauses.*] I asked my mother. She told me to ask my father. I never brought the question up again. No need. No purpose to it. No scream. I began trying then. [*Pauses.*] I've tried . . . to destroy myself . . . more than sixty different times. [*Suddenly, he tries to choke himself, fails, shrugs to audience, in disgust.*] Always spared. [*Pauses. Voice old again, confident.*] When I was four-foot-two, I swallowed a bottle of pills. My mistake, vitamins: E and B-twelve. [*Pauses.*] I grew a foot in seven months, which is to say, I became twelve inches taller. [*Pauses.*] That next year, at five-foot-two, I hurled myself into Lake Quannapowitt. The water was four-foot-two. I was a year late. [*Pauses.*] Caught an awful head cold. [*Pauses.*] The next year I tried fire. [*Pauses.*] Burned all the woods by the West Ward School. [*Pauses.*] Nearly got the little red prison itself. [*Pauses.*] The tree I'd tied myself to was the only one left intact. [*Pauses.*] Horse-chestnut tree. [*Pauses.*] The firemen found me. Bound to it. [*Pauses.*] They

wouldn't believe me when I said I'd tied myself. [*Pauses.*]
Neither did the police. [*Pauses.*] Neither did the Wakefield Daily *Item* or the Boston *Post* or *Traveler.* [*Pauses.*]
Once the rock of scandal rolls out of control, logic and
truth present no worthy obstacle. [*Pauses.*] Tried that
too. [*Pauses.*] Tied myself to an enormous boulder and
tried to roll the West Ward hill. [*Pauses.*] Never got the
stone out of the mud. [*Pauses.*] Ropes held them too.
Didn't surprise me any when all papers, local and national, passed the second story by. [*Pauses.*] Spent one
whole night lying tied in front of a parked Sears and
Roebuck trailer-truck. Driver finally came out in the
morning. Backed up. [*Pauses.*] He couldn't imagine who
had tied up a kid in front of his truck. He would have
called the papers except he didn't much care to have
the world know where he'd spent the night. [*Pauses.*]
Me neither. [*Pauses.*] No regrets now. Not really. [*Pauses.*]
The next year, on March thirty-first, my birthday, I tied
myself to the train track, northbound side. [*Pauses.*]
Twenty-two hours, freezing all night, sweating all day.
[*Pauses.*] The Boston and Maine was on strike. Fare in-
crease threat. Trains didn't run again for six weeks.
[*Pauses.*] Took me the full twenty-two hours to get my
hands free. [*Pauses.*] Opened the knots, finally, midday,
April first. [*Voice to old.*] April Fool's Day. Never
stopped trying. [*Voice to young.*] Simply never, well,
succeeded. [*Pauses.*] Hardly failed. Money, children,
wives, travel, books, several foreign tongues. God *knows*
I've still got my health. [*Pauses.*] I'm an international
ideal. [*Pauses, voice of gangster's.*] Sixty-two and my reputation'd spread beyond repair. I couldn't have sold a
policy to a dying man—*especially* a dying man. [*Pauses,
voice to old.*] Kiss of death. [*Pauses.*] That's what they
called me; kiss of death. Benjy was the first. At an
awards dinner in Boston. The district agent was handing
me my twenty-eighth medal for excellence. He was
searching for an adjective, I suppose. From the audience,
down below, Benjy's voice came booming up: [*Squeaky
voice here*] "Kiss of death! That's what the ghoulish son
of a bitch is: kiss of death!" [*Voice to normal*] The
audience laughed first. Then they clapped. Everybody
knew me. I was a legend all over the country. [*Pauses.*]

Kiss of death. [*Pauses.*] I worked another six months after that, but once a problem has a label that's easy to remember, it's instantly solved, or incurable. [*Pauses.*] Mine was incurable. Everybody knew who I was—and now—*what* I was. [*Pauses.*] No point in going on with it. [*Pauses.*] None. [*Pauses.*] I missed a few. I missed a couple I'd like to have sold. [*Pauses.*] Benjy. I'd pay his premiums myself. Over now. What's the point? [*Pauses, voice to gangster's.*] When I was sixty-four, I met a twenty-three-year-old girl who said she loved me. [*Pauses, voice to old.*] Sixty-five, I moved out here. The house is small, quiet. Just me and a Cairn terrier. [*Pauses, looks around his feet for dog.*] Never knew an animal to be so faithful. Always with me. Wakes when I wake, sleeps when I sleep, eats when I eat. Walks with me. Watches me constantly. [*Pauses.*] I do nothing to deserve such handsome treatment. He certainly doesn't know I'm wealthy. I mean, he can't be in it for the money. [*Pauses. Suddenly shocked, remembers dog is dead.*] Gone now. Hit twice by a Chevrolet. Once wasn't enough. The old lunatic had to back up to see what he'd done. [*Pauses.*] I'd like to think Murphy didn't know what hit him. He did. He knew. [*Pauses.*] Took him sixty-eight days to die. [*Pauses.*] One day for every year. [*Pauses.*] Sixty-eight now. Me. [*Pauses, voice now childlike again, innocent.*] All that time dying. Not fair.

VOICES: [*All speakers*] Poor child. [*Laugh, scream.*]

MAN: [*Voice now old*] During my sixty-fifth year I survived eight known incurable diseases. [*Pauses.*] The most bizarre was called "la Maladie Charcot." [*Pauses.*] The first hint came on March thirty-first, the first day of my first Medicare year. [*Pauses. He struggles with sneaker and succeeds finally in removing it from foot.*] The big toe on my left foot went numb. I wouldn't have known, but for the way I tend my toenails. I've always used that very toe as my barometer. [*Pauses.*] When the nail of my left-hand big toe reaches the innermost point of my left-hand shoe, I clip them all. [*Pauses, makes spitting sound.*] Pttttttttt. . . . [*Sentimental again.*] I was given then to Adidas sneakers, the all-white variety. [*Holds up sneaker next to his face as product in television commercial. Pauses.*] Wore them twenty-four hours a

day. Simultaneously, I was rarely given to cleaning my
toenails, except during manicure. Which is to say *pedi-
cure*. On Tuesday, March thirty-first, at two-thirty P.M.,
precisely, I kicked my alarm clock [*Pauses.*] and heard
the most peculiar sound, like the sound of a toenail strik-
ing a plastic clockface. [*Pauses.*] My left-hand toenail
had poked through my left white Adidas sneaker. I had
heard the sound, but felt nothing. Although the nail was
in every way tip-top, the toe was dead. [*Pauses.*] What
faced me was the dread disease. [*Pauses, removes sock.*]
Thirty days later, the last in April, my left foot was
dead to the knee. By the end of May, my entire leg to
my chest. The whole right leg joined in one fantastic
overnight freeze, in July. By the start of September, I
could do no more than blink my left eyelid for "yes"
and my right eyelid for "no." [*Pauses, winks left eyelid
first, then right.*] Rather flirtatious messages for a man
in my condition. [*Pauses.*] My young doctor, Johnson,
attempted euthanasia. And succeeded. [*To audience.*]
Not me. The hag across the hall. [*Pauses.*] He injected
air into an artery—at least, that's what the paper said.
He was found innocent, of course, and quickly. [*Pauses.*]
On September thirtieth, the last, he bent over as if to
hear my breath. [*Pauses.*] "Do you want a shot?" I
blinked my left lid. [*Pauses, to see if audience remembers
code.*] As soon as the air hit my brain, all limbs un-
locked. [*Pauses.*] Without malice of forethought my el-
bow joint constricted, causing my fingers to clench into
a fist, causing, in Dr. Johnson's groin, a hernia of almost
landmark proportions. [*Pauses.*] When the dust, as they
say, settled, Johnson was unconscious, and every muscle
in my entire body was absolutely functional, except for
those controlling the lids to my left and right eyes.
[*Pauses.*] To this day, I don't blink. I can *force* a blink,
but the normal, everyday state of my eyes is . . . wide
open. [*Pauses.*] The other diseases are hardly worth a
mention. [*Pauses, voice is younger.*] If I could have been
a cucumber.
[*Note: Actor will supply own fresh word here for each
performance. Ex. "If I could have been a "grapefruit."
Also, "Cookie . . ." Or "Cupcake . . ." Chosen word
should not be repeated during run of play. I.H.*]

MAN: [*Pauses, voice returns to normal age.*] Benjy reappeared not more than a year ago. He'd aged; been awfully sick. [*Pauses.*] He wanted me to sell him a policy. I don't know how the hell he found me all the way up here but he did. My reputation, probably. [*Pauses.*] *He* should have known. [*Pauses.*] He named it. [*Pauses.*] I could have. But now that he *wanted* one, I couldn't. To tell you the truth, I was pleased to see his old face. Not that we'd ever actually drunk together, let alone talked. Still and all, there was a face there I'd seen before. And a name with it. [*Pauses.*] I asked him to stay. He did. Three months. Stayed in the back bedroom. Didn't stray out from it much. Stayed in bed, I guess. [*Pauses.*] That's where I found him. Buried him myself out in back. [*Pauses.*] Wasn't much of a talker, Benjy. Never was. Never will be. [*Pauses.*] The thing about Benjy that intrigued me was his height. He had almost none. Couldn't have been more than three-nine, maybe three-ten. [*Pauses.*] Benjy's problem in the insurance game was doorbells. [*Pauses.*] Winters too. Snowbanks. It's hard to imagine what it would feel like to sink in up to your eyes. [*Pauses.*] He had a big heart, Benjy. Never saw a little woman-chaser like that before. He had a lot of style, especially with the tall ones. They used to mother him. [*Pauses.*] Sixty years old and he'd ask 'em if he could sit on their laps. So he could hear better. [*Pauses.*] They loved it. [*Pauses.*] He carried a big knife, Benjy. [*Pauses.*] People used to like to hurt him. Never saw anything like it. I hated to walk on the street with him. People used to come up, out of nowhere, and pinch his cheeks, or poke his arm. [*Pauses.*] "How'd you get so little, fella? Didn'tcha drink your milk?" [*Pauses.*] Then he'd show them his big knife. They moved on. Nobody really liked the sight of a little man with such a big knife. [*Pauses.*] "Kiss of death," he called me. [*Pauses.*] I did. [*Bows head.*] I did it. [*Pauses, voice now young.*] So small. Everything born, dies. Once you see the thing itself, you can't pretend. [*Pauses.*] I never had a son. How could I? [*Pauses.*] Over the years, I lost track of what was real and what was imagined. The distinctions between the two became . . . unimportant. Style was another matter. [*Pauses.*] I'd hoped to tell it well. The beginning was . . .

well . . . not bad. [*Pauses.*] I wish it might have continued that way. Oh, I suffered. But no more, no less,
than . . . well . . . him. He was my father and, as such,
naturally, got to the best and worst of it *before* I could.
But no more, no less, really. [*Pauses.*] It's all the same.

VOICES: [*All speakers: shrill scream*]

MAN: [*Suddenly whacks himself on head with Adidas
sneaker several times in still another suicide attempt. He
fails to die. In shrugged disgust, he throws sneakers
away. He suddenly realizes that he is high on platform
in space and that sneaker is out of reach, low, on ground:
gone. Pauses, voice again old.*] Two days ago, all my
things were stolen. Everything I owned, gone. [*Pauses.*]
Caruso. The handyman. He did it. [*Pauses.*] I knew right
away. He was the one to tell me about the first break-in.
He was shaking. [*Pauses.*] I came home. He was there,
in my living room, with his wife. [*Pauses.*] Bald. [*Pauses.*]
His wife. Erica. Stone bald. [*Pauses.*] She was standing
behind him, with mannish, muscular arms folded across
her enormous décolletage. Quite a contradiction to con-
sider, this union of Caruso and Erica. [*Pauses.*] Caruso
was shaking. He couldn't look at me. His eyes always
kept darting about the room. He couldn't look at me.
[*Pauses.*] The window shutters were whacking and
thumping—the way they do in Yugoslavian movies.
[*Pauses.*] The sofa was gone. So was the chaise lounge,
the desk, the desk chair, the bookcases, and all books
but for a plump book of verse. [*Pauses.*] Caruso was
sweating. "You've been robbed," he said. Then she
punched his arm. They looked deeply into each other's
eyes. Then they either kissed or talked intimately: I
couldn't be sure in that surprisingly inferior lighting.
Then she sang an awful aria in that horrid coloratura
soprano voice of hers. She punched his arm again, they
laughed and left. Later, I noticed that all my lamps had
left as well. [*Pauses.*] The next night, all bric-a-brac;
rugs and carpets, occasional tables, long tables, three end
tables, new, by Drexel. Paintings by all prominent land-
scapists, trash-can and ash-can Americans, and by God,
an early Lipchitz. [*Pauses.*] Four Van Velde lithographs.
Etchings by Baskin, Robbins, Wells, Rich and Green,
Lestrille's famous gouaches, obscure Amy Vanderbilt dé-

coupage, old lady watercolors. Copious aquatints. Frames
for everything mentioned, except the Lipchitz, which
was, of course, a large bulbous statue. [*Pauses.*] No mirrors. Never. Not ever. No need. [*Pauses.*] Insurance trophies—hundreds of them. Some gold, some silver, some copper, some bronze, and a slew in lucite. All
gone. [*Pauses.*] I needn't mention the appliances or every
shred of identity—passport and driver's license, birth
certificate and childhood locks of hair. All gone. [*Pauses.*]
Every scrap moved from its natural place. All order
broken. All gone. [*Pauses.*] Sixty-eight years of careful
accumulation, moved in a mere twenty-one days.
[*Pauses.*] The rhythm boggles the brain. [*Pauses.*] Caruso
and Erica. [*Pauses.*] They must have been obsessed.

voices: [*All speakers: female laugh*]

MAN: By the night of the tenth day, there was nothing left
in the house but my bed and this small revolver, thirty-
two caliber. [*Pauses.*] This morning, shortly after I woke,
Caruso and Erica took my bed. They said nothing. They
simply walked into my room and *she* took it. [*Pauses.*]
I gave up trying to reason with them, days ago. I don't
think Caruso would steal from me if he weren't pushed
to it—by her—the bald wife. [*Pauses.*] I can only guess
at what time the bed left. I haven't had a clock in any
form for more than a week. Ten-thirty, maybe eleven.
At noon or half past twelve, Caruso came into the bedroom, where I was . . . sitting. He still had trouble
looking at me. "Somebody took your bed," he said. I
spat at him. [*He spits.*] He said it again. [*He spits again.*]
"Somebody took your bed." [*Pause.*] He was crying when
she came in. They carried me out of my house and left
me there, at the trellis. I heard them bolt the door
locked, from the inside. [*Pauses.*] The gun was in my
pants pocket. [*Pauses.*] There was no reasoning with
them. [*Pauses.*] I said I was sorry. God only knows what
it was I did. They didn't care. [*Pauses.*] I tried again.
[*Pauses.*] No sense to it. Point pressed into chest. Inside
thumping up to it. Finger still fighting, after all. [*Pauses.*]
Waited for life to pass in front of eyes. Legend faulty.
Never did. [*Pauses.*] Four years old. Woke all shivers.
Mid-July. Nearing dawn. [*Pauses.*] Before me, I stood.
I and my father. Face to face. [*Pauses: voice to old*

again.] Both sixty-eight, both spoiled, both exactly as I
am before you now. I and my father. Face to face. We
touched. [*Pauses, voice again normal.*] Eyes again open.
Mother there. Then still moving. I: all words. [*Pauses,
voice child's.*] "Kiss me, Mama. Hold me gentle." [*Pauses.*]
Down she smiled. "Poor child," she said. [*Note: "Poor
child" exactly as on tape. Pauses, voice young.*] I then
screamed, so shrill and sudden, all sound stopped, all
colors bled. [*Turns away: screams exactly as on tape.*]
Mother's pity joined my scream. Those two sounds would
never leave me. Those and all other sounds would only
float momentarily away. All sounds floating to and from
me, at will, their will, not mine. [*Pauses.*] I could not
continue to hear my returning ignorancies without end.
Voice without end. Sound without end. No pardon. No
amen. No matter how I tried, I could not end it. [*Pauses.
Note: Laughs exactly as on tape.*] Trying since beginning. Five, the first time. Didn't know why. Children
happy. Laughter all around. Me outside. [*Pauses.*] Father
then moving. Mother all ears. Hugs abundant. Talk endless. Food, as talk. Sister, wide-eyed, adoring. Didn't
know why. Gun in pocket, eyes open. Felt the weight of
it. Pushed it in as if to stab. [*Pauses.*] Sounds all empty.
Colors mute. Smells to rancid. Tiny chest thumping.
[*Pauses.*] Lump pricked through. No pain. Full thrust,
no blood. Eyes clenched, no scream. [*Pauses.*] Always
spared. [*Pauses, voice gangster's.*] Spared. [*Pauses, voice
child's.*] Spared. [*Pauses, voice hushed, a whisper.*]
Spared.

VOICES: [*All speakers, a whisper*] Spared.
[*Lights fade to black.*]

THE PLAY IS OVER.

New York, Los Angeles, Waverly (Iowa), Marigot
(St. Martin, F.W.I.), Paris, Hanover, Waltham
1973–1976.

The Wakefield Plays: Addendum

What follows is not at all a planned essay on my work, but a collection of bits and scraps of information about either the plays or their productions that should be somehow insinuated into this first edition of the full cycle of plays.

THE CYCLE

If the plays were ever to be produced as a cycle, they would occupy five theater evenings, in the order that follows:

Evening #1: *Hopscotch* and *The 75th*
Evening #2: *Alfred the Great*
Evening #3: *Our Father's Failing*
Evening #4: *Alfred Dies*
Evening #5: *Stage Directions* and *Spared*

Under certain circumstances, it might be possible to spread the plays over seven nights, separating the paired plays from their mates, and giving them independently on their own evenings.

Casting an Acting Company

It is my hope that a small acting company might service the entire cycle, with performers changing roles skillfully from play to play.

The Quannapowitt Quartet works well with five actors; The Alfred Trilogy might require seven. I should think that eight performers could perform the entire cycle, given an extraordinary director and a long rehearsal period.

The Wakefield Plays is a cycle comprised of The Quannapowitt Quartet and The Alfred Trilogy.

The Quannapowitt Quartet includes four inter-related short plays, *Hopscotch*, *The 75th*, *Stage Directions*, and *Spared*; The Alfred Trilogy includes *Alfred the Great*, *Our Father's Failing*, and *Alfred Dies*.

HOPSCOTCH

Hopscotch had its first public performance in April 1974, at the Théâtre du Centre Culturel Américain, Paris, France, by invitation of the United States State Department, in an English-language production that was directed by the author, with the following cast:

ELSA (a/k/a LORALI) .... Swoosie Kurtz
WILL (a/k/a EARL) .... Lenny Baker

Rehearsals for the French premiere of *Hopscotch* were located at the Manhattan Theatre Club, New York City, where staged readings of the play were offered to MTC subscribers.

Hopscotch was presented on a double bill with *Spared* (Part IV of The Quannapowitt Quartet and Part VII of the complete Wakefield cycle), both at the Manhattan Theatre Club and in Paris.

Subsequent to the Paris production, *Hopscotch* was joined to its proper evening-mate of The Quannapowitt Quartet, *The 75th*, and *Spared* was joined with *Stage Directions*; and *Hopscotch* was then produced in conjunction with the other quartet plays by The Aleph Company, Milwaukee, Wisconsin; by The Changing Scene, Denver, Colorado; at Yale University, New Haven, Connecticut; and by The Cape Ann Playhouse, Gloucester, Massachusetts.

In March 1978, a workshop production of *Hopscotch* was produced by the New York Shakespeare Festival, New York City, under the auspices of Joseph Papp. Woods Mackintosh designed the sets; Jennifer von Mayrhauser designed the costumes; the director was Jack Hofsiss; and the cast was as follows:

ELSA (a/k/a LORALI) .... Mary Beth Hurt
WILL (a/k/a EARL) .... John Heard

Hopscotch will be presented in a rotating repertory of the plays of The Quannapowitt Quartet, New York Shakespeare Festival, New York, during 1979.

The Group Theatre, Stockholm, Sweden, opened *Hopscotch* on July 4, 1978, for an unlimited run.

THE 75TH

The 75th was first presented in a staged reading by The Aleph Company, Milwaukee, Wisconsin, in November 1976, directed by Sharon Ott and the author, with the following cast:

AMY CHAMBERLAIN . . . . Bonnie Dillingham
ARTHUR "COOKIE" SILVERSTEIN . . . . Ollie Nash

Subsequently, *The 75th* was produced at Yale University, New Haven, Connecticut; by The Changing Scene, Denver, Colorado; by The Actors Studio, New York City; and by the Cape Ann Playhouse, Gloucester, Massachusetts.

The 75th was given a workshop production during April-May 1978 at the New York Shakespeare Festival, New York. Joseph Papp was producer; Woods Mackintosh designed the scenery; Jennifer von Mayrhauser designed the costumes; Jack Hofsiss was the director; and the cast was as follows:

AMY CHAMBERLAIN . . . . Elizabeth Wilson
ARTHUR "COOKIE" SILVERSTEIN . . . . Tom Aldredge

In June 1978, *The 75th* was adapted by its author and was taped for *Earplay*, National Educational Radio, for broadcast over five hundred affiliate stations in the United States and Canada. The producer was Howard Gelman; the director was Jack Hofsiss; and the cast was as follows:

AMY CHAMBERLAIN . . . . Rosemary Harris
ARTHUR "COOKIE" SILVERSTEIN . . . . Fritz Weaver

On July 4, 1978, *The 75th* opened at the Group Theatre, Stockholm, Sweden.

The 75th has been optioned for production, along with the other plays of The Quannapowitt Quartet, and will be presented by the New York Shakespeare Festival, New York, Joseph Papp, producer, during 1979.

ALFRED THE GREAT

The first draft of *Alfred the Great* was given an invitational reading at the American Center for Students and Artists, Boulevard Raspail, Paris, on January 11, 1972, under the direction of Henry Pillsbury.

During July and August 1972, the second draft of the play was revised and the third draft was given a public staged reading at the Eugene O'Neill Theatre Center, Waterford, Connecticut, under the auspices of the National Playwrights' Conference. It was designed by Fred Voelpel and directed by James Hammerstein, with the following cast:

MARGARET .... Peggy Pope
ALFRED .... Lenny Baker
WILL .... Kevin O'Conner
EMILY .... Geraldine Sherman

A fourth draft was written after the O'Neill Center reading, which was revised into a fifth draft, presented for public performance at the Pittsburgh Playhouse, Pittsburgh, Pennsylvania (first night: March 17, 1973), designed by Robert Frederico and directed by James Hammerstein.

The cast was as follows:

MARGARET .... Nancy Chesney
ALFRED .... Harry Cauley
WILL .... John Cazale
EMILY ....Carol McGroder

After the Pittsburgh Playhouse production, a sixth and final draft was completed for reading at the 1973 National Playwrights' Conference, O'Neill Theatre Center, Waterford, Connecticut, July 15–August 12, 1973. There, *Alfred the Great* was performed for the first time in conjunction with *Our Father's Failing*, Part II of the trilogy then called The Wakefield Plays. (Now that the Wakefield cycle is complete, *Our Father's Failing* is Part II of The Alfred Trilogy, Part IV of The Wakefield Plays.)

The first public performance of the final draft of *Alfred the Great* was given on November 28, 1973, at the Trinity Square Theater, Providence, Rhode Island. The production was designed by Robert Soule and directed by James Hammerstein. The cast was as follows:

MARGARET .... Nancy Chesney
ALFRED .... Richard Kneeland
WILL .... George Martin
EMILY .... Naomi Thornton

The play toured to the Walnut Street Theatre, Philadelphia, and the Wilbur Theatre, Boston, still under the auspices of the Trinity Square Repertory Company, but with a changed cast. The Trinity Square Repertory Company's text was allowed production in December, 1974, at the University of Saskatchewan, Saskatoon. The author was not present.

Alfred the Great was then set aside for about three years, to allow for work on the other plays of the Wakefield cycle, but for interim readings at the Manhattan Theatre Club (with Michael Moriarty insinuated into the cast, for the first time, as ALFRED, and Diane Keaton as MARGARET, and John Cazale as WILL), and at the New Dramatists Committee, in 1976, when all three plays of the trilogy were read in repertory, with a cast featuring Joanna Miles, Michael Moriarty, Nancy Chesney, John Cazale, Dominic Chianese, and Madeleine Thornton-Sherwood, under the direction of John Dillon.

After the New Dramatists Committee readings, it was decided to put full effort into the completion of *Alfred Dies*, and, once again, *Alfred the Great* was set aside, and the acting company moved, by invitation, to The Actors Studio, West 44th Street, New York City, where *Alfred Dies* was rehearsed and performed. There was in January 1977 an allowed production at Colby College, Waterville, Maine. The author was not present.

At the conclusion of performances of *Alfred Dies*, there was a reading at The Actors Studio of *Alfred the Great*, and an agreement to produce both *Alfred the Great* and *Our Father's Failing* at the studio in the coming season was made with Carl Shaeffer, the executive director of the studio.

It was at this juncture that John Dillon left the company, because of his own father's failing health, and ultimately because of his accepting a job with the Milwaukee Repertory Company as artistic director. John Cazale left the acting company at this time, for reasons of bad health. He died of lung cancer within the year.

During December 1977–February 1978, *Alfred the Great* underwent minor changes to adjust the text to changes made in other plays of the cycle. The final version then was rehearsed and performed, in repertory with *Our Father's Failing*, at The Actors Studio, New York City. Ben Levit was the director, Paul Eads was the scenic designer, and Jennifer von Mayrhauser was the costume designer, with the following cast:

MARGARET .... Jill O'Hara
ALFRED .... Michael Moriarty
WILL .... Paul Gleason
EMILY .... Lois Markle

Real and Invented Background for Alfred the Great

The Quannapowitt Indians once inhabited the Town of Wakefield, Massachusetts. They are all presumed to be dead now, as there appear to be no known descendants, no traces, but for bogus Indians: the Wakefield Tribe of Red Men, a men's social club.

The Wakefield Red Men costume themselves as Quannapowitt Indians and march each Fourth of July in the Independence Day Parade, sponsored by Wakefield's popular West Side Social Club. Wakefield's yearly parade, during the 1950s–1970s, was reckoned to be the largest of its kind in the Commonwealth of Massachusetts.

The majority of marching Red Men played musical instruments and populated the Red Men's Band, creating music and spectacle that was clearly a favorite of Wakefield's children and a high point of the Independence Day fete.

Between the years 1956 and 1966, the population of Wakefield, Massachusetts, allegedly diminished by several thousand people. During precisely that decade, the pregnancy dropout rate among Wakefield Memorial High School's female seniors was alleged to be the lowest in the history of the Town: less than two percent.

The Marching Red Men's band was traditionally led by Wakefield Memorial High School's drum majorettes. Red Men drummers were positioned at the rear of the band, with clarinets in the penultimate slot.

During the 1975 Independence Day Parade, the West Side Social Club itself created a parade float displaying the legend "200 YEARS AGO TODAY—THAT'S THE WAY IT WAS." A burning house was set upon the float, atop a long-bedded trailer truck. A family of Caucasian pioneers, portrayed by West Side Social Club actors, costumed for the occasion in pioneer dress, was set inside the house, play-acting life's final moments. Surrounding the trailer truck and float, on the street, were several other West Side Social Club members, costumed as Indians, armed with bows, arrows, knives, guns, and torches, play-acting the slaughter of the pioneer family and the destruction of their home.

Attendance at the 1975 Independence Day Parade was, allegedly, the highest in the history of Wakefield's annual celebrations.

The Wakefield Memorial High School's drum majorettes also costumed themselves as Quannapowitt Indians. Traditionally, they performed at high school athletic events wearing red suede dresses, beads, and feathered headdresses. Their legs and arms were stained reddish-brown with makeup. Their shoes were of the black-and-white saddle-shoe style. Wakefield Memorial High School's drum majorettes were traditionally Caucasian with traditionally Caucasoid features. One rare exception was noted in the 1950s, when a fullblooded Indian was elected to the drum majorettes' corps. She was alleged to be the stepdaughter of a local family who had been adopted from a Canadian Indian tribe. She allegedly colored her hair blond during her high school years and was not then known to be a non-Caucasian. Her Indian birth was revealed by her, later in life, when she achieved international recognition as a songwriter and performer and had, by then, allegedly, stopped coloring her hair.

(Notes written Paris, France, December, 1971. Revised, Gloucester, Massachusetts, August, 1976.)

OUR FATHER'S FAILING

Our Father's Failing had its initial exposure in staged readings at the Eugene O'Neill Memorial Centre, Waterford, Connecticut, at the National Playwrights' Conference, 1973. The readings were directed by Larry Arrick, with the following cast:

SAM .... Jay Garner
PA .... James Noble
ALFRED .... Lenny Baker
EMILY .... Carolyn Coates

Subsequently, *Our Father's Failing* had its world premiere production in March-May 1976 at the Goodman Theatre, Chicago. The director was John Dillon and the designer Stuart Wertzel, with the following cast:

SAM .... Dominic Chianese
PA .... Joseph Leon
ALFRED .... Lawrence Pressman
EMILY .... Lanna Saunders

In the next season, the play was revised and presented in readings at the New Dramatists Committee (insinuating Michael Moriarty into the cast as ALFRED and John Cazale as PA), and at The Actors Studio. There were several offers by commercial producers to present the play, isolated from The Alfred Trilogy, but it was agreed by the author and the acting company that a full effort would be given to the completion of the text to *Alfred Dies*, in a rehearsal and production period, by invitation of The Actors Studio, New York.

Our Father's Failing was thus set aside until December 1977–February 1978, when the play was presented at The Actors Studio, in repertory with *Alfred the Great*. The director was Ben Levit, the scenic designer was Paul Eads, and the costume designer was Jennifer von Mayrhauser. The cast was as follows:

SAM .... Dominic Chianese
PA .... Sully Boyar
ALFRED .... Michael Moriarty
EMILY .... Lois Markle

Real and Invented Background for
Our Father's Failing

During the years 1964-1974, there were more than two dozen major fires that destroyed buildings in Wakefield, including Castle Clare, in 1974.

In 1930, at age fifty-three, Clarence Hoag began building a castle on the topmost hill on Oak Street, Wakefield. Hoag, a printer with a small shop in Boston's Grain Exchange Building, worked on his castle, Castle Clare, nights, carrying construction materials to his site by hand, by wheelbarrow.

Castle Clare was completed in 1949, although neighborhood people had scoffed at Hoag and his project, labeling Hoag an eccentric, claiming he would never live long enough to fully complete or inhabit his castle. By 1956, it became clear that Hoag would indeed be a long liver.

According to his daughter, Jennie, ". . . he lived so much longer than even *he* expected. All that hard work seemed to extend his life, not shorten it. . . . He put a new roof on the castle when he was eighty, crawling all over the top of the thing."

On October 5, 1974, Castle Clare was razed by fire. Only stone stairs remained. Wakefield's fire chief, Walter Maloney, said, ". . . the fire that destroyed Castle Clare was . . . deliberately set."

(Notes written Gloucester, Massachusetts, August 1975.)

ALFRED DIES

Alfred Dies was initially introduced in a reading at the New Dramatists Committee, New York, during the winter of 1976–7, directed by John Dillon, with the following cast:

ALFRED .... Michael Moriarty
LYNCH .... Dominic Chianese
EMILY .... Joanna Miles
ROXY .... Peg Murray

Ellen Chenoweth, administrative director of The Actors Studio, New York, initiated an invitation by Carl Shaeffer, executive director, and Lee Strasberg, artistic director, for the play to be rehearsed and presented at The Actors

Studio, during the same season. It was agreed that the play would be presented as an open rehearsal of a work-in-progress and was so presented during January 1977.

Ben Levit replaced John Dillon as director; Madeleine Thornton-Sherwood replaced Peg Murray as ROXY; Paul Eads designed the scenery; Susan Tsu designed the costumes.

Subsequently, there were two productions in the same season, both billed as world premiere.

The first world premiere was presented at the Magic Theatre, San Francisco, March–June 1977. The director was John Lion, with the following cast:

ALFRED .... D. J. Buckles
LYNCH .... Irving Israel
EMILY .... Jane Bolton
ROXY .... Linda Hoy

The next world premiere was given in the summer repertory season, 1977, of the American Stage Festival, Milford, New Hampshire. The director was Ben Levit, the scenic designer was Christopher Nowak, and the costume designer was Jennifer von Mayrhauser. The cast was as follows:

ALFRED .... William Meisle
LYNCH .... Patrick McNamara
EMILY .... Etain O'Malley
ROXY .... Ann Patomiac

Finally, a reading of *Alfred Dies* was given at The Actors Studio, New York, in repertory with *Alfred the Great* and *Our Father's Failing*, in February 1978.

The text was completed by the author in June-August 1978.

Real and Invented Background for Alfred Dies

The Catholic population of Wakefield is predominantly Irish and Italian.

The Italian community is located southeast of Main Street, near the border of Wakefield and Saugus, and is popularly known as Guinea Gulch.

Wakefield's Irish population is dispersed throughout the town, joining near the railroad station at St. Joseph's Church, Sundays. Italians have their own churches, all found in their particular community. Wakefield's Irish-Catholic youth is educated, primarily through eighth grade, at St. Joseph's School (founded 1924), commonly known as St. Joe's. For secondary-school education, young Irish-Catholic men seem to choose either Malden Catholic High School or Wakefield Memorial High School (nonsectarian). However, in 1961, Austin Preparatory School for Catholic Boys opened its doors in Reading, Massachusetts, cutting severely into Malden Catholic's enrollment from Wakefield and neighboring towns. Austin Prep is staffed by monks of the Augustinian order, who also staff Merrimack College in nearby North Andover, Massachusetts.

Wakefield's young Irish-Catholic women are usually insinuated into the Nazareth Academy (founded 1947), a Catholic secondary school located on the hill above Wakefield's exclusive Park Section, near the Stoneham town line.

The nuns who teach the young women belong to an obscure order called the Sisters of Charity. Locally, they, as well as the young women themselves, are known as Nazarites.

The Nazarites are in fact an ascetic Hebrew sect, worldwide; excluding, of course, Wakefield, Massachusetts, where they are instead middle-class Irish-Catholic girls.

An emergency fund-raising campaign was held during 1973, to raise several thousand dollars with which to keep the Nazareth Academy in operation during what the Wakefield *Daily Item*'s editor called "these troubled times."

The money was raised and the Nazareth Academy continued operation and does as of this writing.

Little is known about Nazareth graduates.

(Notes written by I.H., Gloucester, Massachusetts, July 1975.)

STAGE DIRECTIONS

Stage Directions was given initial exposure in February 1976, in a reading by student-actors at Brandeis University, directed by Nancy Alexander.

Subsequently, *Stage Directions* had its first public performance in May 1976, at The Actors Studio, New York, directed by J Ranelli, with the following cast:

RICHARD .... Lenny Baker
RUTH .... Laura Estrerman
RUBY .... Nancy Mette

Subsequent productions have been given at Yale University; by The Aleph Company, Milwaukee, Wisconsin; by The Changing Scene, Denver, Colorado; and in London, England, by the Orange Tree Theatre. The play was given a workshop production at the New York Shakespeare Festival December, 1978–January, 1979, under the auspices of Joseph Papp, featuring John Glover, Patti Lupone, and Ellen Greene. The director was Jack Hofsiss.

SPARED

Spared was first performed in a workshop at the Manhattan Theatre Club, New York, March–April 1974, in preparation for its world premiere performances, in Paris, which were subsequently given during April 1974 at the Théâtre du Centre Culturel Américain. The director was the author, with the following cast:

MAN .... Lenny Baker

Subsequently, the American premiere of *Spared* was presented at the Spingold Theatre, Brandeis University, Waltham, Massachusetts, in November 1975, on a double bill with a reading of Horovitz poems, entitled *Misfires from the Canon. Spared* again starred Lenny Baker and was again directed by its author.

A final text was fashioned and presented at Yale University, in production with student-actors, November 1976, and, in that same theater season, in repertory with the other plays of The Quannapowitt Quartet: *Hopscotch, The 75th,* and *Stage Directions*, by The Aleph Company, Milwaukee, Wisconsin, and at The Changing Scene, Denver, Colorado. There was a student production of the play at Dartmouth College, in Hanover, New Hampshire.

The play was presented by BBC Radio-2, London, England, in a production directed by Martin Esslin, 1976.

The entire Quannapowitt Quartet enters a repertory production at the New York Shakespeare Festival, New York, during the 1978–79 season, produced by Joseph Papp.

THE WEBBER-LYNCH FAMILY LINES:

The interrelationships of the two families, as given below, were sorted out by Mary Winn, who was assistant director during the New Dramatists Committee readings and the Actors Studio productions of The Alfred Trilogy.

ALFRED
Emily's husband
Emily's brother
Pa's son
Father of Margaret's child

WILL
Margaret's husband
Margaret's brother
Willie-Boy's son
Sam's nephew
B. J. Lynch's brother
Roxy's son(?)

SAM
Margaret's stepfather (and uncle)
Pa's best friend
Willie-Boy's brother
Will's uncle
B.J.'s uncle
Roxy's lover
No children

ROXY
Emily's mother
Margaret's stepmother
Pa's lover
Two children with Willie-Boy
Will's mother

WILLIE-BOY
Will's, B.J.'s, and Margaret's father
Sam's twin brother
Roxy's lover (two children)
Sophie's (Alfred's mother) lover

EMILY
Alfred's wife
Alfred's sister
Pa's daughter
Roxy's daughter

MARGARET
Will's sister
Willie-Boy's daughter
Roxy's daughter
Mother of Alfred's child
Sam's stepdaughter

PA (TOMMY)
Alfred's father
Emily's father
Roxy's lover (fathered Emily by Roxy)

B. J. LYNCH
Margaret's brother
Will's brother
Willie-Boy's son
Sam's nephew

SOPHIE
Alfred's mother
Pa's wife
Willie-Boy's lover
Bruce's mother

BRUCE
Alfred's brother
Emily's stepbrother

SUPPORT DURING WRITING PERIOD

Special mention should be given to the Creative Artists Service Program, funded by the New York State Council on the Arts; the Guggenheim Foundation; the American Academy of Arts and Letters; and the National Endowment of the Arts, all of which awarded the author grants or fellowships with financial aid during the seven-year writing period of The Wakefield Plays; and to the Eugene O'Neill Memorial Theatre Foundation, The New Dramatists Committee, The Actors Studio, and the New York Shakespeare Festival, all of which presented protected, noncommercial, full productions of The Wakefield Plays during their development.

IN MEMORIAM

By way of a penultimate note, I should like to dedicate the entire cycle of plays to the memory of John Cazale, the Massachusetts-born actor who played in most of my plays, from 1967–1977, including *Alfred the Great* and *Our Father's Failing*. What follows is a eulogy written by me that was published in the United States by *The Village Voice*, March 27, 1978, at the time of Cazale's death.

A Eulogy: John Cazale
(1936-1978)

The great actors give reason to the art of dramatic writing. They change the awful velocity that is life passing. They offer a play's audience spots of perfect time, a life made heroic, and, finally, a system of how to live: a trail guide toward a higher quality of life.

The great actors possess a great patience: to endure great pain or provocation. They possess a great forbearance. They possess a great calm for quiet waiting, for perseverance. They possess a great view of life: to select the moments from a text that are high, out of the ordinary, away from the sour and the soiled. They delicately string these gemlike moments, one after the other, into a gift to the audience, the visible, wearable system of life that is the reason of art. And all of this the great actors must fashion from the dramatist's hopelessly self-centered and imperfect text.

To extract universal truths from the clack and self-pity that is the playwright's private ravings—the play—this is the art of the great actors. To hop from a play's moment of truth, to another, to another, dancing upon each moment lightly, as though they were stepping-stones across a magical pool (ever so careful to miss the stones that are broken and untrue)—this, too, is the art of the great actors.

To perform a laugh, when life dictates a smile, or less; to perform a scream when life dictates a complaint, or less; to perform an action, when life dictates a worry, or less; to perform a dance, when life dictates a stall, or less; to perform a question, when life dictates an answer, or less; this is the art of the great actors.

They make vellum of paper pages.

They make light.

John Cazale was such an actor. His greatness was unquestioned by all who touched him, and by all who were touched by him. Unquestioned. He would laugh at the pretensions of this earnest eulogistic tribute; he would weep for its concern. Such was Cazale's vision: through eyes that always saw the book through its cover.

John Cazale was the perfect blend of Ariel and Bartleby: a sudden laugh stopped by a sudden silence; a perfect silliness that broke dreaded dead-walled reveries. Such was the range of Cazale's perceptions. Such was the delicacy of his St. Francis of Assisi face: to make visible the subtleties of grim and grin, and all between.

Some images from the private life that was the work he shared: Sal, eyes unmoving, fixed, as though they fell from a high place into those unfathomably deep sockets, dotting that unforgivably sweet face; Gupta, the Indian, moving through the jabs and poisoned epithets, to smile with understanding, to touch with love and purpose; Fredo, the perfection of a lounge player, ever hopeful, ever ashamed of his longings, his eyes flickering from down to even lower down; those same eyes now on Angelo's best face, a gaze across to Meryl Streep's supreme Isabella, pulling her around, around, and they would build a love for the rest of his life, and beyond, and we the audience, would notice, we would smile, we would try to learn; Dolan, dangerous, ridiculous, as silly a man as ever drew a sword, now alternatively much more dangerous, much more silly than ever imagined: a fabulous fool; Ui's lieutenant, gimped and sallow, Sal's fixed eye even less moving here, even deeper, a Bartleby *risus puris*, a miracle. Brecht, Coppola, Gorky, Hansberry, Shakespeare—all the lucky writers played by Cazale, improved by Cazale, touched by Cazale. All the lucky writers . . .

John Cazale happens once in a lifetime. He was an invention, a small perfection. It is no wonder his friends feel such anger upon waking from their sleep to discover that Cazale sleeps on with kings and counselors, with Booth and Kean, with Jimmy Dean, with Bernhardt, Guitry, and Duse, with Stanislavsky, with Groucho, Benny, and Allen. He will make fast friends in his new place. He is easy to love.

John Cazale's body betrayed him. His spirit will not. His whole life plays and replays as film, in our picture houses, in our dreams. He leaves us, his loving audience, a memory of his great calm, his quiet waiting, his love of high music, his love of low jokes, the absurd edge of the forest that was his hairline, the slice of watermelon that was his smile.

He is unforgettable.

IN CONCLUSION

As a final note, each of the plays of the cycle is dedicated to a person who was directly involved in sustaining me during the creation of this large work. There are many people, however, to whom plays are not dedicated and whose names do not appear in these notes, who helped also. I hope that such omission is forgivable. It is a fact that a second book as large as this edition of the plays might be created of the facts and details surrounding the productions of these plays, thus far.

The Wakefield Plays, but for the normal trimming and shaping for final production, is complete. (I am amazed to have written the preceding sentence!) These plays exist in tribute to the O'Neill Foundation; to the New Dramatists Committee; to the New York Shakespeare Festival; to The

Actors Studio; to theater directors; to stage directors; to stage technicians and designers; to loving actors; to my extraordinary children, Rachael, Matthew, and Adam; to LuAnn Walther, who stayed by me through the writing of it all—and then some; to my parents; to my friends, small in number, but of towering quality. Interest and respect has been paid to a middle-aged young playwright such as myself, and to a work as complicated and enormous as my Wakefield, Massachusetts, plays.

In this matter, we are grateful.

Israel Horovitz,
Gloucester, Massachusetts,
January, 1979